Frederick A. Ober, Frederick A. (Frederick Albion) Ober

Camps in the Caribbees

the adventures of a naturalist in the Lesser Antilles

Frederick A. Ober, Frederick A. (Frederick Albion) Ober

Camps in the Caribbees
the adventures of a naturalist in the Lesser Antilles

ISBN/EAN: 9783744739481

Printed in Europe, USA, Canada, Australia, Japan

Cover: Foto ©ninafisch / pixelio.de

More available books at **www.hansebooks.com**

CAMPS IN THE CARIBBEES:

*THE ADVENTURES OF A NATURALIST
IN THE LESSER ANTILLES.*

BY

FREDERICK A. OBER.

"To-morrow I sail for those cinnamon groves,
Where nightly the ghost of the Caribbee roves."

EDINBURGH: DAVID DOUGLAS
1880

TO

NATHANIEL H. BISHOP,

AUTHOR OF
"A THOUSAND MILES' WALK," "VOYAGE OF THE PAPER CANOE,"
ETC.,

This Book is Dedicated

BY

HIS FRIEND, THE AUTHOR.

PREFACE.

The islands to which reference is made in the following chapters are those known as the Caribbees, or Lesser Antilles, extending over eight degrees of latitude, between Porto Rico and Trinidad, connecting the Greater Antilles with the continent of South America.

This archipelago, containing the loveliest islands in the western hemisphere, with settlements ante-dating Jamestown and Plymouth, with structure and physical features interesting to men of science the world over, has yet remained, as at the period of discovery, almost an unknown field to the naturalist.

In 1876, under the auspices of the Smithsonian Institution, I undertook the exploration of these islands with the especial view of bringing to light their ornithological treasures. The investigation covered a space of nearly two years, during which time I visited mountains, forests, and people, that few, if any, tourists ever reached before. It was only by leaving the beaten path of travel, and taking to the woods, that I was enabled to accomplish what I did in the way of discovery; for which the curious reader is referred to the Appendix, and to the various catalogues of new birds discovered, published by the National Museum.

While around the borders of each island there is a cleared belt of fertile land, sometimes densely populated, and on the coast are often large villages and even cities, the interior is generally one vast forest, covering hills and mountains so wild and forbidding of aspect that few clearings are made in them save the "provision grounds" of the negroes and Indians. Many tourists and writers have visited these islands, have stopped a while in the towns, have interviewed the natives, and then have hastened off to England or the States, and written books about them. Several naturalists of note have likewise visited the shores of these interesting isles, but, like the writers aforementioned, have never penetrated beyond the line of civilization.

Conjecturing that the public have had enough of descriptions at second hand, from writers who are more ears than eyes, I have hastened away from town and city, and sought an early opportunity for taking my readers to the forest, where everything reposes in nearly the same primitive simplicity and freshness as when discovered by Columbus, nearly four centuries ago.

I took my camera with me, and whenever a new bit of scenery presented itself, a beautiful tree, or cascade, or a composition peculiarly tropical, I photographed it; and my publishers have used as subjects for illustration only these photographs from nature, which have never been presented before. As with the illustrations, so with the sketches in type. I have but photographed the scenes I visited and the people I saw and lived among. Now and then, in following a thread of history that connects these islands and people with an almost forgotten past, I have availed myself of the language of the historian, but in rare instances. My only claim is, that these sketches are original, and fresh from new fields — new, yet old in American history, — and that they are accurate, so far as my power of description extends. They have not, like the engravings, had the benefit of touches from more skillful hands, and they may be crude and unfinished, and lack the delicate shadings and halftones a more cunning artist could have given them; but they are, at least, true to nature.

Though the voyage to and from these islands was fraught with incident, there was little that did not savor of the ordinary sea-voyage, hence it has been left out, and the narrative begins and ends in the Caribbees. Beside this, there yet remains much material which has not been drawn upon, comprising more of pure adventure, which, should public and publishers pass a favorable verdict upon this, may form a volume for another year.

BEVERLY, MASS., October, 1879.

CONTENTS.

CHAPTER I.

DOMINICA.

The Mysterious Ocean Current. — Dominica and Columbus. — Roseau and Anthony Trollope. — A West-Indian Town. — Introduction to Tropical Scenes. — The Mountains. — The First Camp 1

CHAPTER II.

CAMP LIFE IN THE TROPICS.

A March Morning. — Matin Music. — Jean Baptiste. — Sonny. — Breakfast in the Mountains. — Queer Customs. — Delightful Temperature for March. — The Hunt for Birds. — A Day's Duties. — Strange Birds and Scenery. — The "Trembleur." — A Precipice. — An Organ-Bird, the "Mountain Whistler." — Bird Notes. — My Chasseurs. — Land Crabs. — Ardent Assistants. — Twilight 12

CHAPTER III.

IN AND ABOUT MY FIRST CAMP.

The Caribbean Sea, its Deceptive Appearance and Placidity. — My Neighbors, the Mountaineers, their Sayings and Wise Saws. — A French Missionary needed. — The Iguana and its Flesh. — Glimpses of Mrs. Grundy. — A Work of Art. — Cruising for Crustaceans. — The "Grives." — Marie. — Long-Tailed Decapods. — "Where Crabs grow." — "Wait

x   CONTENTS.

there, Monsieur." — Astonished. — Shocked. — The River. —
Drenched. — A Naiad. — A Victim to Science. — Food for the
Gods 25

CHAPTER IV.

THE SUNSET-BIRD. — HUMMING-BIRDS.

The Crater-Tarn. — Temporary Camps. — The "Soleil Coucher." — "Hear the Sunset." — A Bird possessed of the Devil. — The Capture. — A Species New to the World. — Four Species of Humming-Birds. — The Garnet-Throat and Gilt-Crested. — Dan, the Hunter. — Catching Birds with Bread-Fruit Juice. — In Captivity. — Death. — Their Food. — Methods of Capture. — The Humming-Bird Gun. — The Aerial Dance 40

CHAPTER V.

THE BOILING LAKE OF DOMINICA.

A Wild Cat. — Tree-Ferns. — Mountain Palms. — A Rare Humming-Bird. — The Valley of Desolation. — Misled by a Bottle. — Boiling Springs. — Hot Streams. — Sulphur Baths. — The Solfatara. — Building the Ajoupa. — Cooking Breakfast in a Boiling Spring 52

CHAPTER VI.

AMONG THE CARIBS.

Their Peaceful Life. — Fruits and Food. — The Second Voyage of Columbus. — Discovery of the Caribs. — Fierce Nature and Intelligence of the "Cannibal Pagans." — Unlike the Natives of the Greater Antilles. — The Carib Reservation in Dominica. — My Camp in Carib Country. — Two Sovereigns. — The Village. — The Houses. — Catching a Cook. — A Torchlight Procession. — Lighting a Room with Fire-Flies. — "Look ze Cook." — Labor. — Domestic Relations. — A Drunken Indian. — Wild Men and Naked Children. — Carib Panniers. — The only Art preserved from their Ancestors 73

CHAPTER VII.

SOCIAL LIFE, APPEARANCE, AND LANGUAGE OF THE CARIBS.

Happy Children. — Cleanliness. — Primitive Innocence. — A Modest Maiden. — Dress. — Face and Figure. — Flattening the Forehead. — Ugly Men and Women. — Carib Hospitality. — The Basket-Weaver. — Tropic Noontide. — Religion. — The Dying Woman. — A Lost Skeleton. — Burial of the Dead. — The Wake. — St. Vincent Caribs. — Two Dialects. — The Arowaks. — An Agreeable Tongue. — Vocabulary. — Caliban a Carib, and Crusoe's Man Friday. — Crusoe's Island. — Black Caribs. — Weapons and Utensils of Stone. — "Thunderbolts." — Carib Sculpture. — A Sacrificial Stone. — Whence came They? — Their Northern Limit. — A Southern Origin. — Their Lost Arts. — A Dying People 90

CHAPTER VIII.

HOW I CAPTURED THE IMPERIAL PARROT.

Meyong. — My Hut. — A Mixed-up Language. — Departure for the Forest. — Pannier and Cutlass. — Wood-Pigeons. — The Startled Savages. — The Bath. — A Gloomy Gorge. — "Palmiste Montagne." — In the Haunts of the Parrot. — Immense Trees. — Parasites and Lianes. — Wood for Canoes and Gum for Incense. — The "Bois Diable." — Constructing the Camp. — Palm-Spathes. — A Bonne Bouche, the Beetle Grub. — Nocturnal Noises. — Comical Frogs. — A Blacksmith in a Tree. — The First Shot. — The Humming-Bird's Nest. — The Parrot. — An Excited Guide. — An Accident. — Wild Hogs. — The "Little Devil." 112

CHAPTER IX.

A DAY IN THE DEEP WOODS.

The Bee-Tree. — Enveloped in Plants. — Ascending the Giant Tree. — Smoking Out the Bees. — Vegetable Ropes. — Honey *ad libitum.* — A Bite. — A Howl. — The Bee-Eaters. — Carib

Perversity. — Sweet Content. — How to draw a Bee-Line. — The Palm Troughs. — A Bamboo Cup. — A Stroll and an Alarm. — The Carib Ghost. — Traditions. — The March resumed. — An Army of Crabs. — Crabs that Migrate. — Delicious Food. — The Mountain Peak. — Hunting the "Diablotin." — Is it a Myth? — Caught in a Storm. — The Carib Castle. — The Captive's Cave. — Vampires. — The Forest Spirit 130

CHAPTER X.

A MIDNIGHT MARCH, AND WHAT CAME OF IT.

The Apparition. — The Lost Chief. — A Forgotten Language. — The March by Torchlight. — Strange and Distorted Forms. — The Forest Wilderness. — A Mysterious Sound. — "A Tree felled by God." — Virgin, protect Us! — Cooking by Steam. — The Rosewood Cabin. — The Chief Disappears. — Is it Gold? — A Small Boa Constrictor. — A Carib Basilisk. — The Biggest Bug in the World. — It comes in Search of the Naturalist. — The Hercules Beetle. — Centipedes. — Scorpions. — An Unnamed Palm with Edible Seeds. — A Priestess of Obeah. — African Witchcraft. — Its Stronghold. — Prostrated by the Heat. — Fever . . . 147

CHAPTER XI.

A CRUISE IN THE HURRICANE SEASON.

An Experiment in Coffee Culture. — The Pest of the Coffee Plant. — Liberian Coffee versus Mocha. — An African Disease. — Gathering in the Sick. — Down the Caribbean Coast. — The Flame-Tree. — The Orchard of Limes. — Profits of Lime Culture. — The Maroon Party. — The Stampede. — Farewell to Dominica. — Coral Islands. — An Immense Game Preserve. — "The Doctor." — The Jiggers. — New Birds. — A Weary Voyage. — Seasons of the Tropics. — Tempests. — Calms. — Provisions Exhausted. — Turkey or Jackass. — Shark. — Odors of Spices. — The Tornado. — Hurricane Birds. — Pitons of St. Lucia. — St. Vincent. — Palm Avenue. — The Spa. — Hospitable People. — Basaltic Cliffs. — Richmond Vale. — Falls of Balleine. — The Waterspout 162

CHAPTER XII.
A CAMP IN A CRATER.

The Last of the Volcanoes. — The Soufrière of St. Vincent. — The "Invisible Bird." — Ascending the Volcano. — The "Dry River." — Bird's-Eye View of St. Vincent. — The Old Crater. — The New Crater. — The Lake in the Bowels of the Earth. — In the Cave. — Sunset. — Preparing for the Night. — Toby. — Five Days and Nights of Misery. — Fauna of a Mountain-Top. — Exploring the Crater-Brim. — Yuccas and Wild Pines. — Toby in the Cave's Mouth. — A Terror-stricken African. — Jacob's Well. — Snakes and Pitfalls. — Toby's "Stock."— The Soufrière-Bird. — A Mysterious Songster. — Unavailing Attempts to Procure it. — Sought for a Century. — A Dream. — Nasal Blasts. — Searching for the Bird. — The Carib Bird-Call. — The Capture. — A New Bird. — A Plunge into Darkness. — Scared by a Snake. — Toby Desperate. — Departure for Carib Country 184

CHAPTER XIII.
TRADITIONAL LORE. — A MISADVENTURE.

Carib Country. — Sandy Bay. — Captain George. — Captain George's Family. — His Superstitions. — A Carib Romance. — A Love Test. — Courtship and Marriage. — Preparing Cassava. — Farine. — An Indian Invention. — The Obeah Charm. — The Carib Wars. — A Brave Coward. — The Caribs Captured. — Sent to Coast of Honduras. — The Survivors. — The Seminoles. — A Parallel. — Carib Song. — Captain George's Treasure. — A Misadventure. — Balliceaux. — A Search for Skulls. — Battowia. — The "Moses Boat." — The Monster Iguana. — The Cave. — The Tortoise. — A Relic of a Fast Age. — Tropic Birds. — Our Boat Smashed. — A Night on the Beach. — The Southern Cross. — Paul and Virginia. — Church Island 208

CHAPTER XIV.
A MONTH ON A SUGAR ESTATE.

Out of the Forest. — Into a Sick-Bed. — My Good Angel. — Convalescence. — Rutland Vale. — The Happy Valley. — Nocturnal Neighbors. — The Labor Question. — A Planter's Trials. — Coolie Immigration. — The Negro, returning to Savagery. — A Self-appointed Physician. — Government House. — Trees of the Tropics. — Bread-Fruit and Cocoa-Palm. — First Experience with Bread-Fruit. — Its Appearance. — Taste. — History of its Introduction. — Abundance in St. Vincent. — The Palms, their Great Beauty and Utility.— Cocoa-Palm, Palmiste, Groo-groo and Gris-gris, Areca and Mountain Palms. — The Vine with Perforated Leaves. — The Indian Maiden 229

CHAPTER XV.

GRENADA AND THE GRENADINES.

Bequia. — Contented Islanders. — The " Bequia Sweet." — Carib Anecdote. — Union Island. — Canouan. — An Energetic Patriarch. — Cariacou. — On the Ancient Contiguity of the Lesser Antilles. — The Lost Atlantis. — " What if these Reefs were her Monument?"— A Glance at the Map. — An Isolated Geographical and Zoölogical Province. — Grenada. — St. George's. — More Craters. — The Carenage. — The Forts. — The Lagoon. — The "Eurydice."— Iguanas. — Their Habits. — Iguana-Shooting. — Oysters growing on Trees. — Columbus and his Pearls. — Lizards. — A Missionary's Grief. — Food of the Iguana. — The Mangrove. — Cacao. — Its Discovery. — Present Range. — Its Cultivation. — Cacao River. — Cocoa and Cacao. — The Tree. — The Fruit. — The Flower. — Idle Negroes. — Chocolate. — Forest Rats. — Monkeys. — Their Depredations. — An Insult . 245

CHAPTER XVI.

A MONKEY HUNT IN THE MOUNTAINS.

Zones of Vegetation. — Naked Negroes. — The Road to the Mountains. — The Grand Etang. — Quadrupeds of the Lesser Antilles, Extinct and Living. ← The Alco. — Peccary. — Agouti. — Manacou. — Armadillo. — Raccoon. — A Visit to the "Tatouay Traps." — The Forest surrounding the Mountain Lake. — " Haginamah ": Is it a Carib Word? — " Hog-in-armor," not a Carib Word. — " Le Morne des Sauteurs." — The Plantain Swamp. — Signs of Monkeys. — The Monkeys' Ladder. — Habits of Wild Monkeys. — The

CONTENTS. XV

Mammie Apple. — In Ambush. — Feathered Companions. — The Bete Rouge. — An Aged Monkey. — His Caution. — Descending the Ladder. — Monkeys, giddy and grave. — Counting his Flock. — The Monkey recognizes a Brother. — "Shoot! Shoot!" — A Free Circus. — A Man, and a Brother. — The Monkey-Mamma. — Her Terror. — An Impolitic Imp 263

CHAPTER XVII.

SOME SUMMER DAYS IN MARTINIQUE.

From Crusoe's Island, North. — Frowning Cliffs. — Golden Sands. — Birth of a Rainbow. — St. Pierre. — The Volcano. — Our Consul. — "Old Farmer's Almanack," good for any Latitude. — French Breakfasts. — "Long Toms." — The Widow and her Weed.— Patois. — Costumes.— Good Claret. — Poor Calico. — Market-Women and Washer-Women. — Gaudy Garments. — Profusion of Ornaments. — Jardin des Plantes. — The Shrine and the Traveler's Tree. — Creole Dueling-Ground. — Palm Avenues. — The Cascade. — Sago and Areca Palms. — The Lake. — Land-Snails. — Lizards.— Tarantulas. — The Lance-Head Snake. — Venomous and Vengeful. — The Mountain Region. — Hot Springs. — An Extinct Volcano. — A Holy City. — Sabbath in the Country. — Warned of Snakes. — Have Alligator Boots. — The Humble Shrine.— A Shriek.— Narrow Escape.— The Crafty Serpent 280

CHAPTER XVIII.

THE BIRTHPLACE OF THE EMPRESS JOSEPHINE.

Fort de France. — The Park. — Tamarinds and Mangos. — Statue of Josephine. — The Trois Pitons. — Historic Hills. — Coronation. — Inscription.— An Earthquake.— Terror. — Parents of Josephine. — Her Grandmother. — Alexander de Beauharnais. — A Valuable Document. — Marriage Register of Josephine's Parents. — Bungling Biographers. — Musty Memoirs. — Fort Royal Bay.— The Passage-Boat "John."— Trois-Ilets. — The Boulanger. — A Festive Father. — A Dinner in Jeopardy. — A Low Couch. — A High Bill. — Church in which Josephine was Baptized. — A Tablet to her Mother's Memory. — La Pagerie, Birthplace of Josephine. — The Hurricane. — The Roof that Sheltered an Empress. — Ground her Feet had Pressed. — Youth of Josephine. — Another Shock. — The Negro Barracks. — The Empress' Bath. — One Hundred Years ago ! — The Sibyl. — The Humming-Bird. — In Peril from a Serpent. — A Peaceful Scene. — A Rude Awakening. — The River Comes Down. — Earthquake again. — Rags and Melancholy 298

CHAPTER XIX.

ASCENT OF THE GUADELOUPE SOUFRIERE.

Point a Pitre. — The Rivière Salée. — Usines. — Earthquake, Fire, and Hurricane. — A Living Bulwark. — The Caravels of Columbus. — Our Lady of Guadeloupe. — The Caribs. — Basse Terre. — Le Père Labat. — Orphans. — The Cholera Plague. — A Permis de Chasse. — Mixed. — A Horse with Points. — Government Square. — The Convent. — A Summer Retreat. — Matouba. — My Thatched Hut. — Doctor Colardeau. — The Coolie. — The Coffee Plantation. — First Coffee in the West Indies. — Its Cultivation. — Temperature of the Coffee Region. — Blossoms and Fruit. — Picking and Preparing. — The High-Woods. — Their Grandeur. — Giant Trees. — Huge Buttresses. — Lianas, Ropes, and Cables. — Epiphytes and Parasites. — Aerial Gardens. — The Sulphur Stream. — The Cone. — The Summit. — The Portal. — Blasts of Hot Air. — Nature's Arcana. — Sulphur Crystals. — Eruptions. — A Grand View. — Impenetrable Forests. — An Extinct Bird. — Juan Ponce de Leon. — The Fountain of Youth. — The Descent into Gloom 322

ILLUSTRATIONS.

Engraved by John Andrew, from the Author's Photographs and Sketches.

	PAGE
The Island of Cocoa Palms . . . . *Frontispiece.*	
Roseau	9
The First Camp	14
Marie, the Naiad	31
Humming-Bird Hunters	47
Boiling Lake of Dominica	53
The Tropic Stream	59
An Indian Kitchen	81
Carib Girl	86
Ancient Caribs	94
The Sacrificial Stone	107
The Hunter's Bath	117
An "Ajoupa"	121
An Army of Crabs	139
Land Crab	146
The Biggest Bug in the World	155
A Group of Gamins	173

ILLUSTRATIONS.

VOLCANO AND LAVA RIVER OF ST. VINCENT	184
TOBY	206
A FAMILY GROUP OF INDIANS	211
THE INDIAN ZEMI	223
BREAD-FRUIT AND COCOA-PALM	237
THE GROO-GROO PALM	242
SAINT GEORGE'S, CAPITAL OF GRENADA	253
THE LAKE IN A CRATER	265
PALMISTE — GLORY OF THE MOUNTAINS	279
CREOLE COSTUMES AND HEAD-DRESS	286
A MARKET WOMAN	287
THE WAYSIDE SHRINE	289
THE WIDOW AND HER WEED	295
BIRTHPLACE OF JOSEPHINE	302
THE EARLY HOME OF AN EMPRESS	313
POINT A PITRE, GUADELOUPE	323
THE GUADELOUPE SOUFRIERE	341

CAMPS IN THE CARIBBEES.

CHAPTER I.

DOMINICA.

THE MYSTERIOUS OCEAN CURRENT. — DOMINICA AND COLUMBUS. — ROSEAU AND ANTHONY TROLLOPE. — A WEST-INDIAN TOWN. — INTRODUCTION TO TROPICAL SCENES. — THE MOUNTAINS. — THE FIRST CAMP.

ALONG the entire group of the Caribbee Isles, sweeping their western shores, flows a strange, mysterious current. Not subject, apparently, to the laws that govern the winds and tides of this region, it for years puzzled and baffled the ablest navigators and oldest sailors. Among the northernmost of these islands large ships were often sunk, carried by the force of this unseen and unsuspected stream upon sunken reefs or barren rocks. Even so long ago as when Columbus was making his voyages, we have on record that he was detained by this very current among these same islands.

It was not known until a comparatively recent period that it was the outflow of a mighty river — no less than the great Orinoco — that caused all this disturbance of waters, and that dependent upon its different stages was the force of this river through the sea. Though my first experience with this current was in January, when the Orinoco was at its lowest, and the consequent marine flow at its weakest stage, I yet had sufficient proof of its strength to understand how it was that vessels of all sizes were sometimes many days in making ports but few miles apart.

We left the port of St. Pierre, Martinique, for that of Roseau, Dominica, the distance being less than thirty-five miles, and the channel separating the islands but twenty in width. Late in the afternoon we hoisted sail, taking a fair land-breeze from the mountains and getting a fresh blow from the trade-winds drawing through the channel, and at midnight were close under the southern point of Dominica, with a fair prospect, when I went below, of landing early in the morning.

The captain, a good fellow, had given up to me, as the only white man on board the sloop, the only berth the cabin afforded. Into that I crawled, with a lurking fear of centipedes and scorpions, and fell asleep. Soon the wheezy pumps awoke me, and a stream of water trickling through the uncalked deck gave assurance that the water in the hold was being pumped out. As this process was repeated every half-hour, my sleep was not so sound that I did not frequently visit the deck, and at each succeeding visit note with alarm that the land line grew dimmer. Daylight revealed that we were much farther away from shore than at midnight, surely drifting to the north-west, with sail flapping idly and rudder useless.

The sun was late in showing himself, for he had to climb well up the heavens ere he could look over the crest of the mountain-ridge that showed in the distance cool and misty; but as day advanced, and the hour of noon arrived, the cool hours of morning were more than compensated for by the intensity of the heat radiated from the glassy sea, — a heat that made itself felt with a glare that caused every one on board to seek earnestly a shady spot.

And this was the "tropic sea" on-which we were drifting, — the sea so often sung by the poet, the sea we had often contemplated in our fanciful dreaming in more northern climes. Like many an object of the poet's adoration, it is far pleasanter to look upon through his eyes than through visual organs of your own. Though the sun and sea made it painful to look abroad, there was nothing offensively new and glaring about the little sloop, that wearied the eye with bright colors. The prevailing color, in fact, was that of the wood of which it was built, the native wood of the island. The knees were of the natural twist and bend of the native trees; the deck planking and sheathing were likewise of the native wood; the mast, the boom, and the bowsprit were of the native woods of the island; and captain and crew, doubtless, also from the woods, — natives fresh from the native woods of Dominica. There were more than twenty people of color lounging in various attitudes about the deck. They seemed wholly indifferent to the fact that the vessel was drifting with them away from the island; and when I suggested to the captain that he utilize this material at the oars, there was a general howl of indignation. The captain also gazed at me like one who had heard information of a character novel and startling, and informed me that what I proposed was not only useless, but impossible.

Struggle against the current of the mighty Orinoco! Attempt to baffle the wiles of a power unseen, that always had acted in just such a manner, and had carried him over the same course every voyage he had made! It would be preposterous! At night, the land-breeze would come down from the mountains, and he would claw in-shore without any trouble whatever.

Late in the afternoon, however, we descried a speck dancing on the waves, which speck was, of course, a boat; and in that boat, when it reached us, I engaged passage for the shore, my unhappy companions drifting about until the next afternoon, sometimes in sight, sometimes lost to view for a long time. As we neared shore I had time to examine the character of the scenery of the western coast, as one object after another was unfolded, and the mass of green and blue resolved itself into wooded hills, narrow valleys, and misty mountain-tops that reached the clouds. A planter's house gleamed white in a valley; a pebbly beach stretched between high bluffs, with a grove of cocoa palms half hiding a village of rude cabins along its border.

I was approaching an island of historic interest and scenic beauty, of which the events of one and the elements of the other are little known to the world at large. It is the first island upon which Columbus landed on his second voyage. Having been first seen on Sunday, it was called by him *Dominica*, and this event dates from the 3d of November, 1493. Blest isle of the Sabbath day! Many changes has it known since the great navigator first saw its blue mountains and landed upon its fragrant strand.

Does it not read like a fairy tale, this second voyage of Columbus? With three ships and fourteen caravels, containing fifteen hundred persons, he set sail from Cadiz, touched at the Canary Isles, and then shaped his course for the islands of the Caribs, of whose prowess and fierce nature he had heard many stories from the mild people of Hispaniola. "At the dawn of day, November 3d, a lofty island was descried to the west. As the ships moved gently onward, other islands rose to sight, one after another, covered with forests and enlivened by flights of parrots and other tropical birds, while the whole air was sweetened by the fragrance of the breezes which passed over them."

Dominica is but thirty miles in length by eleven in breadth, yet presents a greater surface and more obstacles to travel to the square mile than any island of similar size in the West Indies. Well did Columbus illustrate its crumpled and uneven surface, when, in answer to his queen's inquiry regarding its appearance, he crushed a sheet of paper in his hand and threw it upon the table. In no other way could he better convey an idea of the furrowed hills and mountains, deeply cut and rent into ravines and hollowed into valleys.

"To my mind," says Anthony Trollope, "Dominica, as seen from the sea, is by far the most picturesque of all these islands. Indeed, it would be hard to beat it either in color or grouping. It fills one with an ardent desire to be off and rambling among these mountains—as if one could ramble through such wild bush country, or ramble at all with the thermometer at eighty-five degrees. But when one has only to think of such things, without any idea of doing them, neither the bushes nor the thermometer are considered." In this, as in all his sketches, Mr. Trollope is right so far as he goes; but he does not go far enough. "Filled with an ardent desire," he should have given those woods and mountains the months of camp-life that I did; then would the world be richer in pictures of forest-life and mountain scenery that my poor pen so feebly tries to portray. As one writer, an intelligent geologist, once remarked: "No island in these seas is bolder in its general aspects, more picturesque and more beautiful in the detail of its scenery — indeed, one might be tempted to say, considering its fortunes, that it has the *fatal gift of beauty!*"

At five o'clock, the gun in the fort starts off the bell in the cathedral spire. It is an hour before daylight, and even at six the mists of the valleys cover all, even to the mountain-tops. The sun climbs steadily, though it is eight o'clock before he has shown his face to Roseau, and darts over the mountain-tops to windward his scorching rays. It is interesting to watch the changes that come over the mountain sides and valleys as the sun dissipates the morning mists. Lake Mountain, four thousand feet in height, towers black against the sky; five miles it is from town, yet seems so close as to overshadow it. Its head is veiled more than half the time in mist. Stretching away north and south is a long line of hills, an isolated peak jutting up at intervals. Their summits are blue and purple in the distance. Within this line is a cordon of hills, with valleys deep and dark behind, half encircling the town. These hills are broken and ragged, seamed and furrowed and scarred, yet are covered with a luxuriant vegetation of every shade of green: purple of mango and cacao, golden of cane and lime, orange and citron. Palms crown their ridges, cultivated grounds infrequently gleam golden-brown on their slopes, and dense clouds come pouring over their crests from the Atlantic. North and south this bulwark of hills ends in huge cliffs plunged into the sea. Roseau is seated at the mouth of a valley formed by a river. From the centre of this valley there rises a hill — a mountain it is called here — Morne Bruce.

From its smoothly-turfed crown the view of town and sea is superb, especially at sunset, when the sun sinks beyond the Caribbean Sea, and the cool evening breeze plays through the trees. From it we look upon the town; many palm-trees, few houses, a rushing, roaring river that meets the sea in a surf-line like a northern snowdrift, a picturesque fort, the jail, the government house, and the Catholic cathedral — a building of stone, with arched windows and doorways, short, though shapely spire — with a palm tall and slender, to lend grace and beauty; westward, beyond the shore-line, the Caribbean Sea, its bosom, which glowed so fierily in the sunlight, now cool and inviting in its stillness.

Looking eastward, one can see far into the Roseau Valley, to the wall of mountains, from which dashes out a great waterfall, dwindled to a mere silver thread in the distance. The Roseau River emerges into a plain beneath, a valley filled with cane, containing in its centre a planter's house and buildings palm-surrounded, dashes over its rocky bed with a roar that reaches our ears even at this height of several hundred feet, and runs at the foot of a high white cliff across another plantation into the sea, peaceful enough at the end.

The streets of Roseau are straight, paved with rough stone, and they never echo to the sound of wheels. They cross at right angles and dwindle down to three bridle-paths leading out of the town, one north and one south, along the coast, and one, narrow and tortuous, over the mountains to the eastward. Most of the houses are one-storied boxes of wood, with bonnet roofs, sixteen by twenty feet; many in a state of decay, with tattered sides, bald spaces without shingles, and dragging doors and shutters. Every street, however, is highly picturesque with this rough architecture, and with cocoa palms lining and terminating the vistas. The town is green with fruit-trees, and over broken roofs and garden walls of roughest masonry hang many strange fruits. Conspicuous are the mango, orange, lime, pawpaw, plantain, banana, and tamarind. Over all tower the cocoa palms, their long leaves quivering, their dense clusters of gold-green nuts drooping with their weight.

From the mountains, from the "Sweet River," comes the purest of water, led in pipes through all the streets, and gushing out in never-ceasing flow from the sea wall on the shore. The market, near the south end of the town, a small square surrounded by stores, is the centre of attraction on Saturdays, when it is densely packed with country people, black and yellow, who come, some of them, from points a dozen miles distant, each with his bunch of plantains, or tray of bread-fruit. All are chattering, so that there is a very babel of sounds. Little stalls, temporarily erected, contain most villainous salt fish, ancient and vile-smelling, and every few feet is a table, presided over by a contented wench, who has for sale cakes and sweetmeats of her own manufacture.

Roseau.

Near the market is the fort, a low stone structure, pierced with loopholes, commanding from its high bluff the roadstead, in which, save the trading-vessels and the weekly steamer, there are seldom any craft besides the sugar-vessels. Near the fort is the English church, with a clock in its face, and four magnificent palmistes to guard its entrance. Adjoining is the government house in a garden of flowers; and near, the court-house, of stone, yellow and low. Opposite, on a bluff overlooking the sea, is the public garden, neatly enclosed, tastefully ornamented; a few large trees, many roses, humming-birds, butterflies, and a grand view of the sea. The road leads by a broad green *savane*, near which is a ruined cemetery, down between long rows of lowly cabins, its bed green and grassy, within a stone's throw of the surf on the pebbly beach.

This is Roseau, which I left one March morning for the mountains. Early came the women, who were sent by a kind friend to carry my luggage: heavy boxes and bales they had engaged to carry to the mountains on their heads. It was all the way ascending, but they faithfully performed their duties, nor once complained. Astride an island colt, the loan of another friend, and accompanied by still another, whom I had met a few days before, I left behind me the town, and set my face to the mountains.

Down the street, past the jail, across the river over an excellent bridge, under the cliffs of St. Aromant, into the banana and citron groves that lie at the mountain's base; then up higher and higher, the path growing rocky and slippery, past the lovely valley of Shawford, where the house of my friend Stedman, built upon a small plateau, surrounded by hills, embowered in limes and plantains, overlooks a tropical garden. A mile above, we entered a deep ravine, where are the first perfect tree-ferns on the trail; the gorge is filled with them, and the banks along the path are covered with smaller ones, infinitely beautiful.

Here I first heard the melody of the " solitaire." Long since, the air of the town, hot and parching, had given place to cool and delicious breezes. We went out under the shade of trees, passing many a trickling stream, until an elevation of nearly two thousand feet was reached, when we heard voices, and suddenly came upon a party of mountaineers (half Carib, half negro), naked to the waist, hatless, and armed each with his *machete*, or " cutlass," over two feet in length. They saluted us politely, however, and we passed on until near the " high woods," when we turned to the right and rode down a narrow trail under large trees, and reached finally a narrow gate of bars in a tall hedge of oleander.

Descending rapidly from the forest was an open space of a hundred acres, perhaps, sloping westward, green as a sward of guinea-grass could make it. Over this were scattered volcanic rocks and clumps of trees. This slope terminated abruptly in a cliff so steep that the people living here could not descend except by a long detour. Over this cliff fell the waterfall we saw in coming up. Deep ravines seamed it at intervals, all trending toward the valley wall, and on all sides but this were nothing but forest and hills.

From one of the mountaineers I secured a cabin, one of the seven comprising this little hamlet, and before nightfall had comfortably established myself. My companion then left me alone to what proved but the first of many camps in tropical forests.

CHAPTER II.

CAMP LIFE IN THE TROPICS.

A MARCH MORNING. — MATIN MUSIC. — JEAN BAPTISTE. — SONNY. — BREAKFAST IN THE MOUNTAINS. — QUEER CUSTOMS. — DELIGHTFUL TEMPERATURE FOR MARCH. — THE HUNT FOR BIRDS. — A DAY'S DUTIES. — STRANGE BIRDS AND SCENERY. — THE "TREMBLEUR." — A PRECIPICE. — AN ORGAN-BIRD, THE "MOUNTAIN WHISTLER." — BIRD NOTES. — MY CHASSEURS. — LAND CRABS. — ARDENT ASSISTANTS. — TWILIGHT.

IT is a bright March morning. As I throw open the shutters of my shanty and let in the light of early day, I look out upon a scene of loveliness that it were worth many a day's journey to enjoy.

From beyond the mountains, east, the sun has climbed a little way until he peers through a defile in the hills, and a rift in the cloud masses, and floods only a narrow pathway down the surrounding hills, their northern slopes, a bit of the gloomy valley miles below, and bursts upon the calm Caribbean Sea with concentrated glory. A sail, floating on that sea, drifted hither and thither by strong, unaccountable currents, — which came, perchance, from Martinique or Barbados to the south, or from Guadeloupe or Montserrat to the north, — is ablaze with light, which gives it the appearance of being on fire. No sound comes up from the valley below, nor from the surrounding mountain sides; even the rain frogs and the nocturnal *cicadæ* have closed their concerts and have left it to the birds to usher in the matin hour; and they are singing in low, sweet strains far down in the gloomy ravines below, and in the thickets bordering distant glades.

My first duty is to examine my thermometer. It registers sixty-eight degrees. That recorded, I step out and refresh myself with such ablution as can be enjoyed from a small calabash of rain-water. Soon, a little colored maiden appears bearing a tray with my coffee, and perhaps a cup of milk — oftener without. A cup of coffee and a slice of bread or a couple of crackers, is my only refreshment until noon, when I return from my tramp in the forest.

When I first came to this mountain valley I brought with me a bright, colored boy as aid, fondly hoping he would be of much assistance in preparing my birds, as well as in the culinary line. But, alas! in either profession he was singularly deficient, and save in the preservation of cooked provisions, — in other words, "to keep food from spoiling," — he was of no use whatever. After three days passed in his society, we parted. There was also a question between him and Jean Baptiste (the proprietor of my humble cot), relating to a few small articles that one night disappeared. Now, he was highly incensed that such a thing should happen within the limits of his jurisdiction, and made such a row about it that I concluded that it were best that "Sonny" and I should part, — with no regrets on my part, none expressed on his, — for the laboring class of the West Indies accept stoically whatever fate drops to them as their share. The salary I was paying him was princely, being sixpence a day and "found," while the usual remuneration for such service as he afforded me was *three pence*, and if "found," it was usually after a long search. Baptiste accepted the expression of confidence that this act of mine implied, and took me at once under his protection and care; hence it is that the little maiden aforesaid appears in the morning with my coffee; at noon, when I return weary from the hunt, with a dish of eggs fried in oil and *yam sauvage*, and at dusk with the same, varied with a plate of mountain-cabbage, or salad, from the little wattle-enclosed garden on the hillside.

The First Camp.

The cabin of Baptiste is not far from mine, and my wants are promptly supplied when the hour arrives for meals, even almost anticipated. But there are many things connected with the attendance of my little cook and waiter that, in the light of my early education in New England, seem, to say the least, queer. For instance, when the knives and forks require cleaning, their surplus coating is removed by being brought in close contact with the skirts of her garment. I say *garment*, and use the word in the singular advisedly.

The spoons also are cleaned in the same way, and were it not that my eyes had beheld the process of polishing, I should not believe, as they nestled innocently together on the rough table, but that they had been subjected to the treatment customary in more civilized communities. My tin camp-cup, which has accompanied me in all my camp-life, was often the object of her attention, and at that time it was doubtful to me whether she was washing the cup with her fingers or rinsing her fingers in the cup. At any rate, it shows a laudable desire to have my table furniture in good order, and I do not murmur; but there is a cake of soap and a towel that I keep concealed from her sharp eyes, that, when not observed, I bring into frequent use on those same objects of her devotion. One day I was incautious enough to peer into the culinary department — a palm-thatched structure, black and grimy with smoke which escaped from the fire on the ground, as best it could, through the roof. Only once! I did not wish again to view those ancient pots and kettles, the refuse of preceding feasts, nor to fight my way through the drove of hogs that trooped about the open door.

Occasionally the thought obtrudes itself, "They do not have things like this in the States." This often makes me sad, but I raise my eyes, perhaps, and look out over the green slope, down upon the valley bursting with palms, and beyond the hills to the peaceful sea smiling in sunshine; and I exult in the thought that these enjoyments far outweigh the little annoyances that I have described. And I take down the thermometer and find that it records, if morning, sixty-eight to seventy degrees; if noon, seventy-six degrees; if evening, seventy degrees. And I again reflect, "They can't show all these in the States — in March."

But effectually to escape the train of thought that these observations might give rise to, I take my gun, ammunition, game-basket and note-book, and plunge into one of the lateral ravines that feed the huge gorge below. It is morning. The bread-fruit, mango, and limes that thickly stud the slope above are glistening with dew, and the low shrubs that line the ravine, as well as the taller trees that darken its recesses, are dropping copious showers. I am following the dry bed of a stream that shows, by huge rocks dislodged and excavated banks, what must have been its size and force in the rainy season. Ferns, lycopodiums, and matted and tangled roots conceal the earth and make every footstep a doubtful one, and the loose stones and rocks, with dark holes beneath and beside them, suggest most forcibly the possibility of the presence of snakes. But I am looking for birds (and snakes also, if they come in my way), and do not give them the attention that once I thought I should, when hearing tales of their abundance and venomous character in these islands. As this is a search for birds, the snakes shall be left for some future chapter.

It is well known that each species of bird has its own peculiar haunt, where it feeds, sings, and sports itself. It has also a different haunt for different portions of the day, and the birds of the morning which we find in the ravine may be, in the evening, feeding or singing on the borders of open glades, or higher up the mountain sides. At mid-day you will find all under cover of the densest shade, and silent. It is in the morning that they may be found in localities characteristic of them. The first bird that greets me on the edge of the ravine is the humming-bird, as he dashes here and there from flower to flower, scattering the dew-drops in tiny showers, and reflecting almost prismatic hues from breast and back. There are three kinds here in this mountain valley, the smallest of which has a lovely crest of metallic green; the largest, with a length of five inches, and stretch of wing of seven and a half, has a gorgeous garnet throat, purple back and wings, and tail of green, reflecting most delightful hues. The prevailing hue of the other species is green, with a throat sometimes green, sometimes blue.

I leave the humming-birds to my little *chasseurs*, who with bird-lime catch for me all I want. Of them more anon; let us plunge into the ravine. A movement in the branches of a tall, slender tree claims attention. I look up; see nothing. The broad, glossy leaves vibrate again, and I discern above the lower branches a bird the size and shape of our brown thrush; he has a long, stout beak, a yellow eye, and a glossy, brown coat. He hops from twig to twig, feeding upon the coffee-like berries of this strange tree, silent, engaged in the gleaning of his morning meal. But however intent upon securing those white berries, the husks of which he drops almost upon my head, he does not forget to stop every few seconds and shake his wings and jerk his tail in a most comical manner. A hop, a quiver of wings and tail; a skip, with accompanying shake all over; a jump, with a convulsive shake, quivering and spasmodic twitching of head, wings, and tail. As I watch this interesting bird I am conscious of the presence of another, and of several others also, which when they meet go through the most laughable series of bows, quivering of wings and caudatory vibrations. Well has this bird earned the title — universal, I believe, throughout the West Indies — of *Trembleur*.

And now, the trembleurs having been attended to, I push on till I reach the brink of a precipice. A little stream that falls musically over the rocks and stones suddenly loses itself over the brow of this wall of green, on the summit of which I stand. Cautiously clinging to the trunk of a tree, I look down into the valley. The sight nearly makes me dizzy, for there, five hundred feet beneath me, I see tall trees as little shrubs, bananas and plantains as small plants, and huge boulders as pebbles. The roots I am standing on overhang the precipice, and the tree shoots out far over the dizzy height. Above the sighing of the wind in the tree-tops, and the music of the birds, and creaking of branches, is a roaring of water falling from immense height — a roar that drowns every other noise, and deafens the ear to every other sensation. Wending my way along the brink, clinging to roots and trees, I soon reach a point where I can see, half-way down the perpendicular cliff, a sheet of foam; a hundred yards farther another, falling from a lesser height, yet neither less than one hundred and fifty feet — the higher over two hundred.

They are lost in a sea of green, reappearing farther on as a united stream, which rushes and roars over rocks, through gorges and at the base of mountains, through gardens of figs and plantains, beneath towering, feathery palms, through green fields of cane, at last to reach the sea.

It is while carefully balancing myself on my shaking support of matted roots, that a sound comes to my ear through the roar of a waterfall — a sound strangely sweet, solemn, and impressive; a mellow, organ-like note, clearer than any flute-tone, more thrilling than the solemn chant of sacred song in groined cathedral. It is repeated. I stand entranced, listening to melody that had never fallen on my ears before. The cause I cannot at first ascertain, for the notes seem ventriloquial; and indeed they are so, for I search high and low, the leafy branches above my head, the densely clustered ferns at my feet, and the shrubs at my back, for many minutes, before I find the source of this mysterious music. Balanced airily on a lance-like bamboo that shot twenty feet beyond the brink of the cliff, poised in mid-air, with half a thousand feet of space between him and solid earth, is a daintily-shaped bird, clad in sober drab, save a dash of rouge beneath his throat, and of white here and there.

Unconscious of surrounding things, animate and inanimate, he was devoting his powers to the production of that wonderful music. In the short space I here allot to myself I cannot describe the different notes; surely no flute ever produced such mellow, liquid tones. It was music of unearthly sweetness, that, once heard, would never be forgotten — between the notes a long pause, that made them most impressive. It was not a song — though I discovered later that the little bird had a song — but simply the utterance of a few notes. Soon it ceased, and the bird flew into the near forest, where I soon discovered it busily feeding upon the berries of a tall shrub, to the pendant branches of which it was clinging, now and then dashing at a fugitive bunch, apparently as absorbed in this occupation as in his melodious lay of a few minutes before. Soon he ceased feeding, and commenced preening himself upon a naked limb; then, after smoothing himself out, as it were, and drawing in and stretching out his neck, he suddenly dashed at a single berry, swallowed it to clear his throat, and recommenced to trill. He had uttered but a few notes when he silently flew to a dead branch; a few more and he winged his way to a swinging "liane," where he hung suspended above a little ravine, in which is sunk a tiny stream, whose tinkling waters made music, though not so sweet and liquid as his. Then he disappeared in the dark recesses of the forest, where it would be useless to follow him, but whence came at intervals the ventriloquial music that seemed to float over my head and around me, though the bird was afar.

This bird is called by my mountaineer friends, who have a name, and an applicable one, for everything in the forest, the "*Siffleur Montagne*," or "Mountain Whistler." I afterwards had one in captivity for several weeks, and notes on his behavior, song, and food would fill a column that my readers might think could be put to better use, but which would be valuable to the ornithologist as the first records of an intimate acquaintance with this species.

But let us go on. I will leave the deep valley behind me, with the roar of the waterfall gradually falling, first to a monotonous hum, then ceasing entirely, and climb the bed of another water-course, now dry, waiting for the summer rains. Soon I emerge into a grassy glade, surrounded by mango, coffee-trees, and trees resembling the live-oak. The mangos are bristling with spikes of blossoms — white with them — but not a bird nor a butterfly is hovering above them, though the surrounding trees and shrubs are alive with them. This is a fact I have long noticed, that the mango is ever deserted, though adjacent trees may be vocal with bird-music. But, flitting across this green glade, now bright under the rays of an ever-brightening sun, are many birds; that is, many for this island, for it is not abundant in species, nor in numbers either, save of the humming-bird.

There is a tree full of warblers of strange species—of *Sucrier*, or sugar-bird — a bird resembling our yellow warbler; several of the more strictly fly-catching birds, and a few sparrows, grosbecs, and blackbirds. The three species of humming-bird are well represented, and dash hither and thither seeking their favorite food, indulging in mimic battles and amorous caresses. I push on, after an hour's stop, perhaps, over a rugged trail made by the half-wild cattle as they travel from glade to glade, and crossing another stream, climbing a hill, and descending into a ravine, I climb the steep slopes of the hill on which my cabin is perched. Everything is as I left it five hours before. The door, which is merely kept fastened by a stick braced against it, has not been opened; but I find on the floor a cluster of oranges, a branch of fragrant lime-flowers for my humming-birds, and a tastefully arranged bunch of roses from one of the girls.

While I am putting the finishing touches to my bird-notes, the girl comes in with my lunch, and my little *chasseurs* arrive with their collection of humming-birds. They only hunt at certain times of the day, when I can be near to attend to the little captives, according to my instructions, for they have a cruel way of tying them together if they keep them long. They are finding some new things every day, and as they have got the idea that I am collecting everything in shape of bird, beast, insect, and reptile, they bring me the result of each day's "find." Sometimes it is a snail, a fat caterpillar hideous in its slimy skin, a butterfly, a beetle, or a spider. At one time, from an incautious remark that I made to the effect that I would like a specimen of the curious land-crab which abounds in the ravines and rivulet banks, they conceived the idea of supplying me with the crustacean just mentioned. Each boy and girl on the place resolved to be the first to furnish me with the coveted crab. The consequence was that my place was soon overrun with shell-fish — ugly red and yellow crabs — as large as a man's hand, and from that to the most diminutive. One of the girls in a mischievous mood brought in a crab with a family of little ones, over a hundred, just large enough to be seen, and let them loose on the floor. Through some open window, while I was absent, some giant crab would be dropped on the floor to await my arrival. This was not done in a spirit of mischief, but from an earnest desire to aid me in my labors.

For a week after I could not stir without coming in contact with a shelly creature. I could not put my foot out of bed without a shudder of apprehension. Of nights I would be awakened by a rattling of ale-bottles, and arising would discover that some crab had got thirsty during the night, and had inserted a claw which had caught in the neck of a bottle. Or, as one other night, when my slumbers were broken by a mysterious rattling, and I awoke (thinking that, as Jean Baptiste had prophesied, the "jumbies" had come for me, as they come for everybody who sleeps alone in a strange house), to find another crab vexing his soul in vain endeavors to shin the broom-handle. It may be surmised that I soon informed my corps of naturalists that I could dispense with their services, and now I am again a lone investigator dependent upon his sole endeavors.

In the afternoon I sit down by the loophole that serves as window, (where by raising my eyes I can at any time look off upon the peaceful Caribbean Sea,) gather my birds about me, and, after noting their measurements and other data necessary to aid in their identification, proceed to skin and preserve them preparatory to their long journey to the "States." It is near sunset when this is finished, and after supper I climb into my hammock, or sit on my threshold, watching the sun go down behind the mountains. If I were a little further to the north I could see him down clear to the sea; and, in fact, I often climb a spur of a near hill, where are buried the ancestors of the present residents of Laudat, and watch the sun as he dips below the sea, just gilding with his parting rays the rude crosses that mark the last resting-place of those buried beneath them.

But what I have been most disappointed in as the sun sets, is the absence of that prolonged twilight, which makes our evenings of early summer in the north so delightful; when, after the sun goes down, there remains that blissful lingering of day with night, when the softened light fades so gradually away that we cannot tell at what precise moment, or how, it left us; and when the song of the robin fills the air with melody that many other of our birds keep up in the fields and orchards till late at night. There is none of that here. More than once I have said to myself, as the sun hid his face behind the dark ridge of mountain, leaving the trees sharply outlined against the clear sky — more than once I have repeated, "Now I will sit in the doorway and enjoy the twilight." But I had scarcely found and filled my pipe, and settled myself comfortably in doorway or hammock, when twilight was gone, and the fast-gathering darkness had hid the valleys, and was climbing the western slopes of the mountains. The stars, already out, shine with a liquid brilliancy that causes you to forget the absence of dusk, and you give yourself up to the contemplation of the lighted heavens, losing yourself in thought, wandering perhaps in meditation back to the land you have left, over which the same sky stretches and stars gleam; but not with the clearness of the one, nor the soft brilliancy of the other — at least not at this present season.

CHAPTER III.

IN AND ABOUT MY FIRST CAMP.

THE CARIBBEAN SEA, ITS DECEPTIVE APPEARANCE AND PLACIDITY. — MY NEIGHBORS, THE MOUNTAINEERS, THEIR SAYINGS AND WISE SAWS. — A FRENCH MISSIONARY NEEDED. — THE IGUANA AND ITS FLESH. — GLIMPSES OF MRS. GRUNDY. — A WORK OF ART. — CRUISING FOR CRUSTACEANS. — THE "GRIVES." — MARIE. — LONG-TAILED DECAPODS. — "WHERE CRABS GROW." — "WAIT THERE, MONSIEUR." — ASTONISHED. — SHOCKED. — THE RIVER. — DRENCHED. — A NAIAD. — A VICTIM TO SCIENCE. — FOOD FOR THE GODS.

THE pictures seen from my cabin door are beautiful, but all suggest alike the sea. Detached peaks rise to the eastward and southward, connected by a continuous chain of hills to the sea. Their line is irregular, and very shapely are those mountain-peaks, clothed with verdure to their summits. The broken slope in front of my cabin slants rapidly to the precipice that borders the valley containing the river which hastens to the sea. Outlined against its silvery surface are dark green mountains; a loosely branched tree stands out against it as against the sky; palms, with gracefully spreading foliage, show dark against it. It spreads so far and wide, and seems to climb so high to meet the sky, that it is hardly possible to tell where sea leaves off and sky begins. Every day I am puzzled to ascertain the horizon line.

Every day it blends into sky so softly that all seems sky, or all may be sea. Is the sky blue, so is the sea; is it smoky pearl, the sea is dim, and hides its face beneath a hazy cloud. A cloudy day, with the sun shining on the water from behind the clouds, turning the sea to burnished and glistening silver, is as puzzling as a day with sky of clearest ether, for the sun, reflected from the glowing surface of the sea, dissipates the line of demarkation in the glare of the reflection.

There are times when the sea does not rise up to meet the sky, but spreads out miles and miles, until I almost fancy I can see to Aves Island — that solitary island far west in the Caribbean Sea, where a colony of birds breed on the sands. The best view is obtained at sunset; then, whether the bright orb disappears behind the mountains without a cloud, or whether he leaves a threatening array, clad in armor of gold and silver, the horizon line is well defined. At moonlight also, when mountains and valleys are but gradations in depth of shadow, the sea reposes peacefully beneath moon and stars, content to rest itself as a sea, and claiming no affinity with the vault above.

It seems to me that it changes every time I look upon it — pearl-blue, silver shot with gold, hazy depths, from which no light is shown, and again a sea of deepest ether. It has never been otherwise than calm and placid, though the fierce winds that sometimes sweep down from these mountains and dive into the valleys are enough to ruffle the tranquillity of any sea. Indeed, it is a well-known fact that vessels are often becalmed under the lee of these Caribbee islands for days together, and there is not even a swell to break the monotony of existence on board. I can see white sails, sails of sloops, of schooners, of ships, drifting lazily over the placid sea. Sometimes the morning will reveal the sail of the evening before — the sail that I watched as I swung listlessly in my hammock. It is one of the pleasures of existence here that I can at any time have within my view the still, dreamy, beautiful sea of the Antilles. It is not always so peaceful. In the "hurricane season," when the tempests devastate these islands, it rises in its wrath — not like the miserable Atlantic, though, always in commotion; it is disturbed only by a hurricane — nothing less.

A century ago or thereabouts, there came to this mountain retreat, then unbroken wilderness, (as now it is, save this little clearing) that sanguine Frenchman, Jean Baptiste Laudat. Tradition says he came from his native isle of Martinique or Guadeloupe, and here looked about him for a wife. It is more probable, though, that he brought her with him as a slave, and that she was black; and that there afterwards got admixed a *soupçon* of Carib blood is manifest in the color of these, his descendants. They are not yellow, or bright olive like the Carib, but of a rich brown, with long hair, black and wavy. That the air of these mountains is conducive to health, their size, plumpness and activity prove.

There are but five families, ruled over by the present Jean Baptiste, who inherits his power from his deceased grandfather, as eldest son. With him lives his mother, a yellow-skinned old lady of eighty, who hobbles about with a cane, and is a frequent visitor at the door of my hut. Now, this old lady and her Jean can speak what they flatter themselves passes for English, but their native tongue is the perverted French of their white ancestor. To a Parisian, their perversion of the French verb *faire* would be sufficient to drive him crazy.

For instance, the old lady strives to make intelligible the number of her grandchildren and their respective parents: "My zon, Jean, he make ze enfans seex; Ma fille, he make huit, and *tout les enfans* make seexty." She passed my door one afternoon as I was busy preparing my collections for preservation, and told me confidently that she was going to "make petit walk," but a wail from the house of her eldest son caused her to hurry her old limbs to soothe the child "zat make ze cry." "Me make my sleep," is a common expression.

Jean B. is full of wise sayings, and gives vent to some very strange expressions. One day I returned from a long hunt in a heavy rain, and my worthy friend was greatly exercised that I did not immediately change my clothing. "Who drink ze watah," said he. "It is youselfs feet;" meaning that the moisture had been absorbed into my system. "White man next to God (ze *Mon Dieu*)." "White man not like colored, he no eat ze bones of ze poule." "I tank ze Mon Dieu ef I speaks ze Engleesh." He exercised a sort of paternal sovereignty over me, as the first white man who had honored his little hamlet with his presence, and many a day has he staid from his labor in the mountains to procure something for my table, or some new bird.

One day he brought to my door an iguana, nearly five feet in length, and very ugly. He had seen it basking on a limb beneath the cliff, and had pinned it with a long bamboo, while his brother secured it with a noose made from a liane. I expressed a desire to obtain its skin, and hastened to do so, but a woman was already scorching the scales, which she afterward scraped off in water. It looked quite repulsive, but a piece which they later sent me I ate, finding it sweet, tender, and white, not unlike chicken. This is the season (March and April) when the iguana leaves the rocks and precipices, and takes to the trees. He lives on grass and leaves, principally, if not solely, and only frequents the trees, they say, during the dry season; then he is hunted. During the wet season he lives in his hole, or if he comes out he is hard to find. The dogs of Laudat are trained to hunt this lizard.

I always held that for darning, pure and simple, our good old grandmothers of the good old times held rank *par excellence*. This was conclusively proven one day, when, having made a long rent in the leg of an old pair of trowsers, I took them to Mrs. Jean Baptiste to be repaired. As I turned to go I was arrested by an exclamation, and looking back found her attentively examining them. Now, they were very old; how they got mixed up with the rest of my wardrobe I do not know; but as they were there I made use of them in the woods, intending to leave them there, peradventure they survived.

Years before they had been patched by my grandmother; that maternal relative had a passion for darning perfectly unaccountable. Like Alexander, she would shed tears when there were no more conquests to make in her world of darning, and a new pair of pantaloons, or a coat without a rent, was to her a source of grief. How eagerly she would seize upon a garment that showed signs of dissolution!

Jabbering a few hurried words in patois to a *garçon* who quickly departed, Mrs. Jean Baptiste sat down with the garment in her hands to await the arrival, as I soon found, of the adult female population of Laudat. When they had all arrived she arose and displayed to their united view the broadest part of my inoffensive nether habiliments. At first they were speechless with admiration, but soon broke forth into a chorus of Mon Dieus! each one reaching forward for a closer inspection.

The simple explanation of this is, they recognized the work of a master-hand. Had some connoisseur of paintings found in a garret — as some one is constantly finding in a garret — a painting that, the dust being removed, disclosed a Murillo or a Van Dyke, he could not have been more delighted and surprised. I say delighted, but sober reflection convinced them that such handiwork should not be shown their lords and masters; and they grew troubled lest they should see this masterpiece, and becoming dissatisfied with their spouses' needlework, eventually sue for divorce on grounds of incompetency, or some kindred cause. Then they desired I should teach them; but I protested that I never had taken lessons in that science, and that unless they could puzzle it out for themselves, the art, as an art, must be a lost one to them. Mine host heard of it, however, and to him I gave the garment. And it is said that he has caused to be preserved (by framing or some other way) that design in darning, and, having lopped off the legs for his youngest son, regards the remainder as an art treasure of the highest

MARIE.

value. If his wife gets refractory he has but to point with warning gesture at that specimen of needlework, and she at once subsides.

Even in this wild island, in the depths of the deepest forest, there exists that fear of Mrs. Grundy that smoulders in the human breast in town and city. Though the young people of the mountains go about for days and weeks with nothing on but a single gown or ragged shirt, when the time comes for going to town they must carry with them all they possess in the way of a wardrobe; and they will carry on their heads a large

Indian pannier, or basket, with nothing in it but their best clothes. When they reach the banks of the last stream nearest town they don their finery, and cram their unwilling feet into unaccustomed shoes, and then limp painfully into the metropolis, conscious that they are objects of envy and admiration.

They are really prettier in the more becoming costume of the mountains — a simple dress gathered about the hips, reaching to the knees; and men and boys handsomer in merely cotton pants, with broad breast and muscular arms exposed. I have seen the policemen, when in secluded country districts, walking with their shoes held carefully under their arm. Though improvident of time, these people are very careful of their clothing.

Jean Baptiste came in one day with a bunch of "grives," or large thrushes, which are excellent eating and desirable specimens. At my request he went down into the woods and showed me the tree on which, morning and afternoon, they could be found feeding. It was then noon, and I could not find any; but next morning I started out with the intention of bagging a few. Heavy showers came down every half-hour, but I donned my rubber poncho, and waded on through the wet forest, with my gun securely covered. My course lay down the south ravine. On the hill to the right was a tall *figuier* tree, the fruit of which is liked by the birds. This fruit resembles in shape, size and color, a cranberry, and is attached to the twigs in clusters of two and three.

Now, I could have sworn to the exact position of that tree; yet, having tramped doggedly through the rain for more than half an hour without seeing any familiar tree or shrub, I began to look about me sharply. Though I had noted the direction in my mind's eye when shown the tree, I overshot it in my search and got farther down. A group of tree-ferns I remembered; farther on, across a brook, was a large rock — all right; but where was the ants' nest in a dead tree that I had especially noted? To understand why all my landmarks were small and insignificant, the reader must be informed that in these woods the trees are so large and shoot up so high that their crowns afford no means of identifying them; and all their trunks are so much alike, enveloped in masses of vines and ferns, that other objects must be chosen to guide the hunter in his rambles here. Under thick foliage I went, until the roar of the large waterfall came up to me, and I knew I must retrace my steps, as the tree was on the ridge between the two streams.

At once I was stopped by seeing on the ground before me scattered shreds of *figuier* fruit, and looking up, saw the tree above me. As I had approached from the side opposite to that of my first visit, its surroundings had seemed changed. The rain came down in torrents, but glanced harmlessly from my poncho. It was tiresome waiting, but I secured all I wanted of the grives and went back to the main trail leading to the Boiling Lake, and sat down on a rock in a more open part of the forest, to try to secure a few humming-birds. The rain had ceased, and the sun was shining outside. Yielding to the overpowering influence of silence and solitude, I was indulging in a day-dream, when a voice awoke me:

"*Bon jour, monsieur!*"

I looked up, and saw two brown-skinned maidens. One was a little mulattress, about ten years old; the other was Marie — light-hearted, sunny Marie — in whose veins flowed the blood of three races. The blood of the African showed in her wavy hair and full lips, and told what was the original stock with which that of the Carib was mingled; and that of the jovial Frenchman, who had wandered to these wilds years and years ago, gave the roundness and suppleness of limb, the quick merry eye, the oval cheek, and little hands and feet.

"*Bon jour*, Mademoiselle Marie: where are you going?"

"*Pour chercher les écrevisse*" — To look for crayfish.

Crayfish! Why, just what I wanted; for I had promised one of the professors in Washington to make collections of these very animals. I glanced up through a hole in the leafy roof above me and judged it was about ten o'clock, unless the sun's rays were refracted in coming through.

"Have you anything for me to eat, Marie?"

"Yes, monsieur."

"Then I will go with you."

"It gives me much *plaisir*, monsieur."

"Well, lead the way."

Reader, if you look in a work on natural history for information regarding the crayfish, you will find it there given as a "long-tailed decapod;" and, pursuing the subject still farther, you will see that it is also crustacean — a "decapod crustacean." And thus you might follow the author up to the branch *articu-*

lata, and back again through all its divisions and ramifications, and all you will know about it will be that it is a long-tailed decapod, and inhabits freshwater streams.

Long-tailed decapod, forsooth!

Come with me, reader, and I will show you more of crayfish and their ways than you can learn in a week of books. Follow in my wake, or, as the path is slippery, take good hold of my hand. The way leads up hill and over rocks, wet and smooth, for perhaps a mile. Don't mind the wet leaves that continually flap in your face, or the vines and creeping ferns that vex your feet. Take a good grip and come along. In the language of the immortal bard (who, by the way, never knew of crayfish like these):

"I prithee, let me bring thee where crabs grow."

We may have completed a mile, when Marie stopped: "Stay here, monsieur." I staid, while she went behind a large rock and removed her shoes. Then I was allowed to follow on until the path was left, and we entered the deeper woods to descend to the river. Opposite another huge rock she stopped again. "Wait there, monsieur." Behind this rock she darted with her little companion, and shortly reappeared.

Satyrs and wood-nymphs! I thought these girls about as thinly clad as possible when they disappeared behind the rock, but I declare in all seriousness, they had left a large bundle of clothes behind.

What a mysterious combination is woman! And there they stood, laughing and blushing, in a single dress each, loosely gathered at the shoulders, and at the waist by a girdle. This was becoming serious. If there were any more rocks in our path, I felt morally certain they would dodge behind them. And then how would they appear? My hair began to bristle. I was resolved to stop it at all hazards.

" Look here, Marie ! "

" Yes, monsieur."

" Don't do that any more."

" What, monsieur ? "

" Don't go behind any more rocks; don't take off any more garments."

" Why no, monsieur ; it is impossible ! "

No amount of italicizing or exclamation-points can render the astonishment in her tone as she thus assured me ; and feeling that I could then safely proceed, I gave the order to go on. We reached the river — the stream that flows out of the mountain lake — broad and with gravelly beach, with immense bowlders as islands, and a wall of vegetation on either side that rose straight up a hundred feet. Here my guides left me to my own devices and waded into the stream in search of crayfish. I saw a bird I had not seen before, and pursued it along the shore until stopped by a cascade. It was within shot, however, and at the report of my gun it fell into a little pool. The rocks were smooth as glass, and my great boots, though good protection from the vines and thorns, were but poor aids in clambering over these rocks. The result was that I unexpectedly sat down upon a rock, and very suddenly I came down, too. There was a stream of water rushing over that rock six inches in depth, so that my fall did not hurt me ; but the rapid-flowing sheet struck my back with great force, and climbed up over my coat-collar so rapidly that I was immediately as bloated as a bull-frog. The rain had long ago drenched me, but, though wet before, I did not care to get wet behind.

My half-smothered yells brought Marie to my assistance, and she rescued me and the bird, and then suggested I could wade better with my boots off. Happy thought! The boots were removed. I need not detail, to any one who has had the experience, the pleasure of wading barefoot over stones and rocks for the first time in years. A little torture was enough for me, and in half an hour I was quietly seated, drying in the sun, watching the girls at their work. The stream was broad, with deep pools, and in these pools the crayfish lurked, looking like miniature lobsters through the clear water. I could see only the small ones, but Marie assured me there were large ones out of sight beneath the cascades. I was glad of that, for several severe nips from these small ones had given me enough of crayfish, and I did not care whether my friends in America ever got a specimen.

Erect upon the rock she stood a moment, then plunged head-foremost into a foaming pool, disappearing from sight. A moment later, rising bubbles preceded a round little head, from which hung long, limp tresses; a pair of shoulders brown and bare, and round arms and little hands reaching out for a support. She had a crayfish in each hand, and another, with wriggling legs, in her mouth. These she handed to the little girl on the rock near me, and then climbed out and stood erect, with heaving bosom and parted lips, and nonchalantly gathered up her dripping skirts and wrung from them the water. Outlined against that wonderful background of tropical leaves, with its depths of shade and gleams of light, with the water dashing against the rock upon which she stood, and parting in sheets of foam, what a charming naiad she appeared! Naiad she may have been, but she could hardly have been called a Dry-ad, as the water had caused her garment to cling closely to her shapely figure, and was pouring from it.

Once, breathless and excited, she arose, and came to me with an ugly water scorpion between her fingers, one of which was red and swollen, where the venomous thing had bitten it. Thus we went on up the stream until near the mountain lake, when our way was stopped by a jam of broken limbs. Then we turned down again until halted by a series of wells, worn from the rock by the action of the water, twenty feet deep, into which the flood plunged wildly, ever descending, on its way to the grand leap of two hundred feet into the valley below. While my companions searched a side stream I remained on the banks by the trail. Daylight waned and they came not; the gathering gloom urged me to be up and on my way home; but the trail was obscured, and I was not sure of reaching my hut in the dark without a guide. So I waited, perforce. Everything living seemed to have left the river's banks, and the only companion to my solitude was a gayly-colored lizard, which lay upon a branch and watched me. In the interest of science — but against my better feelings — I held a bottle before his nose, and he walked into it. Then I put in the cork, and later he was having his fill of rum; not the first victim of the bottle — and of science.

Voices reached me not long after, and none too

soon, for we had hardly light enough to reach the main path. Late as it was, however, Marie prepared some of the fish when she reached her mother's house, and sent them to me with some fragrant limes and a spicy pepper. The delicate flesh as far surpasses that of the coarse, garbage-feeding lobster in flavor, as a "saddle-rock" does a coon oyster. With a dripping of lime-juice and a dash of West India pepper, some Peak & Freans' biscuit and a bottle of Tennant's pale ale, I supped so delightfully that all my mishaps were forgotten. I even queried whether crayfish-hunting, with a dusky maiden of sixteen, who extended a helping hand when you slipped, laughed merrily when you fell, talked musical patois as she pattered along, were not better than hunting through musty books.

CHAPTER IV.

THE SUNSET-BIRD. — HUMMING-BIRDS.

THE CRATER-TARN. — TEMPORARY CAMPS. — THE "SOLEIL COU-
CHER." — "HEAR THE SUNSET." — A BIRD POSSESSED OF THE
DEVIL. — THE CAPTURE. — A SPECIES NEW TO THE WORLD. —
FOUR SPECIES OF HUMMING-BIRDS. — THE GARNET-THROAT
AND GILT-CRESTED. — DAN, THE HUNTER. — CATCHING BIRDS
WITH BREAD-FRUIT JUICE. — IN CAPTIVITY. — DEATH. — THEIR
FOOD. — METHODS OF CAPTURE. — THE HUMMING-BIRD GUN. —
THE AERIAL DANCE.

IN all the Caribbee Islands there are volcanoes, many of them still at work, ejecting, not lava, but steam and sulphur fumes. In the mountains one finds numerous tarns of clear, cold water, filling these extinct craters to the brim, and pouring their surplus flood down the mountain sides to form rivers in the valleys below. How came they there, these lakes of unknown depth? Are they fed by subterranean streams, or have the craters become choked, and, instead of vomiting forth water, and gases generated in the center of the earth, become merely receptacles for the drainage of surrounding mountains? Who knows? We only know that we cannot sound their depths with plummet-line, and that the water is pure and tasteless. Ages and ages have they existed here, and he must be more than geologist, and acquainted with the plans of a great Creator, who would answer these questions.

Such an one was the little lake above my first camp in the mountains. Twenty-three hundred feet above the sea, right in the crest of the mountain-ridge, surrounded by the most wonderful vegetation ever beheld by man, it reposed in solitude. On all sides but one the hills rose above it, dipping toward it and forming a hollow through which rushed the trade-winds from the Atlantic to the Caribbean Sea. The trail leading from sea to ocean passed near it, and a cave, hollowed from a clayey bank, gave shelter from rains to the passers-by and to the people from the coast who sometimes came marooning here. A tree-fern, between path and lake, arose above the matted carpet of wild plants beneath.

From my permanent camp I frequently went out into the forest for days, taking with me a young Indian as porter and guide. Leaving this mountain lake, one day, we took a little-used trail along the ridge to the northward. Late in the afternoon we came to another solitary lake, ringed round with giant trees. To my surprise, my guide at once made preparations for a camp, or an *ajoupa*, as he called the primitive structure hastily erected every night to shelter us from the damp.

Darkness settles swiftly in these tropic forests. No sooner is the sun down than night is upon you; consequently we always camped as soon as the sun had set, for traveling after dark in these wilds is a thing impossible.

I objected to camping then, thinking we had at least another hour of daylight, though I could not tell, the forest was so dense, when he quickly demanded: "What! you no hear the sunset?"

I was astonished. "*Hear* the sunset! No, certainly not!"

"Ah, monsieur, me no mean the great sun, *le grand soleil*, but the bird called the 'Sunset-bird,' '*Le Soleil Coucher.*'"

Here was a mystery, an object worthy of investigation — a bird that acted as the forester's clock, that told him the time to go to bed. At once I proposed to go in search of it; but my guide piteously protested, declaring that it was a "jumbie-bird,"— a bird possessed of the devil, — and that to kill it would not only endanger my life, but bring death to the settlement. Half an hour before sunset it utters its peculiar cry, and half an hour before sunrise; during the day it is silent.

"Listen!" said my guide. In a few minutes there rang through the forest a cry weird and mournful, yet having in its notes a resemblance to the words *soleil coucher*—the equivalent in patois for sunset. It was repeated by another bird and another, all around the lake, one answering another. In less than half an hour darkness had covered us, and the cries had ceased.

Grand old trees towered above me, their branches matted together and hung with cable-like vines. In the morning, I listened eagerly for a repetition of the sounds of the night before, and was out and away down to the lake-border with my gun, before my guide was awake, or daylight had made it safe to walk abroad. I was rewarded — "*soleil coucher!*" right over my head. Eagerly I gazed, but saw nothing. The sound was repeated, and by other birds. In the darkness it was impossible to distinguish anything, though never so near.

Impatiently I awaited the coming of dawn, which with its first indications rewarded my search. I saw a dusky body, a bird so small that I concluded it could not be the author of so loud a cry. But in a few minutes I noted it in the very act; and almost before it had finished its note, and while the final cadence was quavering on the air, the sound of my gun announced to my guide that the deed was done, and it was now too late to avert the vengeance of the evil spirits. Regardless of his lamentations, I stood absorbed in the contemplation of the bird now in my hand. That it was a *new* bird I felt certain, and immediately — as soon as my agitation had subsided — I wrote a description of it.

In shape and size it resembles the "king-bird," so familiar to dwellers of the north; it is eight and one-half inches in length; its upper plumage is dark brown; quills brownish-black; under the wings pale yellow; throat and upper parts of breast and sides clear bluish-gray; portion of breast and under parts pale yellow; bill broad and thin, and black like the feet.*

Six months later this bird reposed in the Museum at Washington, and I received from the ornithologists (as I was then at work in a distant island) a notification to the effect that it was a *new* species, and had been named the *Myiarchus Oberi*. Though I afterward discovered many new birds, there was not one with which it would have given me greater satisfaction to have my name identified.

* The reader is referred, for farther information upon the birds captured by the author, to the list of Birds of the Lesser Antilles, in the Appendix.

Standing there by that silent lake, the morning mist enshrouding me, that strange bird in my hand, I fell at once into a train of musing suggested by the thought that this might prove a species new to the world. There is something in such a thought inexpressibly thrilling : to feel that to you alone has been vouchsafed the first glance at a being that has existed for ages undiscovered and unknown ; has lived and breathed and sung, generation after generation of the same type ; and that you, who now hold its breathless form in your hand, are the first to look upon it ! At this age of the world, when man has searched the remotest confines of the globe, to find an animal so high in the scale as this — that has heart and lungs, and in whose veins the blood courses warm and red — is considered an event worthy of chronicling in annals that endure for more than a single generation.

Like these were my reflections that morning, — meditations that caused me to ignore the superstition of my ignorant friend, whose uneasiness regarding the lives of those whom he considered I had placed in jeopardy, was not soon allayed.

Four species of humming-birds greeted me in my first camp in the tropics. They fairly lit up the valley with their gleaming coats; not a bush or tree in flower that did not have one or more hovering above it from morning till night.

Until the New World was discovered, the humming-bird was not known to Europe. Though roaming from the Arctic Circle to the Antarctic, it is ever American, and never extends its migrations beyond the limits of the Western continents. Of all the creations of bird-life this is the most beautiful, the most minute. Depending upon no single feature for attraction, — upon no one plume or tuft of feathers, like the bird of paradise, upon no broad-spread, glaring colors, like the parrot, — it is, in fact, the *gem* of the feathered world. So often have poet and naturalist compared it, in the brilliance of its flashing colors, to the gems of the mineral kingdom, that they have left little to be said, and I can but repeat that it is now a topaz, now an emerald, a turquoise, or a ruby.

East of the Mississippi and north of Florida there is but one species that can be called a regular visitor; this is the well-known ruby-throated humming-bird of the North. As we go south we find them increasing, both in species and in number, until the region of greatest abundance is reached near the Equator.

In Dominica, half-way down the Antilles, and sixteen degrees north of the Equator, I found four species to replace the single one visiting the North, the smallest of which were as large as the ruby-throat, and the largest two inches longer.

This latter is called the garnet-throated hummer, and is five and one-half inches in length, and seven in stretch of wing. It is the most abundant, as well as the most beautiful, and loves the mountain valleys, where are gardens of plantains and fragrant flowers. Its bill and feet are black; a brilliant gorget of garnet extends from beak to breast, each feather of which is semicircular, and of the deepest crimson with gold reflections. It should be seen poised in air hovering above a flower, or preening itself upon a dry branch, with the full blaze of a tropic sunshine glancing from its throat, for one to form an adequate conception of its beauty. The back is black with a blue shade, like blue-black velvet; wing and tail-coverts rich green with bronze reflections; all the feathers, be it noticed, changing with every light that falls upon them. There are two species that measure an inch less in length, that have the crimson or garnet throat replaced by metallic green and violet, and with backs of green instead of blue-black. The fourth, and smallest, is a little fellow, found everywhere, from coast to mountain-top, in the gardens of the town and over the barren hills. From his eccentric motions, he is called the "*fou-fou*," or crazy-crazy, for he darts hither, thither, up, down, round and round, with seemingly aimless purpose. He is sober in hue, and has only a little pointed crest to give him beauty. But this little helmet of metallic green, now shining golden, now purple even, and steel-blue, flashes every ray of the sun from its bright surface. His head is generally carried with the beak pointing downward, so that the crest is always seen to the best advantage. .

There were three little *chasseurs* who used to supply me with every bug and bird within their reach. It takes a boy, especially a boy of the woods, to find out the haunts of the denizens of the forest; and but for these little collectors, my specimens would have been fewer in number. Let us follow little Dan, the eldest and sharpest of the humming-bird hunters, as he goes out for birds. First he goes to a tree called the mountain palm, which replaces the cocoa palm in the mountains, the latter growing only along the coast. Beneath the tree are some fallen leaves, fifteen feet in length; these he seizes and strips, leaving the mid-rib bare, a long, slender stem, tapering

HUMMING-BIRD HUNTERS.

to a point. Upon this tip he places a lump of bird-lime, to make which he had collected the inspissated juice of the bread-fruit, and chewed it to the consistency of soft wax. Scattered over the savanna are many clumps of flowering bushes, over whose crimson and snowy blossoms humming-birds are dashing, inserting their beaks in the honeyed corollas; after active forays, resting upon some bare twig, pruning and preening their feathers. Cautiously creeping toward a bush upon which one of these little beauties is resting, the hunter extends the palm-rib, with its treacherous coating of gum. The bird eyes it curiously, but fearlessly, as it approaches his resting-place, even pecking at it; but the next moment he is dangling helplessly, beating the air with buzzing wings in vain efforts to escape the clutches of that tenacious gum.

The humming-birds brought me alive, I would place in a large gauze-covered box; but they seldom survived many days, notwithstanding great care. If exposed to the light, they kept up a constant fluttering until the muscles of their wings became so stiff they could not close them, and they expired with wings wide outstretched. Some would take their captivity quietly, and though flitting now and then to the front of the box when light was admitted, would sit upright upon the perch, giving an occasional chirp, and dressing their feathers as serenely as if in the open air. They would seem happy and cheerful; but the fact is, they are creatures of light and sunshine, and cannot exist without it. You may give them their favorite food of honey and insects, fresh flowers every day, with the morning dew yet dripping from them, and yet, despite your tenderest care, they will droop and die.

It is touching to witness the death of one of these innocent beings. Though I have caused more than one to lose its life, I never did it without a pang, as though I were committing a great wrong. To shoot a bird at a distance, and have him fall at a distance without a struggle, is not the same as to see him die in your hand. To watch the feeble fluttering of the stiffening wings, the expiring glance of the fast-dimming eye, the painful pulsations of the gentle heart, the last quiver when all is over, — ah! how often has my conscience reproached me when looking upon such a scene. Again and again I have almost resolved never to kill another bird, and only the thought that I was doing this work in the interest of science kept me to my purpose.

The little crested sprite bears confinement less easily than the others, and rarely survives two or three days. Every morning I would introduce a bough of fragrant lime-blossoms, at which they would all dash instantly, diving into the flowers with great eagerness. Sugar dissolved in water, and diluted honey, was their favorite food, and they would sip it greedily. Holding them by their feet, I would place their beaks in a bottle of syrup, when they would rapidly eject their tongues and withdraw them, repeating this operation until satisfied. The long slender tube, at that time, looks like the tongue of a serpent, it is so deeply cleft, or bifurcated. They never displayed fear, but would readily alight on my finger and glance fearlessly up at me, watching an opportunity, however, for escape.

In some of the islands, Martinique especially, the boys shoot the small birds with pellets of clay or hard, round seeds, through hollow canes lined with zinc or glass. They kill a great many in this way.

The week before leaving America for the West Indies I was the guest of a friend, who one day came in with an odd-looking cane in his hand, and said: "This is a gun I am going to give you to use in the West Indies. It is for shooting humming-birds. And you will value it all the more highly when I tell you that it once belonged to Dr. Bryant, who used it in his numerous excursions in the Bahamas." Dr. Bryant, a naturalist of note, and donor to the Boston Society of Natural History of the unsurpassed La Fresnaye collection of birds, spent many years in the West Indies previous to his death, and contributed much to our knowledge of the ornithology of those islands. The gun looked, as I said, like a cane. The barrel was slender, and painted to resemble a stick of mahogany; the stock unscrewed, and could be put in the pocket; and as the ramrod went inside the barrel, where it was secured by a tompion, and hammer and trigger shut down out of sight, this gun made a very convenient walking-stick. Doubly valued by me on account of having belonged to my friend and to a naturalist whom all the world knew, this gun accompanied me in all my wanderings. It was an excellent arm, and I have shot more than five hundred birds with it alone. Not only on humming-birds, but on larger game, did I try its shooting qualities. For hummers it needed but a taste of powder and a thimbleful of dust shot.

Not for the collecting of specimens merely was my mission; I was to obtain all the information possible of the habits of the birds — of their *home* life. It was in this study of them in their forest retreats that I took keen delight, and considered the shooting of them as a necessary evil to procure their identification.

In one of my daily rambles for this purpose, I entered a gloomy glen in the deep forest. Soon as my eyes became accustomed to the gloom, I espied a humming-bird dancing in the air. There was not a flower in sight, and he did not fly as when in pursuit of nectar-bearing flowers, but hovered more on suspended wing, darting sidewise, backward and forward, with the body in an almost erect position. If through the deep shade a sunbeam slanted athwart the glen, his throat gleamed like a ruby. Now, this fantastic dance was not for pleasure, but for food. I ascertained that at such times they are in pursuit of insects; have seen the insect swarms, and so long as there remain any in sight—and even long after they have disappeared from *my* view—the bird darts hither and thither, snapping them up with great rapidity. At such times he does not content himself with a sip here and there and then alight upon some twig or liane, as when gathering honey, but evidently considers the fleeting nature of the prey he is pursuing, and shoots from one hunting-ground to another till he has obtained his fill.

Beneath me, lining the walls of a deep gorge in whose depths a little rivulet tinkled, was a broad area of the plant called by the natives *balisier*, or wild plantain. The leaves of this plant are about six feet in length, broad and green, like the leaves of a banana. From the bases of these leaves shoot up long spikes of crimson and yellow cups, arranged like the flowers of the gladiolus. They are boat-shaped and about three inches in length, and their bright colors lighted up this shady spot like sunshine. Above their broad silken leaves Garnet-throat hovered a moment to scan the interior of these flowers, perchance he might see an insect for him there. A sudden desire came over me to possess the bird, and quick as the thought was formed my gun was at my shoulder, and its sharp report echoed through the silent woods. High and low I searched, but could not find him, until, looking down upon the spot for a final glance, I caught sight of his gleaming throat which a stray sunbeam had lighted on. He lay enshrined in one of those golden caskets, leg uplifted and wings loose spread, eclipsing even those bright tints of orange and crimson in the vivid glow of his gorget.

CHAPTER V.

THE BOILING LAKE OF DOMINICA.

A WILD CAT. — TREE-FERNS. — MOUNTAIN PALMS. — A RARE HUMMING-BIRD. — THE VALLEY OF DESOLATION. — MISLED BY A BOTTLE. — BOILING SPRINGS. — HOT STREAMS. — SULPHUR BATHS. — THE SOLFATARA. — BUILDING THE AJOUPA. — COOKING BREAKFAST IN A BOILING SPRING.

> Dominica's fire-cleft summits
> Rise from bluest of blue oceans;
> Dominica's palms and plantains
> Feel the trade-wind's mighty motions,
> Swaying with impetuous stress
> The West Indian wilderness.
> . . . . . .
> Dominica's crater-caldron
> Seethes against its lava-beaches;
> Boils in misty desolation; —
> Seldom foot its border reaches;
> Seldom any traveler's eye
> Penetrates its barriers high.
>   LUCY LARCOM.

THE record of the weather for a month: showery, cool and delightful. On the coast it was ten degrees hotter; but in this elevated valley, two thousand feet above the sea, the eastern peaks caught the flying clouds from the "trades" and precipitated their burden of moisture.

THE BOILING LAKE.

For two weeks I had been awaiting a change of the moon that was expected to bring a drier season, and one night my friend Jean Baptiste came to my hut with the welcome news, "To-morrow make weddah." As he predicted, the weather cleared. There came to me the sons and nephews of Jean Baptiste (four in number), who were laden, and departed one after the other. François had a large Carib pannier filled with yams, coffee and eggs, a blanket, his never-absent cutlass, and a gun; Michael took my camera, a bag of provisions, cutlass and gun; Joseph, my dark box with photographic chemicals, cutlass and gun; Seeyohl, a large sack of yams and plantains, cutlass and gun. With my game-basket and humming-bird gun, I followed immediately after my guides.

We crossed the three streams hurrying from the mountain to the precipice, where they are compressed into two magnificent waterfalls, and climbed the hills beyond, over a path of interlaced roots, from among which the earth had been washed, leaving a perfect ladder, which served us both in ascending and descending. Past one of the little "provision grounds," where, among fallen and decayed trees, were growing lusty plantains, bananas, yams and tanniers; across another stream and up farther to the crown of the ridge, where the path led through cool and open "high woods," where the sun "can't come," and where *perdrix*, or mountain doves, sprang up from all about us, and *ramiers*, or wood-pigeons, dashed in and out of the tall tree-crowns. At eleven o'clock we reached "La Rivière Déjeûner," where we breakfasted upon boiled eggs and yams, with clear cold water for drink.

Our dogs (we had four curs trained to hunt the

agouti) left us in the middle of our meal and darted into the forest with loud yelps. François followed them, encouraging them with peculiar cries; for these mountaineers have a sympathetic understanding with all animate objects about them, and can guide, hie on and recall their dogs simply by varying their voice. François urged them on, but in a few minutes they came to a stand-still, and their excited yelps assured us that whatever they were pursuing was brought to bay. We thought they had an *agouti* — a small animal, in size between a rabbit and a woodchuck — but the execrations of François a little later, which preceded his appearance from the deep shade, prepared us for the unwonted sight, in these wilds, of a wild cat. It was not a wild cat in the true sense of the word — not a *Lynx rufus* — being only a " *chat maron* " — a cat of the domesticated species run wild. It was gray in color, striped with black, and larger and more strongly made than the cats of the coast, who do not have to forage for a living; showing how, in time, a new species might be possibly the result of this change of life. It lives in the deep woods, preying upon small birds, lizards and crabs, and is as savage and untamable as any specimen of the genus to be found in American back-woods. My men skinned it at my request and wrapped the skin in a plantain leaf, to be hung up until our return. The most weird thing about this animal was the eye; the iris yellow, changing to green, but seen glowering from darkness it was red — blood-red — red as fire, that glaring, glassy red which I have seen in the panther, and which makes the wild *felidæ* so terrible to face in their lairs.

We had here to climb the sides of a steep gorge, the

walls of which were almost perpendicular, where slippery roots and hanging lianes only, enabled us to accomplish the ascent. One portion of our route was through a bowl-shaped depression containing a few acres, in which seemed concentrated all the glorious vegetation indigenous to these tropical forests. Hundreds and thousands of plants of strange and beautiful shapes were massed together in prodigal confusion. Conspicuous among them was the grand tree-fern.

Those who have seen in glass-house or garden of acclimatization, only, the stunted specimens of this plant, can form hardly a conception of the grandeur of these arborescent ferns in their native homes. They are rarely found in perfect development at a lesser altitude than one thousand feet above the sea, and it is in the " high-woods " belt alone that they attain their greatest height and perfect symmetry. They love cool and moist situations, revel in shade and delight in solitude. " If," says Humboldt, "they descend toward the sea coast, it is only under cover of thick shade." I have seen them in these mountains, in the vegetable zone most favorable for their growth — that between fifteen hundred and twenty-five hundred feet above the sea — of a height of thirty or thirty-five feet. Then, truly, were they impressive in their combination of delicately traced leaves and slender stems; essentially children of the tropics. There is sublimity in their expression. There is a suggestiveness of a benediction in those lace-like leaves, which are spread above the head of the observer like outstretched hands, and which only move gently and tremulously, ever pulsating to the slightest breath of air. The light that filters through the cocoa-palm leaves is wonderfully lambent and golden, but cannot compare with the chastened sunbeams that reach one standing beneath this queen of the mountain solitudes; perchance the sun can penetrate to it. There are several species, one of which, with unusually prickly stem (the *Cyathea Imrayana*), is named for Doctor Imray, a resident botanist of the island.

Though the ferns replace, in a measure, the palms, in the ascent from coast to mountain-top, yet there is one species that climbs to as high an altitude as the fern, and is found everywhere on the mountain side until the sub-alpine vegetation is reached. This is the mountain palm, the "palmiste montagne," the "mountain cabbage," *Euterpe montana*. Euterpe, goddess of lyric poetry; no tree of the forest more fitly symbolizes the realm of song over which she presides. In every curve and movement is grace and feeling, whether the long leaves wave gently to the mid-day breeze, or whether they beat wildly their sustaining trunks in the violence of the hurricane. It is not tall for a palm, but is slender and has a lovely crown, and ministers to the wants of the mountaineers in many ways, as will be seen farther on. Inhabiting the same region with the tree-fern and loving the same cool, solitary shades, it accompanies it in its march up the mountains, and ceases with it at the upper edge of the high-woods belt. Two such creations were enough to give these forests world-wide fame; but there are a thousand others which I cannot describe for want of knowledge, nor if I could, for lack of space.

We passed streams every half-mile large enough to turn a mill in the rainy season, but which were then low. Up their rocky beds the trail pursued its way;

rough, slippery work it was, with many watery escapades and some falls — waterfalls. Through dense groups of callas, and other water plants, we were obliged to force our way. At a jam of trees which I was painfully climbing, I saw a humming-bird poised above a flower. I had been sufficiently long in these mountains, I thought, to procure every species; but this was different from any I had shot, and consequently he was at once added to my other victims, and was picked up below by one of my guides, as he floated like a golden leaf upon the stream. It proved to be a rare species, found heretofore only at the mouth of the Amazon, and rare even there; (the *Thalurania wagleri*); and it now rests in Washington, one of the many types of West Indian birds I had the pleasure of sending to our National Museum.

Leaving the stream, we climbed another steep hillside, and traveled along a ridge, on either side of which are valleys leading to the sea and ocean. *Perdrix* and *grives*, or thrushes, started up at intervals. The "*siffleur montagne*" (the "mountain whistler") sent up liquid melody from every ravine; warblers were few, and humming-birds the only ones abundant. These, and even insects, grew rare and finally ceased entirely as the lake valley was reached, and the sulphur fumes, ever increasing in volume, were borne to us in dense clouds. We made a detour and again took the stream, now lessened to a trickling run, where everything was decaying, reeking with moisture, and slippery with confervoid growth. No snakes appeared now, not even a lizard; animal life was absent in this approach to the infernal regions. The trail was barricaded by fallen trees, detached rocks, tangled lianas; flowers were few, the crimson cups of the wild plantain were alone conspicuous.

After three hours of hard scrambling we were rewarded by a view of the first sulphur valley containing the "*petite soufrière*," from which steam ascended in clouds. It is a basin several hundred feet deep, one side of which is broken down, surrounded by steep hills, the valley walls of which, mostly denuded by land-slides, are covered elsewhere by a sparse growth of vegetation. Seeing an opening in the trees, I prepared to descend, though the trail was faint and appeared old. But, being in advance and impatient to get at the wonder below, I ventured alone, and had proceeded but a few rods when I was assured by the sight of a familiar object — a bottle — on a stick. I am not sure but that a sight of it caused me to depart from the beaten path; at any rate, I was diverted, though the bottle was in-verted. A shout from above halted me just as I had reached the brink of a precipitous bank, the earth of which was beginning to crumble beneath my feet. Dejectedly I retraced my steps, my faith in the goodness of mankind somewhat shaken. Months later, while conversing with a good friend — Dr. Nicholls, of Roseau — it came out that he was the culprit; that he had placed the bottle there in the kindness of his heart, as the good Indian is said to have set up a stake in every bog in which he got bemired, as a warning to others.

A warning! In this thirsty land a bottle is as necessary to one's existence as a loaf of bread; and I have met with those who held it more directly essential to the preservation of life than the generally recognized "staff."

THE TROPIC STREAM.

Nearly half an hour's careful work was necessary to descend that steep wall, clinging to roots and stems of small trees, at the end of which we reached a gentle slope facing south, covered with trees of goodly size. Here were the remains of an old encampment, empty bottles and sulphur specimens. A stream trickled near by, which we followed to the sulphur basin, whence sulphuretted fumes ascended that would have choked out the stench of a thousand rotten eggs. This was but the beginning of the valley of wonders, the portal to the enchanted land of mysteries. The basin was covered with rocks and earth, white and yellow, perforated like the bottom of a colander, whence issued steam and vapor and sulphur fumes, hot air and fetid gases. There was a full head of steam on, puffing through these vents with the noise of a dozen engines. There were spouting springs of hot water; some were boiling over the surface, some sending up a hot spray, some puffing like high-pressure steamers. Clouds of steam drifted across this small valley, now obscuring every rock and hole, now lifting a few feet, only to settle again. The silver in my pockets and the brass mountings of my camera were soon discolored to a blue-black hue. Several streams ran out and down, uniting in a common torrent: streams hot, impregnated with sulphur; streams cold, clear and sparkling, only a yard apart; water of all colors, from blue and green to yellow and milk-white.

The heat of a West Indian noon was made tenfold oppressive by the hot, moisture-laden atmosphere. My foot slipped, as we groped our way through the clouds of vapor, and got slightly scalded by breaking through the thin crust that covered the boiling caldron beneath. We descended between huge white rocks and bleached and dying trees to a stream of marvelous beauty, picking our way among volcanic bowlders. At once the scene changed; we entered a ravine through which flowed the streams from above, now mingled in one tepid torrent, along whose banks grew, rank and luxuriant, plants of such tropic loveliness as made me hold my breath in delight and surprise. Everywhere plashed and tinkled musical waterfalls and cascades; from all sides little streams came pouring in their tribute; here a cold and sparkling stream, there another boiling hot, its track betokened by a wreath of steam. There were tree-ferns, wild plantains, palms, orchids and wild pines, tropical vines, lianas, strange flowers, gay epiphytes. Up and down and across stretched the lianas, forming a net-work which my guides were obliged to sever repeatedly with their great cutlasses. Along the bank of this stream and through the water we walked in delight — at least I did — for it seemed a very tropical Eden. And yet on all sides of us was barrenness and desolation; these beautiful forms were all created by the action of hot water upon the scanty soil. Climbing, slipping, scrambling, we at last reached a steep hill-side, where trees of different kinds were growing; and here we rested, for here was the spot selected for our camp.

But there yet remained the Lake, to which all these strange sights were but preparatory scenes. It was but a twenty-minutes' walk, or climb, to the basin. We could hear it roaring behind the hill. Leaving superfluous luggage, and two men to make camp, I started on again with nothing but gun and photographic apparatus. We reached another river, which was tumbling noisily over blanched tree-trunks and sulphur-encrusted rocks, and came out of a large mound of scoriæ and pumice white as snow. Its water was milk-white from the quantity of magnesia held in solution, and steaming hot. Into it poured minor streams of every shade, from white to ochreous, and one black as ink.

Up over large rocks, covered with soft sphagnum, green and white in color; up, over and through rapids and around falls, passing feeding streamlets of hot, cold, mineral and pure water by turns, into a basin (at the immediate base of a high mountain), with heaps of sulphur-stones scattered over a smooth floor of bitumen, with a jet of steam escaping here and there from a hole or fissure in its quaking crust; up the banks of a little stream of sulphur water, subterranean at times, leaving the rivers behind us, and having a steep bank before us, which we quickly scaled, and there revealed to our gaze, lay the Lake.

My first feeling was that of disappointment, for the surface of the lake, usually so turbulent, was placid, save in the center a slight movement — more from the escape of gas than from ebullition — disturbed it, and sent ever-expanding wavelets to the shore. It is sunk in a huge basin, which it has hollowed out for itself. Undoubtedly, it was once a spring, or geyser, which, by the volume and violence of its flow, increased and deepened the aperture through which it escaped, until it reached its present dimensions.

The height of its surrounding walls I estimate at from eighty to one hundred feet, and its diameter at from three hundred to four hundred. As there have been no accurate measurements — indeed, the total number of white men who have looked upon it is not a score — its area will long be a matter of speculation only. The banks are of ferruginous earth, with stones and rocks imbedded, as nearly perpendicular as their consistency will allow, and constantly caving and falling in.

Two streams of cold water fall into the lake on the north, above which rise high hills. Down the bed of one of these we found a place to leap. My apparatus was passed down, and I at once proceeded to secure a picture of the lake. It was then four o'clock, and the sun had dropped very near the margin of the western hills, and just lingered sufficiently to allow me to secure the first photograph ever made in these mountains. Well for me the lake was in a state of quiescence. Well for the success of my picture that the water was not in a wild fury of ebullition, and that its basin was not filled with steam, as it had ever been found before.

Directly opposite the stream in which I stood was the rent in the wall through which flowed the overflow from the lake, when it was at its work, through which at such times poured a stream of sulphur-water that formed a torrent and descended to the coast below. Through this gap I could look away south, across and over green mountains to the shores of Martinique gleaming through the mist in the waning sunlight, twenty miles away, yet seemingly within an hour's row of yonder ridge. This rent is from thirty to forty feet in width at the top, and perhaps fifty in depth.

I descended to the lake margin. The rim of recent subsidence was clearly defined: a belt of black, yellow and gray deposit, some three feet wide. It was narrower on the second day, and the ebullition had much increased, showing that, though I was the first to discover it in repose, it must be intermittent in character, and was then preparing to boil forth again. For this effect I waited long, much desiring to see it in that state, but was not gratified, though the disturbance and noises continued to increase and the water to rise.

The temperature of the water, as far out as I could reach my thermometer, was ninety-six degrees; of the air at the same time, sixty-seven degrees; of the streams falling into the lake, sixty-five degrees, Fahrenheit. Some months previously, Dr. Nicholls, one of the original exploring party who discovered this lake, found it at a temperature of one hundred and ninety-six degrees; and Mr. Prestoe, of the Botanic Gardens of Trinidad, recorded from one hundred and eighty to one hundred and ninety degrees. They also found it fiercely boiling, the whole crater filled with steam, and could obtain only occasionally a glimpse of the water and surrounding walls. They found no bottom with a line one hundred and ninety-five feet long, ten feet from the water's edge. With Mr. Prestoe, I conclude that this solfatara, by widening and deepening its outlet, will eventually lose its lake character and become merely a geyser.

From the high bank above the lake, near the gap through which the waters find egress, is a fine view of the whole northern wall, with the streams falling down from the background of mountain, the hollows and miniature valleys and peaks beyond. The river-bed below is dry and yellow; but huge rocks, tons in weight, that the waters have moved from their beds, attest the force of the current when the lake is at its height. From the north, coming down into another desolate valley, are small streams — yellow, white, green, blue. A spring boils up through a hole three feet across, overtopping the surface eight inches or more. The main volume of hot water comes from higher up the mountains, and there is, I think, another source as large as this, which at present is unknown. The mountains around are green with low shrubs, and from the bank above the lake I secured a giant lycopodium, which is not found elsewhere in any abundance.

We retraced our steps about an hour before sunset, and found on the hillside a comfortable camp, constructed by François and Joseph during our absence. The *ajoupa*, or camp constructed in haste, is a peculiarity of these forests. Regarding the etymology of the word, I am in doubt. Humboldt speaks of the *ajupas*, or kings' houses, among the Caribs of South America, which were used as houses of entertainment for travelers. Whatever the origin of the term, it is now fixed in the patois of the mountaineers to designate a hut thrown up hastily for temporary occupation — what we, in America, would call a "camp." My men first constructed a framework of light poles, tied together with roots and vines, and covered it with the broad leaves of the *balisier*, or wild plantain (*Heliconia behia*). This plant, which grows everywhere in shade and moisture, is one of the attractive features of the vegetation here. Its leaf is like an elongated banana-leaf, but not so wide, and with greater strength and toughness.

Like the palm, this plant serves a great variety of uses. Its root is boiled and fed to hogs, I believe; the mid-rib of the leaf is stripped and split and woven into baskets; the leaves are used for the thatching of huts, as substitutes for table-cloths and plates in the woods, as envelopes in which to wrap anything of soft nature, as butter or honey, — in fact, as wrapping for everything portable, the tissue is so fine and flexible. The young leaves are our substitute for drinking-cups; and it is more convenient to twist off an overhanging leaf and throw it away when done, than to bear about with you a clumsy cup. Its utility, then, is second only to that of the cocoa palm.

They had brought up huge bundles of the leaves from the river below. Slicing the under side of the mid-rib half-way through with a diagonal cut, leaving a barb by which to attach it to the cross-pole, François handed the leaves to Joseph, who rapidly placed them in position, attached to the pole and kept in place by the projecting point, one row overlapping the other. In a short time they had made a thick roof, completely impervious to water, which was good for a week, so long as the leaves remained green and were not split and shrunken by the sun.

A raised platform of poles, all cut with the cutlass, was covered with a good layer of leaves, and upon this I spread my blanket and reposed quietly all night, my faithful boys stretched upon the ground, lulled to sleep by the rushing of the waterfalls.

"La belle," the firefly, illumined our camp in the evening, and an odorous fire of the gum of the flambeau-tree gave both light and fragrant incense. Over this, Joseph, in his French patois and broken English, told the story of the discovery of the lake by Mr. Watt, the one who first surmised its existence, in 1875. This gentleman, a magistrate in the colony, was prone to wander in the mountains in search of adventure. One day he had penetrated farther than usual, by following a valley that led up into the interior, and noticed in the air distinct and powerful sulphur fumes. Later, he set out to ascertain the cause, taking with him two negroes as guides, but, through the pusillanimity of his men, who abandoned him, was lost in the forest for several days. Let Joseph tell the story:

"Monsieur Watt he walk, walk, walk, pour tree day; he lose hees clo's, hees pant cut off, he make nozing pour manger but root; no knife, no nozing; hees guide was neegah [the mountaineers, though some of them negroes themselves, have great contempt for town negroes] ; zey was town neegah, and leab him and loss him. He come to black man's house in ze wood, and ze black man zink he *jombie*, and he run; when he come back wiz some mo' men, for look for *jombie*, Monsieur Watt he make coople of sign, he have to lost hees voice and was not speak, and zey deescover heem."

At daybreak we were stirring. I descended the bank and waded up the stream to take my morning bath. There were two streams, one hot, one cold, which ran in near channels, meeting below. Following the warm one, stepping from pool to pool, I reached a fall about twelve feet in height, surrounded by a wealth of tropical plants, from the depths of which it suddenly appeared. And it was hot — or just as hot as skin could bear — as I sidled under it, first a hand, then an arm, then a shoulder, until the whole volume of warm water fell squarely upon my head. Ah! it was the perfection of luxurious sensations. I essayed to shout aloud in my delight, but the falling water drowned my voice, and I paddled in the pool in silent ecstasy, drawing in long breaths, and allowing the rushing of the water, the delicious warmth of the bath, the flying spray, to lull me to repose. I think I should have fallen asleep had I not been warned, by slipping from the rock on which I sat, that I was becoming unconscious. It was too blissful to leave, too soothing, and I stepped from under the warm douche only to return again and again. Reaching out my hand, I placed it in a stream of cold water, sulphur water at that, while I sat in this tepid bath.

What benefits might be derived by those unfortunates afflicted with rheumatism and kindred complaints, from a dip in these healing waters! They would need a balloon, though, as means of conveyance, for only travel-toughened backs and sturdy limbs can accomplish this journey at present.

My guides boiled coffee, and, that imbibed, we shouldered our traps and marched back on the homeward trail. We reached the first Soufrière — the valley of desolation — and halted, to allow me to take a few photographs, and to cook our breakfast. The sulphur fumes were so strong as to form a coating of sulphide of silver on my negatives, but not to an extent to injure them.

The largest boiling spring is five feet across. As some of these seemingly boiling springs are not in complete ebullition, but have their waters agitated from escape of gases, I took care to plunge my thermometer into all. Several registered two hundred and eight degrees — the lake is more than two thousand feet above sea-level — and many one hundred and forty and one hundred and sixty degrees. One unfortunate experimenter, later in the season, plunged a "store" thermometer into one of these springs, and burst it, as its capacity was not equal to such high temperature.

Perforating the broad fields of calcined stones are little holes, whence issue steam and hot air; very few are inactive. Some, on the hillside, are large as an open grate, and have that shape. Into these you can look deep down into black holes, sulphur crystals in beautiful golden needles lining throat and flue. It required great care not to break through the crust in many places. My guide was constantly warning me: "Have attention where you make you feets!"

While I was preparing chemicals and collecting minerals, my boys were busily cooking our breakfast; and they prepared it without fire, too, and so expeditiously as to cause me wonder. In the forest they had found some wild yams; François had shot a few giant thrushes; there were a few eggs remaining of those we had brought with us.

Curiously I watched them at their work. Tying the yams in a bit of cloth, and tying that to the end of a stick, Joseph thrust them into the large boiling spring. A few minutes later — I do not know just how many — he drew them out completely boiled. The eggs were treated in like manner, and lastly the birds. Then we withdrew to the shade of a near clump of balisiers, on the bank of a clear spring, plucked a few leaves for plates, for cups, for napkins, for protection from the damp earth as we sat down, sprinkled our curiously-cooked food with pepper and salt, and feasted merrily, though half strangled by the sulphur fumes. In watching this cooking process, I could not but think of our own wonderful geysers in the Yellowstone, where explorers caught trout in a stream and cooked them in a boiling spring, without removing the fish from the hook or changing their own positions.

Then we turned our backs upon this valley of wonders — this collection of craters within a crater long ago inactive. My guides placed their loads upon their heads, and we climbed the hills, keeping time to the rhythmic pulsations of a steam-vent, which ejected its vapor with regular puffs, the din of which rang through the forest.

I cannot but feel how poor and meagre is this description of that wonderful Boiling Lake, hid in the bosom of those solitary mountains in that tropical island. The time may come — and it will be better for Americans if it were speedily to come — when the great attractions of these islands will be better known, and I may not be able to say, as I say now with truth, I am the only American who has seen Dominica's Boiling Lake.

We reached Rivière Déjeûner just at dark. I was ahead. And here let me explain how I acquired a reputation as a pedestrian, and why, if you speak of the writer to one of these mountaineers, he will shrug his shoulders and exclaim, "Ah! Monsieur Fred, he walk like ze debbil!" Here is a statement of the reason; and I leave it to any sane person if he would not have done the same under similar cirstances:

Each member of our party had a gun — my four men and myself. In going up and down those cliffs, the guns carried by my guides were sure to point at me, no matter how I would try to dodge them. If I lagged behind, I was confronted by a black muzzle; if I went ahead, two or more pointed at my exposed back. Now, I have carried a gun ever since I could well use one, and for two years have had one constantly by my side; but I never allow one to be pointed at me, if I am aware of it. Going homeward, I stretched my legs to their utmost, and kept ahead, scrambling over rocks and tree-trunks, and swinging myself down steep banks by the roots of trees. My trowsers were torn into shreds; the perspiration started, legs shook, and arms trembled. But I was determined to keep out of range of those dreaded guns; and I did, arriving at my cabin full half an hour ahead of my guides, who had supposed me lost and had detailed two of their number to look me up. Jean Baptiste, my host and forager-for-food, stood in the doorway with a candle, and inside there stood a welcome table with a good supper — yams and eggs and tender mountain cabbage.

Speaking of my hot bath to Jean Baptiste, that jewel instantly exclaimed that he had forgotten to show me the best in the island, situated only a gun-shot from my hut. Next day we visited it. Beneath tall gommier trees stretching down lianes forty feet long, shaded by broad-leaved plantains, was a pool twenty feet across, made by damming a little brooklet with volcanic rock. Its bottom was stone and gravel. A tree-trunk had fallen across the stream, on which I threw my clothes. The runlet was tepid, the pool a little warmer. Suddenly my foot grew hot, as though stung by a scorpion, and I became aware that the pool was heated from below by small jets of hot water forced up through crevices in the rocky crust. How thick was that crust? Down the hillside, into the bath, trickled warm water. A grotto had been hollowed out by the action of these streams, and from this water was spouted in hot spray and jets, heating the bath for a square yard around. This grotto was lined with crystals of sulphur, lime, and magnesia, and in places was green like chalcedony — a most beautiful miniature of some cave I have seen, where stalagmites of every shape were colored by salts of iron.

Floating in this healing pool, in an element delightfully warm, I resigned myself to the unalloyed delight that dripping water, tropical plants, and trees, and balmy atmosphere, all contribute to induce. Floating thus in dreamy sensuousness, I wondered vaguely why this free life of the forest, untrammeled by care or desire of gain, could not always exist for me. It was too irksome to even think an answer; impossible to give it utterance; and it remains unanswered to this day.

CHAPTER VI.

AMONG THE CARIBS.

THEIR PEACEFUL LIFE. — FRUITS AND FOOD. — THE SECOND VOYAGE OF COLUMBUS. — DISCOVERY OF THE CARIBS. — FIERCE NATURE AND INTELLIGENCE OF THE "CANNIBAL PAGANS." — UNLIKE THE NATIVES OF THE GREATER ANTILLES. — THE CARIB RESERVATION IN DOMINICA. — MY CAMP IN CARIB COUNTRY. — TWO SOVEREIGNS. — THE VILLAGE. — THE HOUSES. — CATCHING A COOK. — A TORCHLIGHT PROCESSION. — LIGHTING A ROOM WITH FIRE-FLIES. — "LOOK ZE COOK." — LABOR. — DOMESTIC RELATIONS. — A DRUNKEN INDIAN. — WILD MEN AND NAKED CHILDREN. — CARIB PANNIERS. — THE ONLY ART PRESERVED FROM THEIR ANCESTORS.

IN two of the smaller islands of the Caribbean Sea lives a vestige of a once powerful people. A people with a history; an unwritten and forgotten history, running back unnumbered ages, farther than we can trace it; but beginning to be known to civilized man when the existence of America was first becoming evident to his awakened senses.

Peaceful and gentle, singularly mild and affectionate, they dwell happily in their rude houses of thatch, drawing their sustenance from mother earth with occasional forays upon the sea.

Bananas, plantains, yams, and tanniers are the crops they cultivate, and altogether rely upon. The bread-fruit grows about their cabins, and the mango and cocoa palm, embowering their dwellings in perpetual shade; and the calabash (furnishing nearly all their vessels for culinary use) spreads its gnarled branches, with a wealth of useful products, at their doors. Guavas grow wild, and the berries and buds of the mountain palm, with many other fruits and nuts of the forest, furnish them with food. The many rivers yield to them delicious crayfish, water snails, and limpets. If they can get rum, now and then, they drink it and are happy — they are happy any way, even without this occasional luxury.

In a land that is theirs by right; beneath a sky ever genial, though not always smiling; able to satisfy hunger by little toil in the garden, or exertion upon the sea, or in the river, it is not strange that they should be content with the bounties of the present, nor care to question the precarious prospects of the future.

In the morning the coolness of the bath provokes one to linger, and later the warmth of the sun seems to warn one from much exertion, while the heat of mid-day positively forbids it. The increased coolness of the afternoon, when the sun dips down behind the mountain ridge, leaving two good hours of dreamy shadow, tempts one to give one's self over to the enjoyment of mere existence. Thus the days pass away in this delightful clime. And now, that you, reader, may better understand who are these people whom I would describe in the following pages, allow me to go back a few centuries; let me turn, in fact, to the first page in American history, and let the same great navigator who opened the way for the discovery of our continent, relate the story of the finding of the Caribs.

Columbus sailed away from Cadiz, on his second

voyage, with a large fleet, fully equipped, September 25, 1493. On the second day of November he first sighted land, and in exploring the shores of the island — Guadeloupe — he found the people of whom he was in search. "Here the Spaniards first saw the *anana*, or pine-apple, the flavor and fragrance of which astonished and delighted them. But what struck them with horror was the sight of human bones, vestiges, as they supposed, of unnatural repasts, and skulls apparently used as vases and other household utensils. These dismal objects convinced them that they were now in the abodes of the Cannibals, or Caribs, whose predatory expeditions and ruthless character rendered them the terror of these seas.

"In several hamlets they met with proofs of the cannibal propensities of the natives. Human limbs were suspended to the beams of the houses as if curing for provisions; the head of a young man, recently killed, was yet bleeding; some parts of his body were roasting before the fire, others boiling with the flesh of geese and parrots."

On the following day the boats landed and succeeded in taking and bringing off a boy and several women. From them Columbus learned that the inhabitants of this island were in league with two neighboring islands, but made war upon all the rest. They even went on predatory enterprises, in canoes made from the hollowed trunks of trees, to the distance of *one hundred and fifty leagues.*

Their arms were bows and arrows, pointed with the bones of fishes or shells of tortoise, and poisoned with the juice of a certain herb. They made descents upon the islands, ravaged the villages, carried off the youngest and handsomest of the women, and made prisoners of the men, to be killed and eaten. "The admiral learned from them that most of the men of the island were absent, the king having sailed some time before, with ten canoes and three hundred warriors, on a cruise in quest of prisoners and booty. When the men went forth on these expeditions, the women remained to defend their shores from invasion."

This island of Guadeloupe was their northernmost stronghold. Continuing his cruise northward, toward Haspaniola, and coasting the islands, Columbus discovered the last resident Caribs at Santa Cruz. Here a boat's crew of Spaniards attacked an Indian canoe containing several men and women. The fight was long and desperate. Even after the canoe was overturned the Indians fought in the water, "discharging their arrows while swimming, as dexterously as though they had been upon firm land; and the women fought as fiercely as the men."

"The hair of these savages was long and coarse; their eyes were encircled with paint, so as to give them a hideous expression; and bands of cotton were bound firmly above and below the muscular parts of the arms and legs, so as to cause them to swell to a disproportioned size." Humboldt makes mention of this custom, in vogue among the Caribs of South America, in the early part of the present century.

"The warlike and unyielding character of these people, so different from that of the pusillanimous nations around them, and the wide scope of their enterprises and wanderings, like those of the nomad tribes of the Old World, entitle them to distinguished attention. They were trained to war from their infancy. As soon as they could walk, their intrepid mothers put in their hands the bow and arrow, and prepared them to take an early part in the hardy enterprises of their fathers. Their distant roamings by sea made them observant and intelligent. The natives of the other islands only knew how to divide time by day and night, by the sun and moon; whereas these had acquired some knowledge of the stars, by which to calculate the times and seasons."

This is the account, drawn mainly from Irving, of the discovery and condition of the first cannibals ever beheld by white men. This second voyage of Columbus commenced under flattering auspices: to find at the outset a new people, a new fruit; to add to the language at least two new words — *Carib* and *Cannibal*, — this were enough to satisfy any explorer.

But Columbus was in search of gold. He could not brook delay in a country where the precious metal did not exist; and though the forests were filled with countless trees possessing spicy gums and rare virtues, he could not stop to put them to the test. He sailed away north after capturing some women and children.

The mind of the great admiral was keenly alive to any opportunity for serving his sovereigns and himself. Finding no gold, he looked about for some means of making it. He sent the captive Caribs home to Spain to be sold as slaves. And this is how the great and good Columbus proposed to reimburse his sovereigns for their outlay, and to furnish the colony with livestock. "In this way the peaceful islanders would be freed from warlike and inhuman neighbors; the royal revenue would be greatly enriched, and a vast number of souls would be snatched from perdition, and carried, as it were, by main force to heaven."

Though the gentle and humane Isabella would not listen to this monstrous scheme, there is little likelihood that it would have succeeded with the Caribs; for those old *conquistadores*, though valiant inquisitors, rarely measured swords with these antagonists who loved to fight. Although, a matter of history, the followers of Columbus murdered more than a million of the peaceful inhabitants of the larger islands — Cuba, Haiti, Jamaica, Porto Rico — who were discovered in a state of happiness and innocence, they always evaded encounters with the "Pagan Cannibals." Thus to the prowess of their ancestors are the Caribs of the present day indebted for their existence, when not a vestige remains of the more numerous but peaceful tribes north of them.

But I did not intend, in digressing, to follow the voyages of Columbus; to describe how he converted these fair islands, teeming with happy life, into hells of misery, and left behind him and his monsters a trail of blood and fire. It was merely to begin at the beginning, to bring before you the Carib as he was when found, nearly four centuries ago, and to show, by contrast with his present life, how he has been almost civilized out of existence.

I had been a month in the interior of Dominica, living in the woods, hunting new birds, and enjoying the novel experiences of camp life in tropical mountains. From time to time came reports from the Carib country, that only strengthened the determination I had formed of penetrating to their stronghold. That they lived secluded from the world, held no intercourse with other people; naked they wandered at will in the forest; without houses, they slept on the ground on beds of leaves. Sending my collections of birds to the coast and ordering thence a fresh supply of provisions and ammunition, I left the Caribbean side of the island and marched over the mountains toward the Atlantic, with three stout girls and a man laden with my effects. The journey was to occupy two days, as the rivers were swollen. They had "come down," in the language of the country; but when a river is "down" in the West Indies it is *up* — having rushed down from the mountains, swollen by some heavy rain, and flooded the lowlands.

The Carib reservation in Dominica extends from Mahoe River to Crayfish River, a distance of about three miles along the Atlantic coast, and away back into the mountains as far as they please to cultivate. Though each family has a little garden adjacent to the dwelling, any individual can select an unoccupied piece of ground on the neighboring hills, or mountain sides, for cultivation. All their provision grounds (as are called the mountain gardens where the staple fruits and vegetables* are grown) are at a distance from the house, some even two miles away, solitary openings made in the depths of the high woods. As the soil in general is very thin, and does not support a crop for many successive years, these gardens are being constantly made afresh.

As I rode along, every house seemed deserted; no face appeared, and I met no one save the ancient

* These are, the Yam (*Dioscorea sativa and D. alata*); the Sweet Potato (*Batatas edulis*); the Cassava (*Jatropha manihot* and *J. janipha*); Banana (*Musa paradisiaca*); Plantain (*Musa sapientum*), and Tannier (*Caladium sagittæfolium*).

king, old George, who was named for King George the Third, tottering toward the plantations, to spend for rum some money he had earned. There were two sovereigns, in fact, for the Carib chief held in his hand a golden one, of English coinage. The houses are low and thatched deeply with calumet grass tied in bundles and lashed tightly upon frame-works of poles. Some of them were open at the sides, though a few were built up at sides and ends, with wooden doors and shutters. Near each hut is the cook-house, a roof of thatch supported upon four poles; or again, merely a "lean-to," the roof slanting up from the ground with just room enough for the cook to squat under while attending the fire.

Beneath this roof, on a few stones which support the cooking-utensils, is usually an old iron pot, which serves a variety of uses. Twice a day it is brought into requisition for the household; at other times it is open to the inspection of hogs and strangers. The rudest cabins, but at the same time the most picturesque, were those composed wholly of grass and reeds with wattled sides, looking like the huge stacks of grass one sees on marshes and meadows in America. Even the doors of these huts were made of canes and flags, wattled together with reeds, while the windows were merely loop-holes. The roads, though narrow bridle-paths, are good, as the Caribs seem to take a pride in keeping them in order. Either through fear or pride they obey all the laws imposed upon them by the crown and colony, and always perform their quota of road labor without a murmur.

The path turned suddenly, and at the base of the hill we came abruptly upon the Rivière Saint Marie,

AN INDIAN KITCHEN.

where, sporting in the water, were several naked children, and a girl and woman washing clothes. Of course, there was a general stampede as I crossed the river; and one could not have told, five minutes later, but for the garments drying on the rocks, that there had been a Carib near. I rode up a gentle eminence, and was introduced to the house in which I was to reside for a short time. But one family lived near, an old Carib woman with five children.

The first object conveying a hint of the proximity of Salibia, the Carib village, is a cross — indicating the religion of the people and the site of a cemetery. It stands up lone and majestic, a background of hills giving it prominence, its arms stretched out gaunt and bare, to which the continual trade-winds have given a color, gray and weather-beaten. Palm and plantain crop out on the hillsides beyond, and the former thrusts its head up from the river ravines below. Behind it, hid by the swell of the knoll, are the graves — not many, yet not few, for so small a settlement — simply raised hillocks of earth; and some have upon them a few flowers, which seem to be occasionally renewed. Upon the graves, all the trees have fallen prostrate, or have been felled, to cover them; with limbs stretched at the foot of the cross. I have never been in a cemetery that so appealed to my feelings as this. All is still, and solitude reigns.

From the slight depression of the surface here, nothing is seen evincing human occupancy of the valley, until the foot of the cross is reached. Many an evening, during my six weeks' stay in that lonely valley, have I climbed to the base of the cross and sat there enjoying the silence and solitude. From that point one overlooks the lower half of the valley, which is shut in on three sides by high hills covered with forest, abandoned fields, and provision grounds, alternating. Beneath, the most prominent object is a rude chapel, a loosely-built structure, to which comes monthly a lusty priest, to care for the souls and the silver of the people. Lower still, are the four or five thatched huts comprising the village of Salibia; but one of these is occupied, and the cocoa palms rustle their leaves in a desolate place; and their rustling, with the eternal roar of the ocean, is the only sound heard from morning to night.

There are sea-grapes there in perfumed bloom, among the satin leaves of which dart humming-birds, sugar-birds, and drowsy bees. This is the valley in which I became acquainted with the "Cannibal Caribs" of Columbus, this secluded spot on the Atlantic coast of Dominica, in the month of April, 1877.

As servant and guide I was fortunate in securing a half Carib, named Meyong. At least, Meyong was the nearest English equivalent for his barbarous French name. He was, as I have said, but half a Carib; the other half was black; colors so deftly mingled, so skillfully laid on, that they resulted in a rich olive brown — quite a fashionable shade. Meyong hunted with me, found for me people to do my heavy work, ate my food and drank my rum, and slept. He did everything but work; and yet he was the most faithful, trustworthy servant I ever had, and anything I wanted he would get, or, if too much trouble for him, induce some one to get for me. He studied my wants so closely that I had ever a retinue of willing youngsters at beck and call, all conjured up by Meyong to relieve his labors. His faithfulness and literal obedience to orders are well illustrated by the manner in which he procured for me a cook.

We passed several weeks tranquilly together. My hammock swung in the breeze at night, and I was careful not to hunt in the breathless heat of noon. But there comes an end, sooner or later, to human enjoyment. Our cook, Meyong's sister, concluded, without warning, to visit a friend on the far side of the mountain; and one day, when my guide and myself returned hot and weary from the hunt, the sun at meridian and the parched earth radiating heat like a furnace, there was no breakfast, and no one to get it, either.

The gentleness of that animal, man, when, upon returning to his domicil, he finds a meal unprepared, is proverbial. He has been known to endure without a murmur, for at least three minutes, by the aid of the morning paper; but I had no paper — had not seen one in two months' time — and imagine, if possible, the totality of patience necessary to endure the preparation of a breakfast, while, even at the time your appetite is raging, and hunger gnawing at your vitals, the potatoes and plantains are slumbering on the hillside, and the fish still disporting themselves in their watery element. It is not at all wonderful if I said to Meyong, in my placid intervals, that we must have another cook at once, even if we had to send to town for one. He acquiesced in this decision, but said nothing more, for he was as sparing of speech as of muscle, and soon afterward disappeared.

Thinking he had gone in pursuit of a dove, whose mournful note I had heard above me, I retired to my cabin, after a frugal lunch, to sleep. Later in the afternoon, even after I had prepared all my specimens of the morning, and the shadows of the hills were drawing themselves across the valley, he came not. The sun went down, leaving the valley cool and delightful, and darkness drew swiftly near. The stars came out, and all about my cabin was silent as the grave, and dark. My boy had not returned; I sat in my doorway till late, it must have been nine o'clock, and was about retiring, when my attention was arrested by a noise. It grew louder, and then I saw a light gleam and disappear. I watched for it till again it shone out, at the top of a rising knoll, much nearer, and I could distinguish two torches, held aloft by unsteady hands, approaching through the forest.

What did it mean?

The noise increased, and when the lights flashed nearer I saw there were three persons: two holding the torches, which sent up broad flame and thick smoke, supporting between them another who appeared unable to walk unaided. They were shouting some bacchanalian song, and their unsteady movements convinced me that they were intoxicated. In a few minutes they would be at my door, as they were already at the river, and then there might be trouble; for, though quiet enough when sober, the Carib will sometimes quarrel when drunk.

Acting upon the resolution of the instant, I barricaded door and window, slipped a couple of cartridges into my gun, and retired to my hammock. By this time they were upon me, pounding heavily at my door, and shouting, in unintelligible French, threats, entreaties, imprecations. But I kept silence, which only exasperated them the more, and at last I heard one of them say, " I will see if he is there;" and then, later, when I thought they had gone, my attention was drawn, by a slight rustling, to a crack in the walls, and I saw sailing into the room one after another, tiny sparks of fire, glowing with a greenish phosphorescent light. They did not drop inert, these sparks, nor did they set fire to my thatch, for they were sparks of the animal kingdom, elaters, fireflies, two of which will give out sufficient light to read by.

Would any one but an Indian, a child of the forest, have thought of this original way of lighting an apartment?

These little gleaming messengers increased in number, and the darkness was crossed and re-crossed by fiery trails of light; and still the busy fingers of my assailants thrust them in more and more. At last it became quite light, and by an inadvertent movement I exposed myself. With a shout, they proclaimed the success of their device, and demanded I should let them in. But this I would not do, and they later subsided, after howling themselves hoarse. Before the termination of the entertainment I had fallen asleep, and did not awake until early the next morning.

Carib Type.

Just before the river, which ran near my hut, trickles through the huge rocks to the ocean, it leaves several small pools, hollowed from the solid rock by the waves. The sun rises so quickly in that latitude, coming up hot and glaring from the waves, that a bath, to be refreshing, must be taken at dawn. The morning was cool and cloudy; a few birds were chirping as I stepped from my doorway. I drew back suddenly, saluted by a blast from what I thought must be an asthmatic fish-horn. Peering cautiously out, I ascertained, by the rapidly increasing light, that the noise had a harmless source, though I was correct in my conjecture that it proceeded from a horn, for it came from my Indian friends of the preceding night, who had indeed taken a horn too much. Tracing this mighty snore to its source, I saw that it was produced by the combined efforts of three individuals, who lay stretched upon the grass beneath the palms. There was my boy, and another Indian, and between them, secured by ropes of vines, a girl of about eighteen.

As I was curiously regarding this group, Meyong awoke, and eying me with a look of triumph, exclaimed:

"Ah, monsieur, you no savez; look, ze cook!"

It was too true; the lawless savage had made unsuccessful attempts to hire a cook the previous afternoon, and late, meeting this girl in the forest, had captured her with the aid of his friend. And I, thinking these zealous friends had approached my hut with dire intent, had locked them out and gone supperless to bed.

Among men and women, labor is equally divided. In the house, the woman is supposed to do all the work, but in the gardens and in the woods they work together. She prepares all the food and makes the fires; and, as there seems to exist a perfect understanding on this point, it is not so fruitful a source of discontent as in other and less-favored climes.

The women are generally well treated and loved. An old writer says, the Caribs were noted for their indifference to their women, while the tribes of neighboring islands were excessively fond of their wives. Those other tribes are now extinct; but the Carib character must have most wonderfully changed, for they now treat their wives well, even love them. For certain misdemeanors they claim the privilege, and exercise it, too, of beating them soundly. If a woman quarrel with another, of whom she is jealous with regard to her husband's affections, she is generally treated by her lord to an interview with the stick. But as a community, they dwell together in amity, loving one another, and taking affectionate interest in their children.

One day, upon the solicitations of an Indian, I went to his hut to see a native dance. This man was very drunk; as he approached his hut he darted in and called for his wife. What was my astonishment to see him, instead of pounding her, throw his arm around her neck and kiss her.

I had been among them two weeks before I knew there were Indians in the woods about me, other than those living along and near the road. But one afternoon, in a hunt among the hills, I discovered four huts, the inmates of which, unless suddenly surprised, hid themselves at my approach. They were dressed very meagerly: a shirt for the men, and for the women a torn skirt. In the woods and in the provision-grounds, I met children, from eight to thirteen years old, entirely naked. These people never appear to the white inhabitants; they make a few baskets which their neighbors dispose of for them, but they never leave the woods, not having overcome their original savagery.

Basket-making is the only art they have preserved from the teachings of their ancestors; but in this they indeed excel. Their baskets have such a reputation throughout all the islands that they command large prices, and were it not for their innate laziness, and the scarcity of the peculiar shrub of which the baskets are composed, these people might attain to a degree of affluence. These "panniers," or baskets, are made of all sizes, some large as a common trunk. They are made, sometimes, of a reed called *roseau*, but the best are made from a plant called the *mahoe*, which is now so scarce that the basket-makers have to take long journeys into the forests to obtain it.

By burying it in the ground, and using for some the juices of certain plants, they give to the plaits a variety of colors. There are two thicknesses, and between them layers of the wild plantain, which make them perfectly water-tight. I have one which was in use nearly a year, being constantly carried on the heads of my attendants; and even yet it will, I think, hold water. All the country people desire to possess a pannier, or Carib basket, which serves them as a light and portable trunk.

CHAPTER VII.

SOCIAL LIFE, APPEARANCE, AND LANGUAGE OF THE CARIBS.

HAPPY CHILDREN. — CLEANLINESS. — PRIMITIVE INNOCENCE. — A MODEST MAIDEN. — DRESS. — FACE AND FIGURE. — FLATTENING THE FOREHEAD. — UGLY MEN AND WOMEN. — CARIB HOSPITALITY. — THE BASKET-WEAVER. — TROPIC NOONTIDE. — RELIGION. — THE DYING WOMAN. — A LOST SKELETON. — BURIAL OF THE DEAD. — THE WAKE. — ST. VINCENT CARIBS. — TWO DIALECTS. — THE AROWAKS. — AN AGREEABLE TONGUE. — VOCABULARY. — CALIBAN A CARIB, AND CRUSOE'S MAN FRIDAY. — CRUSOE'S ISLAND. — BLACK CARIBS. — WEAPONS AND UTENSILS OF STONE. — "THUNDERBOLTS." — CARIB SCULPTURE. — A SACRIFICIAL STONE. — WHENCE CAME THEY? — THEIR NORTHERN LIMIT. — A SOUTHERN ORIGIN. — THEIR LOST ARTS. — A DYING PEOPLE.

THE Carib children should be the happiest on earth. Unencumbered by clothing, they wander over the hills and along the shore as they feel disposed. The rocky rivers give them delightful retreats from the sun, where they paddle in the pools, hunt for crayfish, and sleep upon the broad bosoms of the rocks. Either from habits of cleanliness or love of the water, every member of a household takes a daily bath in the river. They are consequently always clean, and, though ragged, are entirely free from those odors which make the sable brother so offensive. If their garments get soiled, they soon remove them, even if they have to wash them while themselves naked, and wait in the shade while they dry in the sun. In washing they use their hands in scrubbing the clothes, and do not belabor them with clubs, as in the more civilized districts, and in Martinique, where the *sound* of the washing is loud in the land.

The prettiest picture of Indian life I have seen was during a hunt in a secluded nook among the hills behind the settlement of Salibia. The Rivière Collette tumbles over and among great rocks, through narrow chasms shaded by tree-ferns and mountain palms. Many water plants grow in clumps, and little pools are formed among the rocks. As I was leaping the stones, in crossing, I heard a low murmur of song, and looking up, saw a young girl of sixteen sitting on a large bowlder, mending a handkerchief. Around her, drying in the sun, were her clothes, which she had washed — probably all she possessed. She was so absorbed in her work, so carelessly happy in the freedom of this wild seclusion, that I had nearly crossed before she observed me, when, with maidenly modesty, she covered her face with the handkerchief.

The majority of the people go about lamentably ragged. There are few shoes and stockings in the community, and those who have them only put them on upon great occasions, when they appear ill at ease, cramped and uncomfortable. So it is with regard to dress; while, with a dress well made and fitting nicely, the women consider themselves magnificently arrayed, to me they appeared at a great disadvantage. In short frock descending to the knees, gathered about the hips with a twist of lialine, or forest vine, their hair contained in a simple kerchief, or, better, flowing in luxuriant tresses down their backs, as they appear when going to labor in the forest, they are in perfect character.

This brings me to speak of the appearance of the Caribs, of their form and color, which make them different from people of other nationalities. Through the changes of climate and residence, and the greater changes wrought by intermarriage with other tribes and with the negroes, the true Carib type is likely soon to be lost. It is, however, lighter in complexion than that of the North American Indian, — so light, that, from their peculiar cast of golden-brown, they have acquired the name of *Yellow* Indians. From my photographs it will be seen that the type is more of the Mongol than of any other. A peculiar instance came under my observation in one hamlet, where a Chinaman — pure Mongolian — had married a yellow Carib. Their progeny, a numerous family of children, could not be distinguished from the Indian children around them. One beautiful feature about them is their hair, which is abundant, long, and purple-black; it is finer than that of our Indians, though not so fine as that of the Caucasian type.*

Though early losing the grace and symmetry of form of childhood, through labor in the fields, exposure to the sun, and a natural tendency to corpu-

---

* "That cacique that was a stranger had his wife staying at the port where we ankored, and in all my life I have seldom seene a better favored woman. She was of good stature, with blacke eies, fat of body, of an excellent countenance, her haire almost as long as hirselfe, tied up againe in pretie knots." — SIR W. RALEIGH'S *Discovery of Guiana.*

lency, both men and women preserve the shapeliest of limbs. The arms of the men are extremely muscular, and their breasts huge knots of muscle. The head is well shaped and gracefully poised. This, as well as the straightness of the back, and backward throw of the broad shoulders, may be owing to the universal practice of carrying every kind of load upon the head. The custom of flattening the forehead by compression, which was universal until the commencement of the present century, is not now practiced.

Let me subjoin a description of a boy and girl, made as they stood before me, in the primitive garb of innocence and virtue, two years ago. The boy, aged eleven or twelve, had a face round, with chin of good shape, and small; nose rather flat; mouth small; ears small; eyes almond-shaped, with black silken fringe; the forehead broad and prominent; hair purple-black, abundant, cut short above the eyes and flowing behind; the shoulders straight — a plumb-line dropped from the junction of cervical and dorsal vertebræ would touch the heels; back hollowed; abdomen full; legs straight; hips not large but powerful; breasts well rounded. The girl was an exact picture of the boy in the features above described; the mouth was daintily cut, with thin lips; and grace and lithesome freedom were in every turn and motion.

It almost gave pain to think that these sprightly little beauties would develop into coarse, full-bodied men and women, like those about them. But it undoubtedly would be so; and this little boy, though retaining longer the shapely limbs which would develop into muscular and brawny members, would eventually become as wrinkled and flabby as the ugliest man in the village; and the careless little maiden, not many years later, almost as soon as her shape and limbs were rounded and perfected, would begin to acquire that grossness that mars maidenly beauty, and, if married at eighteen, at twenty-five or thirty she would be old, though vigorous, and resemble those middle-aged females about her.

ANCIENT CARIBS.

A writer thus describes the Dominica Caribs in 1795: "They are of clear copper color, and have sleek, black hair; their persons are stout and well made, but they disfigure their faces by flattening their foreheads in infancy. They live chiefly by fishing in the rivers and the sea, or by fowling in the woods, in both which pursuits they use their arrows with wonderful dexterity. It is said they will kill the smallest bird with an arrow at a great distance, or transfix a fish at a considerable depth in the sea. They display also very great ingenuity in making curious-wrought panniers, or baskets, of silk-grass or the leaves and bark of trees."

None of the old writers mention the hospitality of the Carib, which at the present day is a virtue he possesses in perfection. I recall one of the many excursions made through the environs of the hamlet into the forest in my search for birds. The day was hot, but a cool breeze from the ocean, which always blows from ten in the morning till 'six in the evening, tempered the heat. Bordering the forest was a little open space, in the center of which, on a spur of the hills overlooking the sea, was a small thatched hut, inhabited by one of the few families of Caribs who have remained uncontaminated by negro blood. As I emerged from the forest I was met by a robust damsel with laughing eyes, who brought for me a wooden bench and placed it beneath the grateful shade of a mango. Then appeared her father, who welcomed me to his habitation, and then disappeared. A little later, when he re-appeared, he was driving before him a flock of fowls, and singling out the largest and plumpest, he requested me to shoot it. Thinking I had not understood him, I hesitated, but, at a repetition of the request, fired and tumbled the fowl in the dust. There was an instant scattering of the others, but the old man picked up the slain one and marched off with it to his wife. Then he knocked down a few cocoa-nuts, and, clipping off the end of one, brought it to me, with its ivory chamber full of cool and refreshing water, apologizing that he could offer me no rum or gin, which it is customary to mix with it.

In an hour or so I was invited to the hut, where, on a clean table, was spread a substantial meal of bread-fruit and yam, with the chicken I had so recently shot. This last was a luxury the Indian seldom treated himself to; and when I reflected to what extent my host had deprived himself, and upon the recent, the very recent, demise of the chicken, I could scarcely eat. My friends refused to sit at table with me, but attended upon my wants, bringing me fresh cocoanut-water, and mangos and guavas for dessert. To be sure, there was neither fork nor table-knife; but one living in the woods is never without his pocket-knife, and a fork can be quickly whittled from a palm-rib. After the repast I retired to the shade of the mango; the father gathered about him his materials for making baskets, and the daughter wove for me a curious cone of basket-work, used by the children in their games, which, being slipped over the finger, cannot be removed so long as it is tightly drawn.

The sun at noon is very powerful in that climate, and one quickly feels its somnolent influences. The people are up early, and work a little in the morning, but in the heat of the day little is done. No traveler passes, unless some one on a long journey; and no one works except the basket-maker, who can do so under the broad-spreading shade of a mango or tamarind. Even he, as noon draws nigh and breakfast is disposed of, stretches himself upon a board and dozes for an hour or two. Everything is hushed in universal calm, and even the insects and birds feel the influence of the solar rays and are silent, drowsy, and indulging in mid-day siestas. *Dolce far niente* is the life these people lead; the sweet-do-nothing more than is absolutely necessary.

Hospitality such as I have mentioned is not exceptional. If an Indian takes a liking to you, henceforward you are his *compère;* all he has is yours —

and what you possess, also, is reckoned as his, if he want it. When he offers to you his house and all in it, it is no idle custom without meaning, for even his household furniture, if there be any, is at your disposal.

The ancient Caribs, if we may credit the statements of early writers, believed in some sort of a future state, and also that their departed friends were secret witnesses of their conduct. "The brave had the enjoyment of supreme felicity with their wives and captives; the cowardly were doomed to everlasting banishment beyond the mountains. This was their next world. They dimly recognized a Divinity, a great creator of all things, and vaguely offered their homage and sacrifice."

It is supposed that each person had his tutelar deity; it may have been a tree or a rock. The northern tribes, the Arowaks, had their *zemes*, or household gods, when discovered by the Spaniards. "The Caribs erected a rustic altar of banana leaves and rushes, whereon they placed the earliest of their fruits and choicest of their viands, as peace-offerings to incensed omnipotence. They could not be insensible to the existence of a great ruler, when the convulsions of nature were so great as they witnessed in the earthquake and hurricane."

In religion, at the present time, the Caribs of Dominica are Roman Catholic, and are very observant of the rites of the church. Upon the occasion of the priest's monthly visit, nearly all flock to hear him, even if they do not obey his injunctions; and the sick are brought, and the dying, to obtain the sacrament. At the close of service, one Sabbath, word was brought the priest that Madame Jim, a middle-aged woman, was dying, with a request that he would hasten to administer the last rites of the church. But the priest was anxious to be away; his house was a dozen miles distant, and half-way there, at the house of a friend, a dinner was awaiting him. With impatience, then, he commanded that she be brought to the chapel; and the dying woman was placed in a hammock suspended between poles, and carried to the priest, over a mile of rough, steep road, patiently suffering, anxious only to receive extreme unction before she passed away.

The same Sabbath there was buried at the foot of the cross the oldest inhabitant of the nation, a very old Carib woman, whose death I lamented, as I was awaiting her recovery to secure from her a vocabulary of Carib words. My grief was only alleviated by the thought that an opportunity might occur for exhuming her skeleton, which would prove a valuable acquisition to the Smithsonian Museum.

Formerly, the Caribs buried their dead in a sitting posture, in order (as an old Indian told me) that they might be all ready to jump, when the Spirit came for them; and facing the sunrise, to see the light of morning. When the master of a house died, they buried him in the center of his hut, with his knees bent to his chin. They then left the hut and built another, some distance from it.

Eight days after the death of Madame Jim, the neighbors had a sort of wake, or " praise "; until midnight, the girls sang hymns. After twelve o'clock, all the younger people formed themselves in groups and played games until morning, while the wicked

Meyong, and a few more of the ungodly — who had amused themselves by tickling the ears of the choristers with straws and palm-leaves, in vain attempt to upset their gravity — improved the hours so assiduously in imbibing the new rum furnished by the husband of the departed, that the morning light saw them thoroughly fuddled. The whole settlement attended, old men and women and children, even to babes at the breast. The expense to the bereaved husband must have been great; and his reflection upon this fact, coupled with the equally saddening one that the wife of his bosom would never again labor for him in the garden, or relieve him of the burden of domestic duties, must have caused him to regret her departure.

Eight months later, I was in the island of Saint Vincent, in latitude thirteen, north, two degrees and a half south of Dominica. Here reside (with those of the latter island) the only remaining Caribs north of South America. While those of Dominica speak a perverted French, these speak an equally corrupt English. The former are Roman Catholic in their faith; the latter, Church of England. Two weeks I lived with these Caribs, in a little wattled hut thatched with leaves, which was given up to me by a young colored man who had recently married a Carib wife.

In St. Vincent, the Caribs made their last stand against the English, in the latter part of the last century, and there are more abundant evidences of ancient occupation, and the traditions are better preserved than in Dominica. It was for the purpose of securing a vocabulary of their ancient language, to compare with one I had formed in Dominica, and to ascertain if any difference existed between the Indians of the two islands, that I visited them.

In Dominica there are but twenty families of pure Caribs; in St. Vincent less than six; and but a few, of the older men and women, can speak the original language. In a few years — another generation — the Carib tongue, as spoken by these insular people, will be a thing of the past, of which there exists but an imperfect record, speaking which there will be no person living.

The source of my information in Dominica was a woman, who had, I have reason to believe, purer speech than my informant in St. Vincent, who was a man. Humboldt observes, quoting Cicero: "The old forms of language are better preserved by women, because, by their position in society, they are less exposed to those vicissitudes of life, change of place and occupation, which tend to corrupt the primitive purity of language among men."

I found, however, a greater difference than the mere supposition of difference of sex, or the interval of a hundred and fifty miles between their respective habitations, would create. I found, in fact, that this people spoke *two* dialects, in confirmation of which my vocabulary, from which I can quote but briefly, will testify. For certain things they had two words entirely different. In the construction of sentences, though there would be close analogy, there was a difference in the opening or closing words that was at once noticeable. In the following, for instance, where the woman expresses a wish for a fish for dinner: "*Noó-iz, há-ma-gah, oó-do.*" And the man: "U-I-DI, *há-ma-ga, oó-do.*" Almost invariably, a word commenced by the man with a *B*, by the woman was begun with an *N*.

Although I could surmise the cause of this discrepancy, which in some instances was even more marked, I could not be satisfied to trust to my own inexperienced reasoning, but turned to the greatest authority upon any such subject in his day — the immortal Humboldt. Some light was thus afforded, for he had noticed the same peculiarity. "The contrast between the dialects of the sexes is so great that to explain it satisfactorily, we must refer to another cause (than difference in sex), and this may perhaps be found in the barbarous custom practiced by the Caribs, of killing their male prisoners, and carrying the wives of the vanquished into captivity. When the Caribs made an irruption into the West Indies, they arrived there as a band of warriors, not as colonists accompanied by their families. The language of the female sex was formed by degrees, as the conquerors contracted alliances with the foreign women; it was composed of new elements, words distinct from the Carib words, which in the interior of the gynecæums were transmitted from generation to generation, but on which the structure, the combinations, the grammatical forms of the language of the men, exercised an influence."

Seeking farther, I found in an ancient volume, a French work published in 1658, conclusive evidence in place of what was with Humboldt mostly conjecture. It says: The Caribs have an original language peculiar to them alone, like any other nation, which they speak among themselves. The men have many peculiar expressions which the women understand very well, but never utter; and the women have likewise their own words and phrases which the men never use except in ridicule. The savages of Dominica relate that when they came to live in these islands (the Lesser Antilles) they found them in possession of a nation of Arowaks, whom they entirely destroyed, except the women, whom they married. Thus, the women having preserved their own language, taught it to their children. Having been practiced until the present time, this language remains different in a great many respects from that of the men.

But the boys, after they attain the age of five or six, although they well understand the speech of their mothers and sisters, follow their fathers and elder brothers in the formation of their language. In proof of what they relate, they allege that there is some resemblance between the language of the female Caribs and that of the Arowaks of the main-land (South America).

The Caribs had also a certain form of speech which they used among themselves in their councils of war, — a gibberish very difficult to understand, of which neither the women nor children were permitted to have any knowledge; nor even the young men, until they had given some proof of their bravery, or of zeal in the common quarrels of their country against their enemies. It is owing to this fact that their designs were never prematurely disclosed, and their invasions of an enemy's territory always so unexpected. They have in their native tongue few terms of abuse, and about the most offensive is: "you are no good," or, "you are no livelier than a turtle." Again, they have no equivalent word for virtue, which even at the present day is rare indeed. In counting, they cannot express themselves above twenty, and then only by means of the fingers and toes. Among the Seminoles of Florida I found a system of numeration perfect up to one thousand. Their pronunciation is soft and agreeable, and their language abounds in those figurative expressions which make the speech of our aboriginal tribes so interesting.

Like the northern Indians, they use the expression moon for month : *nóo-no*, moon, and *ká-ti*, month, meaning the same. My wife is "my heart"; a boy is a little man; an idiot, a person without light, or unillumined; the fingers are the little ones, or the babes, of the hands; the rainbow is God's plume. To signify that a thing is lost, they say it is dead. Their first white visitors they styled "children of the sea," because they came to them in ships from over the sea.

Though different writers have sought to prove by comparative vocabularies affinity between the Carib and the Jew and the Tartar, it has not been conclusively proven that this people descended from either. There is, however, whatever the origin of the language, a striking significance in their designating appellation — Carib, or Cannibal, which are epithets referring to valor and strength.

We have seen that they received this name from Columbus, or his associates, who had heard it as applied to them by the inhabitants of Hispaniola, the year previous to the discovery of the Caribbees. Humboldt relates that the Caribs of South America called themselves Carina, Calina, Callinago, Caribi; and that the name Carib is derived from Calina and

Carifoona. The word *Carifoona* was given me, both by the St. Vincent and Dominica Caribs, as the ancient name of the tribe; so there can be no doubt of the origin of the latter term.

In this connection, the author of "Myths of the New World" has propounded a curious and by no means improbable theory: "The mythical ancestor of the Caribs created his offspring by sowing the soil with stones, or with the fruit of the Mauritius palm, which sprouted forth into men and women; while the Yurucares, much of whose mythology was perhaps borrowed from the Peruvians, clothed this crude tenet in a somewhat more poetic form, fabling that at the beginning the first men were pegged, Ariel-like, in the knotty entrails of an enormous bole, until the god Tiri — a second Prospero — released them by cleaving it in twain. . . . . . It is still a mooted point whence Shakespeare drew the plot of 'The Tempest.' The coincidence mentioned in the text between some parts of it and South American mythology does not stand alone. *Caliban*, the savage and brutish native of the island, is undoubtedly the word *Carib*, often spelled *Caribana* and *Calibani* in older writers, and his 'dam's god, Setebos,' was the supreme divinity of the Patagonians when first visited by Magellan."

As another curious fact, which inseparably links the Carib with our best fiction, as well as with our early history, let me mention that Robinson Crusoe's "Man Friday" was a Carib; and the island of their adventures is not in the Pacific Ocean, but lies among the historic isles of the Caribbean Sea. It is, in fact, the island of Tobago, which I visited, and in which I had many and varied adventures.

From the same old Carib who aided in enriching my vocabulary I obtained many quaint tales and traditions, which, in another chapter, are related to show that the Caribs, though wanderers, robbers, and cannibals, were not without their fireside stories and superstitions. Like the African, like the North American Indian, the Carib is very superstitious; the woods, shore, rocks, and trees are peopled with *jumbies*, or evil spirits, who can, if they please, work them harm; the spirits of men and women who once lived among them, and who, they firmly believe, still inhabit this earth. Anything of odd shape or mysterious aspect is believed to be possessed of a jumbie. The owl, from its nocturnal habits and soft flight, its large, staring eyes and boding cry, is the chosen bird for the terrestrial abode of the spirits, and bears the appellation of "jumbie-bird" in every island. But a jumbie may appear in the shape of anything animate or inanimate, and it may happen that now and then an animal is wrongly accused of being possessed of a jumbie.

To the ethnologist, the Caribs of St. Vincent present an attractive subject for study, for there is among them a people formed by the union of two distinct races, the American and the Ethiopian. They are called "Black Caribs," to distinguish them from the typical or "Yellow Caribs." Various reasons are assigned for the cause of this mixture. One tradition is to the effect that the Caribs attacked and burned a Spanish ship, in the sixteenth century, and took its freight of slaves to live among them; another version, that a slaver was wrecked near St. Vincent, and the Africans, escaping, joined the Caribs. The Yellow

Caribs received them as friends, but eventually the negroes possessed themselves of the best lands and drove their benefactors to the most worthless. Having intermarried with the Yellow Caribs, they departed from the negro type in a few years, but sufficiently resembled the slaves, beginning to be introduced into the island by the French in 1720, as to cause them alarm, and they took to the woods and mountains, living there for quite another generation. They also adopted the Carib practice of flattening the foreheads of their children, so that succeeding generations differed generally from their fathers. They now form a small community on the northwestern shore of St. Vincent, at a place called Morne Ronde.

Throughout the island of St. Vincent I found traces of occupation by the ancient Caribs. These were in the shape of implements of war and utensils for domestic use, of the rudest description: hatchets, axes, battle-axes, gouges, chisels, and spear-heads, of stone, generally classed under the head of "celts." The negroes, ever superstitious, attribute to these stones, which they occasionally find in the fields, a celestial origin, declaring they are "thunderbolts," and that they come down from the sky during thunderstorms. This they prove to their entire satisfaction, by citing the fact that they are always more abundant after a rain. This is evident from the fact that rain washes away the earth from these ancient stones which have lain so long buried.

The Caribs did not possess that advancement in civilized art that enabled them to produce such sculptured works of intricate and beautiful design, both in stone and wood, as the Spaniards found among the

THE SACRIFICIAL STONE.

inhabitants of Cuba and Haiti at the time of their discovery. They confined their efforts to the production of axes for hollowing out their canoes, and the manufacture of implements of war. They made pottery, but I doubt if the cotton found in their huts by Columbus was of their own weaving. It is more probable that it was taken from the Arowaks of the greater islands.

In the forests there are yet more striking evidences of aboriginal occupation, which would tell us that there once existed here a people different from those of the present day, were there no written or traditional chronicles of their existence. In a valley of the Caribbean side of St. Vincent is a large rock covered with incised figures, which are undoubtedly of great antiquity, and the lines or grooves are so nearly obliterated that I will not hazard a guess as to their meaning. The central figure, however, a face enclosed in a triangle, seems to resemble rude aboriginal representations of the sun. It is conjectured that this was a sacrificial stone used by the Caribs, or their predecessors, the Arowaks; and this statement would seem to be confirmed by the various channels leading from the attendant satellites to the central figure. The rock at present lies with its face slanting to the southwest, owing to the excavation of the earth beneath it by a small stream that runs near. A few miles below is another and smaller rock, having carved upon it a face surrounded by scroll-work. In the island of Guadeloupe is a large rock having upon it a figure of more intricate design; and it is said that there are sculptured rocks in the island of St. John, one of the Virgin Islands. Owing to the rugged conformation of the islands chosen as their home, it is not possible to discover such evidences of their handiwork as in islands of more level surface.

As the only remaining Indians between the continent of South America and North America, between Guiana and Florida, these Caribs possess an interest attaching to no other tribe living. Having visited the southernmost resident Indians in the United States, the Seminoles, offshoots from the Creeks, I was enabled to note more intelligently the differences between the two tribes; and, aside from these and other reasons, I do not think the Caribs ever reached the continent of North America. This statement may be met with the counter one that the Seminoles, at the time of Carib supremacy in the Lesser Antilles, were residents of the country north of Florida, and that a different tribe, the Yemassees, inhabited the peninsula.

Very naturally arises the question, whence came this people? This must remain unanswered until our *savants* have determined the origin of the entire race of which these Indians are but a fragmentary portion. They may trace them to Jew or Tartar, to Malay or Phœnician, for their remote origin; but to the ethnologist who believes in an original American civilization, that there was for ages an emigration from South America northward, a little light may be afforded by tracing the confines of the Carib.

Considering the Esquimaux and the North American Indians to be an "immigrant element" from Asia, we must look to the South for the origin of those other tribes more advanced than they in civilization. The Mound-builders of the Ohio and Mississippi valleys, and the Cliff-dwellers of Colorado and Arizona, may be traced to Mexico as the country from which they sprung. The Aztecs, in the height of their power when discovered by the Spaniards, pointed to South America as the land from which they had invaded Mexico. Those learned men are not few who trace a connection from these peoples to that wonderful race that built the aqueducts of Peru and the roads of the Incas; and who maintain further that American civilization had its beginning in the elevated valleys of Peru.

These Caribs have no affinity with the people who built such wonderful cities and wrought such works of art as now lie scattered throughout the vast forests of Honduras and Central America; but that they originated in the same continent of South America, there seems to be abundant evidence to prove. We can trace them from South America northward, killing and devouring as they went. In the time of Columbus the people of Porto Rico were beginning to feel alarm from their incursions; and the Spaniard may be consoled by the thought that if he had not murdered his millions, the Caribs would have eventually depopulated these peaceful isles. We have seen that they had gained possession of all the Lesser Antilles, coming up from the south, and probably were the same who possessed Jamaica from the west, coasting the shore northward from Darien and crossing the intervening sea. According to the Spanish writers of the sixteenth century, the Carib nation then extended over eighteen or nineteen degrees of latitude, from the Virgin Islands, east of Porto Rico, to the mouths of the Amazon. It seems, then, but a question of time when they would have possessed every island in the Caribbean Sea.

It is not my purpose to attempt to trace ancient American civilization, but merely to describe the northern limits of a people contemporary with the more civilized Indians. Their warlike character and unyielding nature is fully shown in their resistance to the yoke of slavery the Spaniards sought to put upon them, when they perished fighting rather than yield to the oppressors.

How changed are the Caribs of the present day! They have intermarried with the negroes to such an extent that their individuality is nearly lost. Their free mode of life, their long journeys by sea, their language even, are all things of the past. This remnant of a race, living so quietly in these islands, hemmed in between forest and ocean, peacefully cultivating their gardens and weaving baskets, quietly breathing away existence, are slowly but surely passing on into the great gulf of forgetfulness. Already have they forgotten the deeds of their fathers, the dread prowess of their ancestors. The bow, the hatchet, the war-club, mighty weapons in willing hands, are lost. In all their settlements one cannot find a bow. Here, then, are people who have lost language, prestige, tradition, ambition; and it is a matter of comparatively little time ere they will have ceased to exist, and the forests and rivers, the cool, fern-shaded baths and tropic streams, no longer know their presence.

CHAPTER VIII.

HOW I CAPTURED THE IMPERIAL PARROT.

MEYONG. — MY HUT. — A MIXED-UP LANGUAGE. — DEPARTURE FOR THE FOREST. — PANNIER AND CUTLASS. — WOOD-PIGEONS. — THE STARTLED SAVAGES. — THE BATH. — A GLOOMY GORGE. — "PALMISTE MONTAGNE." — IN THE HAUNTS OF THE PARROT. — IMMENSE TREES. — PARASITES AND LIANES. — WOOD FOR CANOES AND GUM FOR INCENSE. — THE "BOIS DIABLE." — CONSTRUCTING THE CAMP. — PALM-SPATHES. — A BONNE BOUCHE, THE BEETLE GRUB. — NOCTURNAL NOISES. — COMICAL FROGS. — A BLACKSMITH IN A TREE. — THE FIRST SHOT. — THE HUMMINGBIRD'S NEST. — THE PARROT. — AN EXCITED GUIDE. — AN ACCIDENT. — WILD HOGS. — THE "LITTLE DEVIL."

"It was a land of rills
And birds, and giant hills
Rose westward; eastward thundered the broad main."

WALLS of reeds and roof of flags, a small hole looking eastward for a window, a larger one for a door. Leaning against the door-post is a Carib youth of eighteen, a gun resting in the hollow of his arm, a coarse cotton shirt and trowsers his habiliments. Upright, in a hammock swung from two corners of the hut, sits a sleepy American, thrusting his fingers through his long hair; he is the only white man in that region. Reader, consider yourself introduced to my Indian guide, to my hut, and to myself.

Meyong, my faithful servant and henchman, was christened Simeon in the little chapel over the hill;

but that was a name too long and savoring too much of English for these idle aborigines, and he was at once and forever rechristened.

"Meyong!"

"*Oui, monsieur.*"

You must pardon Meyong for frequent lapses into French, and for saying, "*Oui, monsieur,*" instead of "Yes, sir." The fact is, he has no language he can call his own. Though born a Carib, he never heard the Carib tongue, save from some very old woman or warriors. He was born under English rule, but never learned the English language. His parents spoke a degenerate French, but never owed allegiance to the French government. Meyong, then, speaks a patois, or dialect of his own, derived from the French, who once owned this island. His speech is abominable alike to cultivated Frenchman and Englishman.

"Are you ready, Meyong?"

"*Oui, monsieur.*"

"And Coryet?" Coryet is his inseparable companion, with whom he roves sea and forest.

"Coryet come long time, m'sieur; he come ebryting."

"Very well; then bring me my coffee."

While he was preparing my coffee I drew on my boots and hastened to the river to bathe. Darkness still covered everything, but the low, uneasy twittering of birds gave token of the near approach of dawn. Crickets and locusts and all the nocturnal insects had hushed their chirpings, and all the valley was wrapped in the silence that preceded the break of day.

Each of my young hunters had a large pannier strapped to his shoulders, like a knapsack made of basket-work, filled with the essentials for our journey. In them they had stored yams, tanniers, and "farine" of cassada, two bottles of native rum, my blanket and rubber poncho. One of them also carried a very heavy iron kettle, and the other a large calabash. Why Coryet chose thus to burden himself with the heavy kettle was explained by Meyong, who said that the kettle was the only article of kitchen use owned by his friend, and that he wished to display it as much as possible in going through the Indian gardens. When we reached the forests he would bury it and exhume it for exhibition on our return. Nearly everybody has some pet foible. Some display it in neck-ties, others in gloves; but Coryet's took the shape of a pot of iron, black and battered.

I forgot to add that each boy carried a great *machete*, or cutlass, two feet and a half in length and two inches broad. I had grown so accustomed to seeing them with this weapon that I almost considered it a part of themselves. Meyong also carried his gun.

There were but three things he cared for in this world more than rum and sleep—his cutlass, his gun, and his friend Coryet. Night and day they were together. He did, I think, entertain a high regard, approaching to love, for me, and he certainly feared the priest; but the consideration of other things never disturbed his soul.

We climbed the hill, and had reached the ridge forming the semicircle that hemmed in our valley before the sun appeared. He came up from the ocean with a bounce and darted at us hot beams; but we were then walking beneath tall trees, where he could not enter, and we laughed at him. The trail we were following was one thread of a net-work of secret paths known only to the Indians, that had extent all over the island, traversing the forests only, from shore to shore. Our path was crossed by other trails, but my boys infallibly selected the right one, and we marched on swiftly.

We were skirting the innermost of the Indian gardens, but soon left them and plunged into the woods, where the trail followed mainly the crest of a tortuous ridge. *Ramiers*, or wood-pigeons, were cooing all around us, and Coryet and I went for one. He saw it first, and tumbled it from its high perch among the leaves to the ground. After an hour on the ridge we began to descend. The hill was very steep, and I had to cling to roots and rocks in going down. Soon we passed through a garden owned by Indian Jim, whose wife we saw "toted" in a hammock, the week before, dying, to the village to receive extreme unction from the priest on his visit. Poor woman! her last task is finished on this earth, and never again will she look upon this solitary spot so often the scene of her daily toil. It was a dell most secluded and wild, and ground, rocks, and trees were covered with ferns.

As we waded along knee-deep in ferns, a couple of *perdrix*, or mountain doves, got up; one alighted in the loop of a swinging liane some forty yards away, and I dropped him into the ferns, stone-dead. Meyong saw an agouti, but too quickly he penetrated the forest of ferns for us to catch him. Suddenly I heard the music of falling water — the most liquid melody in the world — and opportunely, too, for we were tired and thirsty. Rapidly we descended, as fast as loosened rocks and earth furrowed by the rains would allow us, to a shady valley, where a foaming brook came down to join the large river that entered the sea two miles below. But another sound greeted our ears, other than that of water laughing over mossy stones; it was the rumbling of loosened rocks and rolling of stones caused by the hand of man. We stopped to listen, and then Meyong went on ahead. He beckoned and I followed, to see, as I peered over the bank, a naked Indian running about in and out of the brook; a magnificent man, with brawny shoulders and long black hair. Just ahead of him was a woman, his squaw, clad in a ragged skirt. Both were intently searching beneath the stones for some object, the man overturning large rocks in his way.

What was this thing they seemed so eager to find? It was not gold, for they do not know it in its virgin state. It was something more valuable to them, for present needs, a shell-fish for their breakfast and supper. The crayfish, the fresh-water lobster, makes its home beneath the rocks of the mountain streams. Being so excellent, it is much sought by these people, who have no guns, no bows nor arrows, and few dogs with which to hunt. It is their chief reliance when the seas are heavy and they cannot go out in their canoes to fish.

Pressing too near the bank, I dislodged a pebble which fell with a splash into the stream. Hardly had it touched the water, when, with a wild cry of alarm, the startled Indians darted into the forest; we could hear them as they ran in their fear, for some minutes. At the river we stopped to lunch and drink its pure water. Crossing the stream we entered an abandoned provision ground, where we disturbed two girls and a boy gathering yams and tanniers. They shrieked and fled, without staying to answer our *bon jour*. We then marched up the gravelly bed of a brook near the river bank, our path overhung by wild oranges and

THE HUNTER'S BATH.

coffee trees, until we came abruptly upon a perpendicular wall of rock directly across our path. It was black and frowning, dotted with lovely ferns and long drooping leaves of the wild plantain. Swerving aside, we found that we must cross the river, and that the channel was too deep to wade, and we must swim it.

There are two things forbidden by the laws of health in the tropics: eating fruit when the body is hot, and bathing when in the same condition. But Meyong said it would not hurt us if we would remove our clothes and sit in the sun a while to dry the perspiration; which we did, and then plunged in. It was icy cold, and the current was so swift we could hardly stem it, for the river flowed between huge walls of rock — a narrow gorge. Into the deep black chasm we at last ventured, where the sun could not reach us, and essayed a peep into the cavernous depths beneath the cliffs. Suspended from a swinging rope, a liane, we hung upon the surface of as black and dismal a pool as I ever saw. The water fell from a great height into the farthest recesses of the chasm and created a sort of whirlpool where we dared not venture, and then it flowed out through a narrow opening into the daylight and sunlight, falling over a broad ledge one sheet of foam.

The lianes gave a strange effect, hanging from the heights to the water like loosened ropes; but the most beautiful and strangely-attractive forms were those of the tree-ferns, which sprang out of the crevices in the rocks, and spread their broad, lace-like leaves above us.

Refreshed by the bath, and by the contemplation of this grand work of nature, we dressed and prepared to scale the cliffs on the other side. A little stream fell musically over the rock, where it had worn a channel for itself in the solid stone, and up this brooklet, assisted by tree-ferns and lianes, we climbed and climbed. It was now mid-day and the sun gave us a warm reminder of his strength, so that we gladly hailed the first sight of a mountain palm. As it is never found at less than two thousand feet above the sea, its presence assured us of cool breezes; and not only of cool breezes but of possible approach to the region of the parrots.

The great Imperial Parrot, the "Cicero" of the Indians, the *Chrysotis augusta* of ornithologists, delights to feed upon the seeds of this tree. We did not, however, hear any cry or noise betokening their presence, for at noon in the tropics all animal life is silent.

We went up and on for several hours into a region of palms and "gommier trees," and at last halted beneath towering trees, on a carpet of green, where we threw ourselves upon the ground. My boys were soon refreshed and sprang up again to seek water, far down the hill.

While they were gone I lay upon my back, studying the forms of the various trees above me. They formed a perfect canopy of green which the sun could not pierce. Exceeding all others in height, as well as in usefulness, is the tree known to the natives as the "gommier," or gum-tree (*Bursera gummifera*). Some of the trunks are eight feet in diameter, throw out huge buttresses on all sides, like the wall-supports of a Gothic church, and rise into the air one hundred feet. The seeds of this tree are favorite food of the parrots and wood-pigeons. Its branches and trunk are completely hidden in a wealth of parasitic growth and lianes. This is the tree used by the Caribs, even at the present day, for their canoes. From a single trunk they hollow out, by means of fire and axe, a canoe in the rough. This is most often done far in the mountains, and the hollowed log must be dragged, with great labor, to the shore. There it is placed in the shade and filled with water, to open it; a strip is nailed along the top for a gunwale, knees put in to strengthen it; it is finished smoothly with the axe, and then makes a strong, buoyant boat, which floats lightly on the water, and rides gracefully heavy seas. In such a boat the ancient Caribs made war excursions of more than three hundred miles. From the bark of this valuable tree exudes a gum that burns freely and with such grateful odor that it is used in the Romish churches as incense. This gum is wrapped in bark in an ingenious manner by the Indians, and made into torches, or *flambeaux*, three feet long, which are used by hunters and fishermen at night. Hence the tree is also known as the "flambeau tree."

Another very useful tree is the "*bois de bonté*," the young saplings of which are used in making the ajoupa, or hut. It is tall, of lesser height than the gommier, with fine ovate leaves. Upon the seeds of this tree, also, the parrots feed, and its abundance here induced my boys to select this site for our forest camp. But the most interesting thing about it is the property of the bark, which, when steeped in tea or in rum, has a warming effect upon the human system, and has probably some medicinal qualities. Winding among the branches of this tree are those of another called "*bois diable*," or devil's wood; it is much used in making charcoal and flambeaux.

They returned from the spring after a long absence, with the calabash and a section of bamboo full of water. Meyong started a fire with a flake of gommier gum, and then departed for covering for the house, which he and his companion were now to erect. It was very near dark, and I did not think they could put a roof over our heads before sunset; but when I mentioned this doubt they smiled and told me to rest quietly. Coryet then cut about a dozen saplings and drew them up to the fire. Across two crotched uprights, some eight feet high, he placed a pole about twelve feet in length for the ridge-pole of the house. From this front pole he extended three other stout limbs to the ground, and across these again at right angles he lashed ten others about a foot and a half apart. Thus he had the frame-work of a roof in less than half an hour, and every pole was lashed securely without a single rope, and fastened firmly without a nail.

It was interesting to watch him at this work. When he had placed the poles in position he left them and went to a tree near at hand, and drew down from its branches, sixty feet from the ground, several hundred feet of lialines and lianes, the latter large as grape-vines, the former small as fish-lines, and so lithe and tough that a hard knot could be tied in one without its breaking. With these he fastened the framework together.

By this time Meyong had returned with a back-load of strips of thin white bark. They were about six feet in length, and looked like great flakes of slippery-elm bark. Upon examination I found that they were the sheaths or layers from around the terminal bud of the mountain palm. This bud, which is much sought as a delicacy, and cooked like cabbage, forms the apex of the stem of the palm; and this rare vegetable, forming only enough for a meal for a small party, is only obtained by cutting down one of the stateliest trees in the world. It was from a fallen palm that Meyong had stripped these layers, which he now threw upon the ground.

With his cutlass he shaved away the middle of each, thus making the central portion so thin that it could be spread out flat. Each piece was then about four feet broad and six to seven long; and two breadths of four pieces each completely covered the skeleton shape of the roof and made a water-tight covering. The lower course was laid first, with the upper overlapping it, like two rows of shingles. Across each course was laid a pole, fastened at either end to the poles projecting on each side underneath. In less than an hour we had a good roof over us, impervious to water. A few palm leaves were fastened at the sides, and a huge back-load of small and springy leaves thrown on the ground for a bed. Over these I threw my poncho of rubber silk and a warm gray blanket to protect me from the night air. Thus we had house, and food at hand, all obtained from material on the spot, with no foreign aid save a single cutlass.

I say food, but forgot to specify what it was and how obtained. Meyong had brought us a luscious morsel from that same palm, in the shape of a great, fat grub, large as my finger, which he proposed to fry at supper time. With characteristic generosity, he offered me the whole of it, but I declined, and he and his friend smacked their lips in anticipation. This grub was from an egg laid in the decaying heart of the palm by a black beetle, which always chooses such a place of deposit for its eggs. The ramiers were plucked and dressed, and some potatoes and yams boiled. The former made a fine stew for supper, after which, as we were all very tired, we sought our couch of palm leaves. I threw a large piece of gum upon the fire before retiring, and sat a while watching the curling smoke and inhaling the sweet incense.

There was a moon, a bright moon shining in the heavens, but I could not see it through the trees; it only turned the darkness of night beneath the foliage into dusky gloom, and twinkled through the leaves a single diamond ray.

The voices of the night are many, but principally issue from frogs and nocturnal cicadæ. The most conspicuous is the "crak-crak," which continually repeats the two syllables forming its name, from sunset to sunrise. There are several frogs also that give utterance to the most comical sounds; but the one that made me laugh was a small frog, like a rain-frog, and what he repeated all night long was this: " Rig a jig jig, rig a jig jig, amen ! "

Soon, the many voices blended into one, and I was asleep. Wrapped in my blanket, my gun by my side, and my two Indians stretched in slumber near me, I slept long and soundly, nor stirred till near morning. It may have been an hour before daylight, as I lay in that half conscious state that sometimes precedes awaking, I heard distinctly the ringing of steel upon steel, echo through the forest. Listening dreamily, I heard it again — *cling, clang!* Instantly I was transported to another clime, and the forest and its tropical wonders faded away. I was in a little New England town, in the shop of the village blacksmith, with the old mare I used to drive waiting for a shoe. It was a hot, sultry day in July, the hay-makers were sweltering in the sun, and the leaves on the trees stood still. *Cling, clang, cling!* I saw the old blacksmith smiting the shoe as he fashioned it, and heard the metallic ring as the hammer fell with a half-blow upon the anvil. *Cling!* — " Monsieur ! "

" What — what's the matter ? "

" Monsieur," — it was Coryet who spoke — " you no hear ze blacksmit ? "

" The blacksmith ! ah, yes ; but where is he ? "

" Oh, m'sieur, he no on ze *terre*, he *en haut* in ze tree."

" In the tree ! A blacksmith in a tree ? "

" Oui, m'sieur, *mais* he no blacksmit veritable, he inseck ; he make ze noise wiz hees weeng."

Now I saw it clearly, it was one of those cicadæ, or a cricket, which produces such a noise by rubbing together the heel-plates of its wings. Thus was my pleasant dream dissipated. It was now about sunrise, though it would be long before the sun could penetrate our leafy grove. Meyong made but little fire, just enough for the preparation of our coffee, for the wary parrots would detect our whereabouts, and depart farther up the mountain. We heard the faint cry of one, answered by another, far down the mountain-side, and this stimulated us to extra haste in departing.

Coryet and Meyong were to descend by a ravine to a valley, while I was to follow along the ridge a mile or so, and take my stand beneath a tall tree which was accurately described. I preferred going alone, as I ever do when hunting, not only from the fact that less noise would attend me, but that then I could indulge to the full that communion with nature which the presence of a companion always interrupts, or rudely breaks.

It was still gloomy in the forest; a shower had fallen during the night, and leaves, vines, and ferns were heavy with moisture. Noiselessly I pursued my way, indulging in that sweet reverie which solitude in a great forest always excites. Suddenly there broke upon the stillness the faint report of a gun. This at once stirred the blood in my veins, as my boys had promised not to shoot at any other bird than the imperial parrot, and I hoped that this announced the capture of one. Impatiently resting beneath the huge tree, and concealing myself in a bower of orchids and hanging ferns, I waited for something to appear. Soon the harsh screams of parrots broke upon my ear, and a flock of ten or twelve swept through the woods like a whirlwind, just beyond range. They were the small green parrot, another species, but equally desirable with the larger. Then all was still again, the deep silence broken only by the call of the wood-pigeon.

Turning my attention more closely to the vines that enclosed me, to be satisfied that there were no poisonous centipedes or scorpions lurking there, I unexpectedly beheld a vision of loveliness seldom vouchsafed to dwellers of the icy North. Close at hand, within two feet of me, sat a tiny humming-bird on a downy nest, which was fastened upon a twig no larger than a pencil. During all my stay it had sat there, gazing upon the first object of human kind, probably, it had ever beheld. Fearlessly it glanced at me with its bright, black eyes, and curiously it followed my every motion with its shapely little head. Involuntarily I stretched forth my hand to touch it, but at once drew back for fear it might take alarm and fly away. A buzzing of wings attracted my attention, and I beheld the mate of the one on the nest, who darted at me with unmistakable fury, his glittering crest erected and anger shooting from his eyes. Verily! had this pigmy's body been in proportion to his heart, I should have been destroyed. Satisfied that he could not drive me away by darting at my eyes, he rested himself a moment upon a twig near the nest, where he was at once joined by the female, who seemed to endeavor by caresses to soothe his ruffled temper and to assure him that my intentions toward them were not evil. Touched to the heart by this exhibition of trust and love, I would not have harmed these little innocents for a fortune. Exposed for a moment, as the female left the nest, were two eggs, white as snow, diminutive as seed-pearls.

For several hours I watched without even a sound

to reward me, and during my stay those humming-birds watched with me, the male darting off upon frequent forays for insects and honey, the female snuggled cosily in her dainty nest. The little husband now looked upon me as an intruder, to be tolerated only upon sufferance, and at my slightest motion he would dive at my face; at which exhibition of bravery the little wife would twitter with delight and swell with pride.

Finally I retraced my steps, as it was near noon. I had nearly reached camp when I saw a puff of smoke and heard a loud report, and directly Coryet, who had espied me, ran forward with animated gestures. Interpreting their meaning, and obeying his directions, which he jabbered in broken French, I directed my attention to an immense gommier tree a few hundred feet away. At first I saw nothing, but approaching I gradually resolved the mass of foliage into its component leaves and twigs, vines and air plants, and caught sight of a glowing body clothed in purple and golden-green.

In the cloud of smoke from my gun it disappeared, but only to gleam again athwart the leafy space ere it fell with heavy thud to the ground. To recover it was the work of an instant with the excited Indian, whose enthusiasm almost equalled mine as he placed in my hands this largest of all the parrots of the Indies. Their first shot in the morning had been ineffectual, but the second had wounded the mate to this; and it was its loud cries that caused my bird to remain so long in a place fraught with so much danger.

At last I had secured this valuable bird! And I

had the satisfaction, several months later, of learning that mine were the first ever sent to America. Does it not seem strange that though Columbus, in 1493, when he approached this island of Dominica, especially noticed the "flights of parrots and other tropical birds," nearly four hundred years should elapse before one of these parrots should reach the continent he was the means of discovering?

This bird is peculiar to the island and is found nowhere else. Its cry is harsh, somewhat resembling the cry of the wild turkey. It does not, like the small parrots, associate in flocks, but is always found in pairs; once mated, they are sundered only by death. Morning and evening, when feeding, they cry out noisily, but at other times are silent; though if a gun be fired within their hearing, or a tree fall, they will all scream loudly and harshly once or twice, and then subside into perfect silence. They are shy and wild, since in the autumn months they are much hunted, being then fat and delicious. In size, they are nearly as large as a fowl, being twenty-three inches long and thirty-six in extent of wings. In color, they are bright green above and purple beneath, with metallic reflections. Rarely does it descend to the valleys, as its favorite food is in the mountains. Its nest is made in the broken shaft of a palm, very high from the ground. The young, if obtained early, will readily learn to talk.

While the two Indians were away looking for more parrots, an accident happened to one of my birds which greatly excited my ire. I had skinned both birds and plentifully besprinkled them with arsenic, and had left them on a log near the ajoupa, while I went in search of some dry moss with which to stuff them. Returning, when some distance away I heard a low grunt, and looking up saw a large hog, black as night and gaunt as a wolf, snuffing at the log. I darted forward with a cry, but not before the sable fiend had seized one of the birds by the head and started to run. Thinking only of my specimen, I pressed him so closely that he turned at bay, showing fangs long as my fingers. Then he started again, as I hesitated a moment, and ran more swiftly than before. In running, he stepped upon the trailing wing of the bird and wrenched the head from the body, but kept on, crunching the bones between his powerful jaws, and disappeared in a clump of bamboos. As I had neither gun nor knife, I was powerless to avert this catastrophe, but was obliged to bottle my wrath until Meyong's return. He then informed me that there were hundreds of wild hogs in the woods, but that we would require dogs to hunt them with.

It was at once decided that Coryet should return to the coast on the morrow with my birds, procure more provisions, and two hunting-dogs belonging to old Joseph, a chief. Upon his return we would move higher up the mountains, and seek reparation for my bird from the droves of wild hogs there roaming the forests. At the same time it was possible I might add to my captures that inhabitant of the upper volcano, the *Diablotin*, or " Little Devil," which had not been seen for thirty years.

CHAPTER IX.

A DAY IN THE DEEP WOODS.

THE BEE-TREE. — ENVELOPED IN PLANTS. — ASCENDING THE GIANT TREE. — SMOKING OUT THE BEES. — VEGETABLE ROPES. — HONEY AD LIBITUM. — A BITE. — A HOWL. — THE BEE-EATERS. — CARIB PERVERSITY. — SWEET CONTENT. — HOW TO DRAW A BEE-LINE. — THE PALM TROUGHS. — A BAMBOO CUP. — A STROLL AND AN ALARM. — THE CARIB GHOST. — TRADITIONS. — THE MARCH RESUMED. — AN ARMY OF CRABS. — CRABS THAT MIGRATE. — DELICIOUS FOOD. — THE MOUNTAIN PEAK. — HUNTING THE "DIABLOTIN." — IS IT A MYTH? — CAUGHT IN A STORM. — THE CARIB CASTLE. — THE CAPTIVE'S CAVE. — VAMPIRES. — THE FOREST SPIRIT.

EARLY the next morning, Coryet departed for the coast, taking with him nothing but his cutlass, his pannier, and a cooked tannier to eat on the way. He left us barely enough provisions for a day, but Meyong reckoned upon finding some wild yams, and shooting birds and agoutis. He went a little way with his beloved friend, and then returned to the ajoupa.

After the customary coffee had been prepared and brought me, he returned to the fire and proceeded to collect together four or five brands some two feet in length, with blazing ends, and bind them firmly into a flambeau, with tough lianes. Knowing it was unnecessary to question him when he had unrestrained power to do as he pleased in the forest, I watched him as he fastened on his wicker pannier, and lined it with broad leaves. This once strapped to his shoulders, he took up the calabàsh, the cutlass and blazing brands, and bade me follow him. I did so, carrying, of course, my gun (my never-absent friend), and swinging on my game-basket, with a supply of cartridges.

He then led the way down the hill, and stopped almost in sight of the smoke of our fire in camp. It was beneath a tree of vast size, which shot up from a wilderness of fallen trunks and limbs, a gommier, towering aloft in kingly majesty, enveloped in lianes which hung from every bough and limb, thickly covered with broad-leaved parasites, orchids and wild pines, its base throwing out strong buttresses like the cypress of the South, but higher and broader, its upper limbs jagged and weather-beaten, stretching their multitudinous fingers heavenward two hundred feet above us. It was beginning to decay, and this forest monarch of centuries, perhaps, was almost ready to totter on his throne.

Meyong pointed to a dark spot as large as my hand, some sixty feet above, and said, "You no see um?"

"See what?"

"Ze bees!"

Then I fully understood the meaning of his preparations, which I had till then hardly surmised. This was a *bee-tree*, the home of a swarm, one of the numberless progeny of some bees from Europe, which went wild a hundred years ago.

Laying his gun at the foot of the tree, and lopping off a few leaves from a parasite overhead, to protect it from the damp, Meyong seized hold of a large liane, cut it from its attachment at the base, and climbed up into the tree. Remember, there were no limbs for eighty feet. About twenty feet up he rested a moment, and requested me to attach the bundle of smoking fagots to a liane; he then drew it up to him and stuck it into a crevice.

Then he went up again, — he didn't "shin," by clinging with his arms and legs; the tree was too broad, and the mass of vines and plants too enormous for that, — but he just seized a liane, like a rope, between his toes, the great toe and the one next it, and *walked* up, hand over hand, and toe over toe. The pannier fastened to his shoulders, and the cutlass dangling behind from his belt, gave him the appearance of a hump-backed monkey, as he ascended rapidly, half enveloped in smoke. Great parasites, with leaves like cabbage leaves, and orchids large as peonies, came crashing down, sprinkling me with water from their inverted calyxes, as he went on steadily climbing.

At last he reached a point just beneath the hole, at a height equal to the mast-head of a brig, and then, holding on with one hand, he drew up the firebrands and thrust their unlighted ends into a crevice a little below the hole. He signaled me to attach the calabash to a lialine no larger than a fish-line, which I did, and awaited further orders. Detaching a brand from the bundle, he thrust it into the hole previous to putting in his hand. He was almost hidden by a cloud of angry bees, who, stupefied by the smoke, did not seem to recognize in him an enemy, and hundreds alighted upon his shirt and pantaloons, and many on his bare legs. The hole was too small, and Meyong enlarged it with his cutlass; previously, however, he had formed a staging upon which to stand, about four feet beneath the aperture, by thrusting a stout pole through the lianes, and lashing it with a lialine. The fagots, to which he had secured a piece of punky wood, were smoking bravely, and he now signaled me to send up the calabash. First, however, he filled his leaf-lined pannier, or basket-knapsack, with great flakes of wax, throwing away the first crust, which was brown and dry, and very soon had it full to the top with honey-laden wax. Detaching it, he lowered it down by one of the living ropes which surrounded him, and drew up and filled the calabash. I laid the wax dripping with honey upon some long and broad leaves of the wild plantain, three feet long by one foot broad. At every successive descent of the vessel it contained more and more liquid, and at last came down with but little wax, nothing but golden and fragrant syrup.

What should I do? There was no bowl or pan to put it in.

Meyong saw my perplexity, and shouted down for me to collect some of the boat-shaped spathes of the mountain palm, the sheaths that protect and overhang the seeds and flowers. A palm lay prostrate near me; two of its spathes, exactly like the half of a pea-pod in shape, five feet long and two feet wide, were quickly drawn to the tree. They were clean and freshly washed by the dews of the morning, and into one of these I poured the honey fast as it came to me from the tree above.

An exclamation caused me to look up, and I saw my friend in agony, grimaces passing swiftly over his face, as he endeavored vainly to dislodge an intruding bee, whose success in finding a vulnerable place on

Meyong's skin was proclaimed by that worthy in a howl of dismay.

Meyong was a good boy and generally very tractable, but he would never listen to my advice and wear his shirt inside his pantaloons. He said it was the *fashion* to wear it outside, and used an expression equivalent to that in so common use among the ladies: "To be out of fashion is to be out of the world."

I argued with him and entreated him, but in this he would have his own way; and I really believe that if every man in the Carib nation were bitten by a bee every day in his mortal life, he would still persist in displaying a flag of distress above his nether coverings.

And thus he went on, with alternate howls and exclamations of sweeter character, such as *miel douce*, (honey sweet,) until the great palm troughs were full enough and I concluded it would be well to desist.

Early in the proceedings he had whistled shrilly several times, and when I asked the reason, he said it was to call the *mal fini*. "Mal fini" was the name given to the hawk, from its cry; but this applied to a small bird of the fly-catcher family, which would come and eat the bees and thus diminish the number of Meyong's assailants. The bird came, a small, shy, gray bird, which approached cautiously, evidently astonished to see a human being up in a tree surrounded with smoke, and another at the foot of the tree. But he did not stop to speculate, but worked assiduously, and soon he was joined by others; though their united efforts failed to lessen perceptibly the angry swarm.

Supplied with all the honey I cared for, I sat contentedly upon a fallen log, with my feet thrust down

A DAY IN THE DEEP WOODS.

among tangled twigs, exposed to the gaze of ants, centipedes, scorpions and what not, and calmly munched the waxen cells, expressing from those hexagonal receptacles their delicious burden of honey, by a process the most primitive, but also the most satisfactory, known to man.

As I sat there a picture of sweet endeavor, Meyong prepared to descend, and brought with him as he swung down, hand under hand, a cloud of bees, who, attracted by the cargo of honey in the spathes and by my sweet countenance, left the boy and traveled in my direction. Entangled as I was in the meshwork of branches, I furnished a scene for the hardened Meyong, who, still smarting from recent stings, was a most joyful witness of my discomfiture.

Though never an apt scholar in mathematics, I learned a lesson from the bees that day, and described, as accurately as the nature of the ground would allow, a *bee-line* for camp. I think the most stupid student in school would be able to understand that a straight line was the "shortest distance between two points," with a swarm of angry bees after him thirsting for his blood; especially, when at one of those points was safety, and at the other bees.

In the afternoon I went out hunting and was successful, bringing back several pigeons. Meyong meanwhile had not been idle, for he had, ready-cooked, the cabbage of a mountain palm, and two hideous grubs nicely browning over the coals. Now we had vegetables, meat and honey, but there was no utensil for dipping out the latter from the troughs.

"Come wiz me," said Meyong.

I went with him a few rods to a clump of bamboos

— the same in which the hog had disappeared the day before. Selecting a long reed an inch and a half in diameter, he cut it off with his cutlass. The joints in this reed were about four inches apart, and it was a hollow tube partitioned at the joints; upon the outside of each grew a lateral branch. Trimming off the small shoot and cutting the larger part off about three inches each side of it, he had then a double-ended cup with a firm handle, divided in the middle. Upon our return to the village, Meyong covered this cup very neatly with basket-work; and I have it now before me as I write.

Towards night, I took my gun and wandered a little way from camp to try to shoot some of the immense vampire bats that haunted the forest. My attention being taken up with the many objects about me, I wandered farther than I had intended, and darkness fell about me at a distance from the camp. If the days are glorious, the tropic nights are grand; impressive in the deep brooding silence, until the insects of the night break the stillness, or the hoot of the owl, or the shriek of the diablotin, disturbs it.

I had been seated a little while and it had grown quite dark, and I was about returning, when, as I moved, a stick crackled sharply, thrilling me through with a strange feeling of fear. It was nothing but a dry twig upon which I myself had stepped, yet an unaccountable dread of moving possessed me at that moment, as though I felt the presence of another person near, whom I could not see. As I walked, I peered all about me, but could see nothing. Yet, during all that short walk I felt as if in the presence of a powerful man about to lay his hand on my shoulder.

This feeling I could not shake off; but I reached camp without harm, though my face must have betrayed me, for Meyong noticed my agitation and remarked: "Ah, you meet jumbie, eh?"

Jombie, or jumbie, is the name by which are known the evil spirits who walk the earth.

"No," I replied, "I have seen nothing." I did not care to show to Meyong any such foolish fear as had just before possessed me.

"You no see him, but he see you; something make you 'fraid." This I could not deny; and then Meyong launched into the story of the ghost that haunted this mountain, which he fully believed. Stretched upon my bed of palm-leaves, I listened as he talked.

"If 'crak-crak' bawl one kind way, some person go to dead. Me sinks me hear zat to-day. Long agone, in old Carib time, one berry cruel man say he must to be bury like he sit down, he must to be put in he grave just like he sit on bench. Well, zey make him so, and not long all ze person get walloping; zey know not who make it, but if a man only so speak of ze man buried and say, 'Ah, poor fellah,' he shu to get him skin well wallop. It make ze person most fright to dead, and if zey but go near he hut where him bury in ze night, zey must to see him jumbie and get blow on ze head. Soon again, he jumbie take to go in ze canoe all about ze coast; when zey go fishin' he always to be dah: he whistle, he sing, an' ze canoe men use to him an' not mine him. One day ze canoe swamp an' ze jumbie make to drown, but ze Carib men he no drown; zey see him no mo'. Person say he come up to ze mountain, zat I sinks myself. After zat, no mo' Carib bury like him sitting down."

By the time this was finished I was asleep and knew no more till morning. Instead of waiting for Coryet on the third day, Meyong proposed that we should make an easy march up the mountain-side, leaving a sign for his friend to follow when he should reach the camp. Our route lay through a region similar to the one we left, only constantly becoming more and more elevated and consequently rugged.

It was during this march that we met one of the most curious processions ever seen in this land of wonders. Climbing the steep hill-side, and clinging by one hand as I climbed, giving all my attention to my work, I suddenly became conscious that I was surrounded by moving objects, whom I could hear as they rustled over leaves and rocks. I rubbed my eyes and looked around. Meyong was behind, but saw them at the same time I did, and eagerly shouted, "*Gardez!* Ze crabs!" It was true, there was *an army of crabs*, and we were in the midst of it. It behooved us to get out of the way at once, for these crabs (as large as a good-sized crab of the sea-shore) have a disagreeable way of climbing up and over everything in their course, and of using their powerful claws upon the slightest provocation.

Well, we got behind a large tree, and my guide made side forays upon them as they went by (for they are most delicious eating), until we had collected as many as he could carry.

And how, think you, did he secure them? Why, he just tied their claws together with a lialine, a small cord-like root, and then placed them in a heap at his feet. Fortunate for us that this was a small army, otherwise I don't know how soon we could have pursued our way, for they sometimes travel by thousands. A very old French writer gives the only account that we can find of these crabs; and were it not that I had seen them on the march, there are some things he says the truth of which I should be inclined to doubt.

They live not only in a kind of orderly and quiet society in their

AN ARMY OF CRABS.

retreats in the mountains, but regularly once a year march down to the seaside in a body, some millions at a time. They choose the months of April and May to begin their expeditions, and then sally out from the stumps of hollow trees, clefts of rocks, and from holes which they dig for themselves in the earth.

The sea is their destination, and here they cast their spawn. For this purpose, no sooner has the crab reached the shore than it eagerly goes to the edge of the water and lets the waves wash over its body to wash off the spawn. The eggs are hatched under the sand, and soon after, millions of the new-born crabs are seen quitting the shore, and slowly traveling up the mountains. In going down, they turn neither to right nor left; even if they meet a house, they will attempt to scale it. The procession sets forward with the precision of an army. It is commonly divided into battalions, with the strongest in front. The night is their chief time of traveling, but if it rains by day, they improve that occasion. When the sun shines, they make a universal halt till evening. In the season of moulting, they retire to their burrows to cast their shells, filling them with grass and leaves.

My native boy's account of their habits agreed substantially with this, and he added, moreover, that if there was any one thing better than another, it was the flesh of these same crabs; a statement I can cheerfully verify, as that night we feasted on crab on the half-shell, crabs' claws, crab fricasseed and crab roasted.

As the camp we had left was at a good height above the sea-coast, we were now in the upper regions of the mountains. The vegetation had already changed to a great extent and had more of an Alpine character. As we walked along we could now and then catch glimpses of the sea at a distance, and obtain a view of the nearer sea of trees, spread over the fair valleys below us. In the afternoon we were painfully scaling the precipitous sides of one of the two peaks which form the double summit of Morne Diablotin. We were now in the region especially appropriated as his home by the *Diablotin*, or "Little Devil;" and anxiously we searched, as we scrambled over the loose rock, for some trace of the hole in which he lived.

Wherever I had been in the island I had heard of the diablotin, and my curiosity was excited to such a degree that I determined to clear away the mystery which surrounded it. For thirty years it had remained unseen. Many treated as a myth this story of a bird living in the mountains (for it is a bird) so long a period without appearing to human vision. But sufficient proof existed, in my opinion, to warrant a search for it. The older people of the island had distinct remembrances of seeing it, and attributed its disappearance to the depredations of the "manacou," a marsupial animal like an opossum, which hunted it from its holes and devoured it and its eggs. No two persons agreed as to its color, shape, or size; but I had seen in an old French work, written by a Catholic missionary to these islands some two centuries ago, — the Père Labat — a good description of the bird. This description, doubtless translated bodily, I also found in an old history of Dominica, published in 1791. It says: "The *diablotin*, so called by the French from its uncommonly ugly appearance, is nearly the size of a duck, and is web-footed. It has a big, round head, crooked bill like a hawk, and large, full eyes like an owl. Its head, part of the neck, chief feathers of the wings and tail, are black; the other parts of its body are covered with a fine, milk-white down. They feed on fish, flying in great flocks to the seaside in the night-time, and in their flight make a disagreeable noise like owls, which bird they also resemble in their dislike of the day, when they are hid in holes in the mountains, where they are easily caught. This is done by stopping up some of the holes which lead to their hiding-places and placing empty bags over the rest, which communicate underground with those stopped. The birds, at their usual time of going forth to seek their food in the night-time, finding their passage impeded, make to the holes covered with the bags, into which entering, great numbers of them are caught."

Though hardly accepting the statement by the mountaineers that a bird so far-flying could be exterminated by a merely local disturber, I was obliged to admit that it no longer inhabited its old homes. For two hours we prolonged the search, cold and wet, but found nothing to reward us. We saw, to be sure, many cracks and crannies in the rocks where a diablotin might have hidden, but no long holes, such as those made by the "Mother Cary's chickens" in the Bay of Fundy. There, five years previously, I had drawn many a petrel from the end of a long, winding hole, as it sat quietly upon its single egg; but this other petrel (for it is a giant petrel, probably the *Prion Caribbæa*) was not to be found, and I departed sorrowfully down the mountain, to look for shelter.

We were at such an altitude that mist and rain constantly surrounded us. The fierce wind, that always blows from the eastward, nearly swept us over the narrow crest. Thunder boomed beneath and around us, and rain fell in torrents at times, and the view I had hoped to obtain of the fairest group of islands in the Southern Sea was hidden by a veil of mist and fog. It was nearly dark, though perhaps not very late; but the cloud of mist aided approaching night, and I was apprehensive that exposure would result to our injury, especially as there was no roof to cover us and no material for making a fire. My implicit faith in the resources of my guide was not unrewarded, for we had descended but a short distance when he cried out, pointing to an immense rock as large as a church, just in sight farther down, "You no see ajoupa?"

It was, as I said, a huge rock, so delicately poised upon a spur from the main ridge that it seemed ready to fall. We seemed surrounded by an almost interminable forest beneath, while above towered the twin mountain-peaks, bare and gray. As those near peaks were more than five thousand feet above the sea, we were now in a region cold and bleak, forty-eight hundred feet above the coast. Meyong had called this rock an ajoupa, and there must be, I knew, some reason for it, as he was one of those matter-of-fact persons who call a spade a spade. Just as we reached an angle of the rock he turned abruptly from the trail and dived beneath another rock into a hole about breast-high. Following him, I found myself in a spacious cavern hollowed out of the rock, with an entrance on the mountain-side just large enough to admit a man conveniently.

The sudden transition from the howling of a tempest to comparative silence, from the fury of a pelting rain to the shelter of a roof, was bewildering, and I looked about me in wonder. While I stood in the semi-darkness that wrapped everything in gloom, the water dripping from my saturated garments, Meyong drew out from a corner of the cave a manufactured flambeau and lighted it. By the glare it shed around I could see that I was in a smoke-blackened chamber large enough to contain fifty men, with high vaulted roof and rude seats hollowed out of the rock near the floor, which latter was covered with a thin coating of earth. There was a large heap of dry wood near the entrance, from which Meyong drew enough for a fire, which was soon blazing cheerily, the smoke escaping through some crevices in the roof.

My first care was for my beloved gun; and having taken off the barrels and inverted them near the fire, I oiled the locks and steel parts of the stock, and, later, the barrels themselves; then stripping myself of clothing, I drew a blanket over my shoulders and waited for my garments to dry. Huge bats, disturbed by the unwonted light, flapped above us with regular beats of their broad wings, some of them large as pigeons, known as vampires, true blood-suckers. A small variety also flew softly about, hundreds of them playing in the space above our heads and darting at us.

"Zis old Charaib caverne," said Meyong.

"What, the one to which the chief carried the governor's wife?" demanded I quickly.

"*Oui*, ze rock veritable."

A long time ago, — nearly or quite two hundred years, — when the Carib was known only as the cruel, untamable cannibal, these Indians made long cruises in their canoes to procure victims for sacrifice at their feasts. One hundred miles north of Dominica lies the lovely island of Antigua, at that time thinly settled. To this island the Caribs made frequent predatory raids, always returning well rewarded. In one of these excursions the chief of the tribe captured the wife of the governor of Antigua, who lived in a secluded nook in that island, near the sea. She was brought a prisoner to this place, to this very cave, Meyong says, and held, contrary to their custom, for ransom. I will not try to depict the wrath and despair of the husband, nor the details of the pursuit he at once organized, but merely state that he sought her out, traced her to the Carib retreat by fragments of clothing torn from her by cruel thorns, and eventually succeeded in returning with her. She had been weeks in captivity, but had been well treated.

This, then, was the cavern in which that delicate lady lay captive, nearly two centuries ago! Truly, it was a poor retreat for a tenderly nurtured woman, but a grand one for Meyong and myself. After the fire was well going, Meyong made a large torch, which he stuck in a crevice outside as a guide to Coryet in his ascent. The crabs, which the sly fellow, with wise forethought, had deposited in a heap by the rock as we had ascended, were then brought in and some of them roasted; and these, with some cold boiled yam, made a grateful repast. We sat over the fire till late, then spread our blankets upon the earth and lay down to sleep.

Several hours later I was awakened by a disturbance, and rolling over quickly, saw Coryet standing in the doorway. But it appeared more like his apparition than himself in flesh and blood, as he stood there shaking with cold. The dogs, which he held in leash, as soon as released slunk into a corner with their tails between their legs, uttering low whines.

The fire had burned low, and it was only by its fitful gleams that I saw this strange vision. Meyong touched me, and whispered, "Coryet see jumbie."

So it was; he had seen the visitor of whom I had but felt the presence. Looking upon this event, or chain of events, in the light of subsequent revelations, I laugh; but at that time I almost believed, with my boys, in the existence of a forest spirit.

CHAPTER X.

A MIDNIGHT MARCH, AND WHAT CAME OF IT.

THE APPARITION. — THE LOST CHIEF. — A FORGOTTEN LANGUAGE. — THE MARCH BY TORCHLIGHT. — STRANGE AND DISTORTED FORMS. — THE FOREST WILDERNESS. — A MYSTERIOUS SOUND. — "A TREE FELLED BY GOD." — VIRGIN, PROTECT US! — COOKING BY STEAM. — THE ROSEWOOD CABIN. — THE CHIEF DISAPPEARS. — IS IT GOLD? — A SMALL BOA CONSTRICTOR. — A CARIB BASILISK. — THE BIGGEST BUG IN THE WORLD. — IT COMES IN SEARCH OF THE NATURALIST. — THE HERCULES BEETLE. — CENTIPEDES. — SCORPIONS. — AN UNNAMED PALM WITH EDIBLE SEEDS. — A PRIESTESS OF OBEAH. — AFRICAN WITCHCRAFT. — ITS STRONGHOLD. — PROSTRATED BY THE HEAT. — FEVER.

DRAWING the well-nigh exhausted Coryet into the cave, Meyong quickly revived the fire, and assisted him to disburden himself of his load of provisions. Weak and trembling, the boy sank to the earth; and not till a drink of rum had been poured down his throat could he tell us the cause of his alarm. With us as excited listeners, he then gave a story, of which the following is the substance:

He arrived at the camp late in the forenoon, and, finding we had left for the cave, followed on at once. Burdened with his load and the care of the dogs, he was obliged to travel slowly, and it was dark long before he left the high-woods belt and struck the upper trail. He was not afraid, however, as the dogs gave him company, and he walked cheerily on, until a low growl from one of his canine companions caused him to look around. Then he saw, creeping stealthily through the low trees on his left, a figure which to his excited imagination seemed clothed in shining white. He was so terribly frightened, that, notwithstanding his heavy load, he darted forward over the rocks at a rapid pace. The rattling of the stones set adrift by his feet, as they bounded down the steep mountain-side, impressed him the more that the spirit was pursuing him, and he ran with all his might. The flambeau that Meyong had prepared to guide him was now but a flickering brand, and he did not see it until close upon it. By its presence, however, he was enabled more easily to find the cave, in the mouth of which he stood as before described.

He had barely finished this recital when a loud exclamation from Meyong caused me to look up, and I saw in the place so lately occupied by Coryet another apparition. This time it was surely the ghost. He was not clad in white, however, but in tattered garments of skin, and his long hands grasped the top of a staff such as no spirit could wield, assuredly. As soon as we had recovered from our surprise I sprang forward and aided this tottering figure to the fire. It was an old man, a very old Indian, who, if he could speak, I thought, might be able to tell us of the capture of that fair lady who was imprisoned here so many years ago. He uttered no word, made no sign; but we did not need either to inform us that he was starving and perishing. Again the rum was brought into requisition, again did my faithful Meyong bring forth from the ashes the tender crabs for our unexpected guest.

Without a doubt, this was the jumbie that had given both Coryet and myself such a fright. This harmless, pitiful old man, who had approached us in the dire extremity of want, had nearly perished through being taken for a visitor from the spirit-world, which he manifestly so soon would reach. This assurance was not necessary to induce my boys to tenderly care for him, and we soon had the satisfaction of seeing the poor creature resting on the ground in peaceful slumber. After this event nothing occurred to disturb our rest, and we all slept well, the spirit laid that had alarmed us; and not one of those to whom this cave belonged in olden time did trouble us.

We stayed there all the succeeding day, and renewed our search, though unsuccessfully, for the *Diablotin*. Our guest slept till nearly noon, but when he awoke he seemed greatly refreshed, and strove to make us sensible of his gratitude. The words he uttered were those of an unknown tongue, but we knew that he fain would express his thanks, and tried to assure him that we understood him.

It was finally concluded between Coryet and Meyong that this old man was a crazy chief, who, refusing to submit to English rule, had fled to the mountains more than fifty years ago, whence he sometimes visited the Indians of the coast by stealth. For several years he had not been seen, and it was thought that he was dead. He had been insane for many years. Towards night he became restless, and late in the evening he insisted upon going outside. Finally, his desire to depart grew so strong, and his gestures to us to follow so violent, that, after consultation, my boys were convinced that it would be best to follow him. The night was dark, as the moon had not then risen, but it was clear. When the old man learned that we were willing to accompany him he seemed content; but whether joy or sadness overspread his features, it was all one with the expression of them, so sunken and wrinkled were they. The boys prepared torches and collected our luggage, and then we started off. The old Indian struck a brisker gait than we had supposed him capable of, and we followed by the light of the torches.

There is a weird solemnity about a night march in a great forest. On either side of you is a wall of inky blackness; before, behind, the same enclosing gloom, against which the torches send a feeble glare. By the time we had reached the high woods, where the trees were completely enveloped in masses of vines, our surroundings assumed an aspect wild and terrible. That hanging liane, twisted and contorted, took the shape of a serpent ready to dart at us as we passed. The flickering play of the light upon the leaves of trees and parasites, alternately bringing to view and leaving in shade strange forms, gave to everything a startlingly living appearance. It was as if all had been changed into animated beings, especially noxious insects, like scorpions and spiders, which, one and all, seemed crawling in our direction.

At last we came into a more open forest, a densely wooded plateau, the home of the wild hog and the resort of runaway slaves in olden time. Very few, even of the hunters, visited these dark woods we were now traversing. We penetrated the dense shade, following now our guide, for the boys were wholly at loss. Suddenly there boomed through the forest a thunderous sound that waked the echoes of the entire region, accompanied by a shock as of a slight earthquake; then all was still as death. Startled, I seized Meyong by the arm, and inquired the cause of that noise. He replied, with a shrug, that it was "a tree felled by God," and crossed himself devoutly.

A tree felled by God! A monarch old and weather-beaten, that had outlived centuries of storm and hurricane, only to fall in the dead of night, when the breeze stirring would not have wakened a bird! Is there not something grandly awful in this?— something that causes a thrill of awe and makes one regard with veneration the great Being who created all these wonders, which are to us so great, to Him so small? It fell so close that, as it went crashing through the trees with the force of a thunderbolt, the wind created by its fall fanned our torches into brighter blaze.

With indignant and frightened howls our curs broke away from Coryet and disappeared in the darkness, carrying with them our hopes of capturing the wild hogs of the forest. Scarcely had I recovered from this shock when there came borne upon the still night air, the faint puffing of steam, like the sobs of an engine in from a long run. It grew louder and louder as we advanced; and as neither of my boys knew the cause of it, and the old man spoke nothing but Carib, to us as Hebrew, we were forced to march on in ignorance, myself in doubt, the boys in trepidation, muttering prayers to the Virgin. At last our guide halted right on the banks of a deep ravine and threw a great stone into the depths below us, from which howled and sputtered escaping steam. Immediately upon the throwing of the stone there was an increased force given to the noise, as though it had struck in a small pipe and been forcibly ejected. The noise then for a moment ceased, and the old man beckoned us to follow quickly, as he plunged into the ravine and scrambled over great rocks and across a roaring brook.

It was long after midnight when he finally stopped at the side of a great rock, against which was built a low cabin, the sides of logs, the roof of thatch. To gain entrance we were obliged to penetrate a deep thicket of low trees which completely screened it. As the light from the torches revealed the dingy interior, I involuntarily shrank back and thought wistfully of the comfortable cave we had so lately left. Resigning myself to the bed made for me, I was soon wrapped in slumber.

The old man, who had disappeared, re-appeared in the morning with a good repast, — yams, iguana, and land crabs — but all *boiled*. This circumstance, together with the absence of fire, led me to investigate his cuisine; and, if the reader has not already anticipated it, I can tell how this poor Carib utilized the forces of nature and made them do his bidding. Following him to the ravine, I saw, in a small opening in the ground whence issued puffs of steam accompanied by loud reports, the source of all the noises of the preceding night. Near this steam-escape was another hole whence the water bubbled up and over, flowing off in a hot stream. Into this boiling spring my friend lowered a tannier-root fastened at the end of a lialine. The tannier is, when boiled, of greater consistency than a potato, else he would have lost his breakfast. In a few minutes the vegetable was completely cooked, and he drew it out. Meat he lowered down in small baskets made of tough roots. A small cold stream flowed near by; and thus this rich-poor man had, with the game of the forest, everything he wanted right at hand.

Returning to the cabin, my attention was called to the logs of which its walls were built. They were solid rosewood, which once grew wild in these forests. Could they have been transported to the coast, they would have brought a good price. The cabin was one of those built by some of the Maroons, or runaway slaves, some forty years ago, when they escaped to the mountains and formed so formidable a body that troops were required several years to capture and subdue them. The space we were in was shaped like the bottom of a shallow bowl, surrounded by high hills, the dry crater, probably, of an extinct volcano. There were many evidences of the residence of the runaways, in dismantled cabins, and gardens, and fruit-trees. It is thought that the wild hogs roaming about the surrounding hills were from their stock.

We were much puzzled to account for the mysterious visits the old man paid now and then to a gloomy gorge, into which he would not allow us to penetrate. My boys related the story, prevalent some ten years previously, that the old man had a lovely grand-daughter, only survivor of the family he took with him to the woods. They thought she must be, at the present time, about thirty years old; and they described her as being as beautiful as the old man was ugly, which was saying a good deal. But we did not at that time see this fair Carib, nor did we even obtain conclusive proof of her existence. There was, however, much in the old man's behavior that gave us the impression that he had a hidden treasure near of some kind; he seemed as anxious to get rid of us as before he had been to have us come with him.

When the old Indian visited the gorge again, Coryet was on his track, at a distance not to be observed, yet near enough to note his movements. He followed the bed of the stream running through the hot-spring basin until it was narrowed to a rivulet flowing between high converging walls of rock. A narrow ledge, sometimes in, sometimes above the water, afforded a pathway through, after following which for a few hundred feet, the old Indian disappeared in an opening in the rock. It was just wide enough for Coryet to squeeze through, but soon opened into a wide chamber-like passage so dark that the boy was terrified and soon beat a retreat. He could hear his guide, however, as he scrambled over loose rocks and stones, penetrating deeper and deeper into the cavern. He lighted a match and examined the rock, but discovered nothing save that it seemed veined with sparkling metal. He brought me a fragment containing this ore, but whether it was gold or pyrites I could not tell at the time. I tried to save it for examination when I reached home, but it was lost. Whether the old man took the alarm or not we could not tell, but he did not appear at all that day.

In the afternoon Meyong came in with a snake, a species of boa, and the only one peculiar to this island. He called it a "*Serpent tête chien*," or Doghead snake. It was twelve feet in length and looked capable of crushing a sheep to death — as indeed I was told it could. The little inoffensive agouti and birds are its prey, and it lives in holes in the earth and beneath loose piles of stones. It is a terror to the negroes and Indians, who fear contact with its slimy skin more than they dread the Lance-head, a poisonous and deadly serpent of Martinique. Fortunately, though rather abundant in the forests, they do not willfully attack man, and seldom do harm more than to pay occasional visits to the hen-roosts of sequestered settlements.

This must be the serpent of which the Caribs had a tradition, two centuries ago, when the island was in their possession, and white men rarely visited it except as prisoners. But when a white man did visit them he was joyfully received, and a feast was prepared, of which, though in his honor, he did not partake, but only *formed a part* of it. They used to relate to strangers the story of a great and frightful serpent, which had its lair in the deep forests of the island. It had upon its head a brilliant stone, like a priceless carbuncle for brilliancy, which was usually covered with a movable skin like the eyelid. When it descended to the streams to drink, or when in sportive mood, it would withdraw this skin and flash forth such a dazzling light that no one could look upon the fiery rays without losing his sight.

The day passed quietly and the night came on. The old Indian did not return, and we did not expect to see him again, and decided that we would make an early start next morning for our sea-coast camp. A fresh bed of leaves was made up, and we retired early within the cabin with rosewood walls. When it was quite late and very dark, I was awakened by a rustling among the leaves as of objects crawling over them. I put out my hand to ascertain what was there, but drew it back with a tremor of horror. It had come in contact with the *biggest bug in the world.* Its back seemed hard as iron, and its mandibles were as long as my fingers. I had always boasted my immunity from bed-bugs, and that the greatest army of them could not make me afraid. But now they were coming to convince me of my mistake. I could hear them burrowing through the leaves, could feel them crawling over me, and, unable to endure it longer, sprang up with a cry and rushed out into the open air. The perspiration rolled off me, and my hands twitched nervously, for I was pretty thoroughly frightened. At my command, my boys lighted a torch and examined the leaves; and when they drew out three huge beetles almost as large as my hand, and I stood regarding them with horror, they burst into fits of laughter.

"Ah! Monsieur very fear, he 'fraid jumbie, he 'fraid razor-grinder."

"What do you call them?"

"Person say he 'razor-grinder.'"

"Does he grind razors?"

"Oh, no! *mais* he make noise like he make to grind."

"Hark zat noise!" said Meyong, raising his hand to command silence. Through the forest came a sharp, whizzing sound, like that produced by the wheel of the perambulating razor and knife grinder.

"Zat make by heself."

"How does he make it?"

His answer was to this effect: The beetle is provided with two long mandibles, articulating like the thumb and forefinger, placed immediately above the mouth. They are smooth and hard, and furnished with protuberances, or notched, while the upper man-

The Hercules Beetle, (*Dynastes Hercules,*) Life Size.

dible is lined on its under surface with velvety hairs. The beetle would seize hold of a small branch of a tree, exactly as we would grasp it between the thumb and forefinger. Then it would, with its wings, whirl itself round and round, slowly at first, but increasing, so rapidly as to produce a continuous buzz or whir. This it would keep up until the limb was severed.

The reason for this I could not find out. The beetle lives on rotten wood, it is thought, and in cutting into these branches it may be in search of food. But the most plausible reason is, that it is calling its mate. This is strengthened by the fact that the females are not furnished with these mandibles. It flies high in the air among the trees at night; it burrows in the ground, beneath leaves and in decayed wood, in the daytime. Being strictly nocturnal in its habits, it is seldom found, unless, as in the present instance, it goes in search of the collector.

It is the largest known beetle in the world, the specimen in my possession being six and one quarter inches in length. The only species approaching it in size is the Goliath-beetle of the African coast, which is broader than this, but not so long. Guiana is the home of this beetle, and he has never been found out of South America except in this one island of Dominica. Well is he called the Hercules, for that is his name, *Dynastes Hercules*; and modestly he bears his title, for he does not presume upon his size and strength to annoy man or ill-treat his insect neighbors. He is a strict vegetarian, and leads a happy, careless life among the tree-tops at night, and upon the ground during the day.

The only specimen I was able to bring with me

to America was a full-grown male. The proboscis and whole forward part are jet-black, the legs and under parts rich brown, the wing-cases, which cover the back and sides, greenish-olive dotted and streaked with black. It is altogether one of the most attractive entomological specimens I secured during my trip.

Further search among the leaves revealed several centipedes, which were more to be dreaded than the beetles, as their bites will throw one into a fever. A scorpion, also, was turned out from his lurking-place beneath a log. Both these pests prefer old dwellings and decaying ruins for their abodes, and though not so abundant in Dominica as in Martinique and St. Lucia, are often the cause of alarm, and sometimes of sickness, to the inhabitants. Their bites rarely prove fatal.

To escape annoyance from these insects, I always, when practicable, slept in my hammock; they did not then have so open a field, and I only ran the risk of having one drop from the roof or a branch above me.

Owing to the disturbance just mentioned, we were up long before daylight, and started on the homeward trail before the woods were fairly alight. The "Sunset bird" (*Myiarchus Oberi*) sent his tremulous cry through the forest, as we turned our backs upon the boiling springs and commenced descending a gentle plain well studded with trees. We had probably seen the last of our Indian friend, and though we felt rather conscience-stricken at leaving him without a farewell, we reflected that his seclusion was of his own seeking.

Our yams and tanniers were quite finished, and we

were obliged to use as substitute the seeds of a species of palm, a tall and slender tree with drooping leaves. It is a species not yet described, I think, and is either a *cocos* or a *geonoma*. The seeds are dark and shining, and grow in clusters at the bases of the leaf-stalks. They are edible, and constitute an important portion of the food of the forest Caribs.

A beautiful plant, which nearly covered the trees along the streams, was the *Hillia longifolia*; it had white, star-shaped flowers, and glossy laurel-like leaves. Every old stump and decaying tree was covered with a fuchsia-like plant with lovely pink and scarlet flowers, the *Alloplectus cristatus*, which enveloped every disfigured tree in a garment of beauty.

We reached without adventure the great river, and followed it down to its mouth, where was an abandoned plantation in the possession of negroes. A dilapidated hut was pointed out to me as being occupied by a famous sorceress, a priestess of *Obeah*, who could give one a charm that would kill one's enemy, or cause a robber to restore stolen property. Her fame extended beyond the confines of the island, and she was visited by many credulous negroes from other places.

Obeah, a relic of African witchcraft, has strong hold upon the ignorant blacks and Indians. Salibia, the valley in which I camped for more than a month, was once the stronghold of the priests of Obeah. For years they held sway there, and many people are supposed to have been killed by their poisons. The laws of the English government are severe in its punishment, but it is practiced to a greater extent than is generally known.

It was the middle of the afternoon when we reached

the fording-place; the heat had been increasing since ten in the morning, when first we were brought to feel its force. Having eaten little that day, I was weak at noon, and experienced violent pains in the head. On the river bank I halted and would gladly have slept, but my boys urged me on. The water was only about knee-deep, and I waded in; half-way across, the current nearly swept me off my feet, and I grew faint and dizzy, and had barely reached the bank when I fell to the ground.

Beneath a guava bush my boys stretched me out and watched while I slept; and at dark they awoke me and assisted me to a house. Here the kind mistress attended me for nearly a week, until the fever had somewhat abated, when, leaving my collections and camping equipments to be forwarded by Meyong, I took a coasting vessel from a near port for the Caribbean coast.

11

CHAPTER XI.

A CRUISE IN THE HURRICANE SEASON.

AN EXPERIMENT IN COFFEE CULTURE. — THE PEST OF THE COFFEE PLANT. — LIBERIAN COFFEE VERSUS MOCHA. — AN AFRICAN DISEASE. — GATHERING IN THE SICK. — DOWN THE CARIBBEAN COAST. — THE FLAME-TREE. — THE ORCHARD OF LIMES. — PROFITS OF LIME CULTURE. — THE MAROON PARTY. — THE STAMPEDE. — FAREWELL TO DOMINICA. — CORAL ISLANDS. — AN IMMENSE GAME PRESERVE. — THE "DOCTOR." — THE JIGGERS. — NEW BIRDS. — A WEARY VOYAGE. — SEASONS OF THE TROPICS. — TEMPESTS. — CALMS. — PROVISIONS EXHAUSTED. — TURKEY OR JACKASS. — SHARK. — ODORS OF SPICES. — THE TORNADO. — HURRICANE BIRDS. — PITONS OF ST. LUCIA. — ST. VINCENT. — PALM AVENUE. — THE SPA. — HOSPITABLE PEOPLE. — BASALTIC CLIFFS. — RICHMOND VALE. — FALLS OF BALLEINE. — THE WATERSPOUT.

A MILE from the town of Roseau are the cliffs of St. Aramant, above which is the snug little country seat of Dr. Imray, one of the oldest residents of Dominica. A friend and correspondent of Sir Joseph Hooker, he is an ardent botanist, and has several of the native plants named in his honor. For a generation, the good doctor ministered to the sick and afflicted; for more than thirty years he was the leading physician of the island. At last, feeling the need of rest, well advanced in years, though in robust health, he delegated his authority and practice, with all needful pills and potions, to a most worthy successor, Dr. Nicholls, a young Englishman, full of love for his profession and energy in the practice of its duties, and with the aged doctor's botanical predilections. These two gentlemen, then, active in everything pertaining to the welfare of the island, cultured and with scientific tastes, are of inestimable value to the inhabitants, and a blessing to strangers.

Dr. Imray is devoting all his time to the reintroduction of coffee into the island. Years ago it was cultivated to such an extent that it acquired a name and reputation; in the latter part of the last century there were over two hundred coffee plantations, giving an annual yield of three hundred thousand pounds; but with the abolition of slavery its culture languished, valuable coffee estates were abandoned, and at present the island does not produce sufficient for its own consumption. About forty years ago there appeared a blight upon the coffee-plant that ruined whole crops and aided in the abandonment of its culture. This was in the shape of a *coccus*, a scale insect that fixed itself upon the leaves and buds, causing them to shrivel. This undoubtedly came of neglect, and increased until it acquired the mastery over the entire island. In Guadeloupe they have the scale insect, but it has never gained ascendency over the planters, as more attention has been paid to the trees. Acting upon the theory that the leaf of the Mocha variety was too tender to resist the attacks of the insect, Dr. Imray has successfully introduced the Liberian variety, the epidermis of the leaves being thicker and tougher. At the time of my visit he had a little plantation of trees about three years old, some of which were in flower and bearing.

Upon my return to Roseau I was suffering from a low fever that would not be shaken off; and upon the advice of the two doctors I decided to rest for a month, either in the mountains or at some point on the western shore. The young doctor was going down the island to visit a distant town, and it was decided by my friends that I should occupy a seat in his boat until he reached Battalie, Dr. Imray's lime orchard on the Caribbean coast.

Aside from a large and constantly increasing practice, Dr. Nicholls was burdened with the duty, almost self-imposed, of medical superintendent of the Yaws hospital. The name *yaws*, or *yaw*, is of African origin, and is said to be derived from the resemblance of the fungoid ulcers or tumors, which cover the skin in this disease, to a raspberry, or strawberry, of which *yaw* is the native African name. To present a description of this disease, unknown in America and Europe, I quote from the doctor's annual report for 1878.

"The disease Frambesia, or Yaws, was introduced into the West Indies by negro slaves imported from Africa. The date of its ingress into Dominica is unknown, but it existed in the island early in the present century. It did not, however, make any great headway before emancipation, for each estate of considerable size had its 'Yaws-house,' and the infected patients were there segregated and treated by a nurse, under the direction of a medical attendant. Upon the abolition of slavery, and the consequent impoverishment of many estates and the total abandonment of others, the medical surveillance of the negroes came to an end, and the number of persons affected with yaws increased considerably. The rugged conformation of the country of Dominica, the smallness of the population as compared with the area, the facilities for 'squatting,' and the absence, until recently, of a medical service, all tended to favor the spread of the disease. About eight years ago the number of cases had increased to such an alarming extent that measures were taken for the repression of the disease. Hospitals were established, yaws patients were admitted and cured, and it was hoped that the disease would be extinguished; but the system adopted was stopped too soon, and the malady reappeared and spread with great rapidity. The government, in a few years, had to grapple with a contagious disease, which was present in every district of the country, and which held hundreds of victims in its grasp.

"Fortunately the disease is one amenable to medical treatment, and the yaws hospitals, now in full working order, are fast removing the blot which has existed upon the public health for so many years. That the disease will be finally eliminated from Dominica is disbelieved in by many, but I see no reason why this desirable event should not really occur. In former days the disease existed in all the islands of the West Indies, but now it is confined to few." .

Empowered by the government to gather in and isolate all persons found afflicted with the yaws, undismayed by opposition from the ignorant or by the accumulation of filth in these Augean stables, this young enthusiast went to work with a zeal and intelligence that presaged success, to eradicate the disease. Under his direction the police of the island scoured the neighborhood of the villages, and brought into the hospitals the filthiest offscourings of humanity. Of course there was much difficulty in the way, not only from the patients themselves, who preferred hugging this living death and communicating it to others, to separation from their friends, but from rabid philanthropists of the "Exeter-Hall" type, who saw in this an infringement upon the negro's liberty.

The disease is engendered and propagated by a filthy mode of living and insufficient diet; hence, the most important agents in effecting a cure are cleanliness and good living. No one would suppose the natives would object to that, but they do, and neglect no opportunity for escape from the hospitals; thus the doctor's position is one of thankless labor and vigilance.

It was a five-hours' row to Prince Rupert's, and half that to Battalie. We left Roseau in a long dugout, rowed by four men and guided by a cockswain, and rapidly glided along the Caribbean coast. Reclining beneath an arched canvas, we could look out upon a swiftly-gliding shore, green sugar plantations, bluff headlands, narrow valleys. Being June, when all the flowering trees are in bloom, and when the fruits are ripe and ripening, it was a pleasure to note the vegetation. Conspicuous above all foliage was the *Flamboyant*, the "flame-tree," with its broad umbrella-shaped top, one mass of flaming crimson. Without a leaf at the beginning of the season, its twigs and branches are covered with gorgeous flowers. So far as you can distinguish any object on shore, you see the flame-tree, its bright coloring making it as prominent at a distance as bright-plumaged birds, which, as in the case of the " pink curlew," I have recognized when mere specks in space.

At dark we entered a crescent-shaped bay and ran the boat upon a pebbly beach, which was pierced by two rivers as they entered the sea. Overhanging them were cocoa palms, shading them almost to the sands, while sea-side grapes hung above wave-worn rocks and rounded pebbles, and a forest of lime-trees filled a narrow valley enclosed between high cliffs. The manager of the estate welcomed us with a good dinner and comfortable beds in the doctor's own house, which always remained ready for his occupancy, though he rarely visited it. The next morning we whipped the streams with poor success, and attacked the sea-birds with scanty returns; in the afternoon, my fever returning, and the doctor continuing his journey, both fish and birds had a rest.

The valley of Battalie is one great field of lime-trees — a smooth sea of verdure — hiding beneath its surface golden fruit that is constantly dropping to the earth, and being carried to the stone mill beneath the cliff. Twenty years ago Dr. Imray conceived the plan of converting a poorly-paying sugar plantation into an orchard of limes, and he thus made of a narrow valley, riven from gigantic rocks and strewn with volcanic bowlders, a garden of profit and delight. The majority of the trees are fifteen years old; they first bear at three years of age, and yield good crops at five years. Since the first full crop he has realized a large income from these trees, his manager informing me that during two seasons the returns amounted to two thousand pounds sterling each. The trees are thickly planted so as to shade the ground, and after they acquire their growth need no clearing beneath.

A corps of boys and girls gather the limes as they fall to the earth — they are never picked — and carry them to the mill, where they are passed between two upright rollers, such as were in use when the sugar cane was raised there. The expressed juice is conducted to evaporating pans and boiled down to the consistency of molasses — to a density of one-tenth — and then run into fifty-gallon hogsheads for shipment to England. It was worth, in 1877, about twenty pounds sterling per hogshead, and has brought thirty pounds; and the plantation has yielded from seventy to eighty hogsheads in a season.

The juice is used in making citric acid, and is shipped in its concentrated form to reduce freight. It would seem possible to further reduce this item of expense by the complete crystallization of the juice. Such an experiment has been tried in Florida, though without complete success. There is not there a sufficient quantity of limes, though, from the experience of Dr. Imray, it would seem more profitable to raise limes than oranges. I do not, however, think the lime will flourish so luxuriantly, nor produce so much juice, in Florida, as in the rich soil of the West Indian islands. The trees are without fruit during two months only in the year — February and March — and at other seasons are fragrant with fruit in various stages of growth.

One day, two or three weeks after my arrival, the priest of a neighboring village, Père Michel, came over to the plantation for a little recreation, and gathered some of the people together for a *partie rivière*. By different names do the residents of these islands call these gatherings in the open air, which in other places are denominated picnics. *Partie rivière*, the French name, has a suggestiveness about it that picnic has not; and to go on a " maroon party," as they sometimes style it, transports one in imagination at once to the wild forests.

In the afternoon we were all gathered at the upper end of the valley, beneath a great mango; cloths were spread on the ground, and upon them were placed our eatables : roast pig, chickens, and vegetables, with ale, claret, and sherry. The père and myself were the only members of the party who were not, in a manner more or less remote, connected with the immortal Ham; but that did not mar our enjoyment of the festivities. Before the spread had been well discussed, a sudden shower came down with fury — as showers are apt to do in the summer season — suspending operations and driving us to shelter. As we were on the upper bank of the river, and the stepping-stones were covered a foot deep in fifteen minutes, we were all obliged to wade the turbid stream, in great discomfort.

These June showers, though lacking the force of those of the later months of the year, are nevertheless of frequent occurrence. They warned me away from an island so mountainous, and but a week passed before I was speeding north to an island of lesser elevation, and consequently less rainfall.

Furnished with letters of introduction from the president of Dominica, Mr. Eldredge, I visited the islands of Barbuda and Antigua, spending there two months, shooting deer, pigeons, doves, and wild guinea-fowl.

These islands are of coral formation, and the former is a perfect preserve, being abundantly stocked with game. Two gentlemen lease it from the crown, though it formerly belonged to the ancient Codrington family. Its horses are celebrated throughout the islands, being descended from imported Arab stock.

The climate of Antigua is perceptibly warmer than that of the mountainous islands, though a cool breeze freshens a great portion of the day. It is hot in the morning from seven to ten, when a breeze springs up. At noon it is intensely hot, but in the shade the cool sea-breeze makes it bearable. Another oppressive spell is near sunset, before the evening winds set in; but by eight o'clock the air has cooled, and the nights are endurable. In July and August, when I was there, there were frequent showers; rain fell for an hour or two quite unexpectedly, and as quickly ceased. The wind blows nearly always from the east, and when it changes to the west, a hurricane may be expected.

In Antigua, alone, I suffered from mosquitoes, and was obliged to protect myself by a net. Fleas, also, disturbed my rest at night; and not the universal flea only, but a cousin of his, which can "discount" the common insect largely. I allude to the "jigger," or *chegoe*, which, not content, like his relative, with a hop, skip, and a bite, penetrates the skin, and lays its eggs beneath the surface.

I awoke one morning with an itching of my toes, which frequent rubbing failed to allay; and examination revealed four white tumors. They were as large as peas, and in the center of each was a little black speck. Ignorant at that time of the existence of such creatures, I called my boy, William, who at once pronounced them jiggers. How to remove them was the next question. William soon settled that, for he called in the first old negress that happened to be passing, and she turned those jiggers out of their nests with an adroitness that showed long practice.

Care must be taken that none of the eggs remain in the wound, as the larvæ hatched from them burrow into the flesh, and eventually create painful ulcers. The eggs and insect are contained in a sac, which must be turned out with a pin or needle with great care, and the cavity filled with tobacco ashes to destroy any remaining germ. After I had got rid of my unwelcome tenants, there was a hole in each toe large enough to contain a humming-bird's egg. This, my first experience with the *pulex penetrans*, was so satisfactory that I carefully guarded against the development of any more eggs of those loathsome insects. A few hours are sufficient to give the jigger a hiding-place, and as the sensation he causes is a rather pleasant itching only, for a time, he is sometimes not discovered until a painful sore is formed. The negroes are very negligent in attending to these sores, which increase to such an extent as to endanger their limbs; negroes with all their toes eaten away are daily met with, and I have seen several who have lost a leg from this same cause.

It was my intention to visit St. Kitts, with a view to obtaining some specimens of monkeys residing there, but an invitation to an island in another direction caused me to abandon it. Though St. Kitts may be very interesting in many other respects, it is especially so to a naturalist, as it contains great numbers of monkeys, being one of three islands in the Antilles honored by these quadrupeds as their abode. Barbados is said to have very few, and Grenada has large troops of them. Those of St. Kitts are numerous and do much injury to the crops. It is related that they have access to a passage under the sea, to Nevis, a distance of six miles.

Before leaving Antigua I met an old acquaintance, a dentist, who had sailed in the vessel in which I took passage from New York, and who had left me at Martinique, the first island of the chain at which we touched. Though he had never taken a degree, he was generally known as "The Doctor." He was an apt manipulator of the forceps, and had accumulated, during the six months we were separated, twenty-five hundred dollars, extracted from the innocent islanders. Now, the doctor was a genius. He had a genius for making money, and a special tact for taking care of number one. Leaving New York with but sixty dollars and his stock in trade, he landed in the West Indies with his cash greatly augmented, and with the captain, mate, cook, in fact the whole crew, deeply in his debt. That I escaped with a whole tooth in my head I attribute to some special interposition of Providence. The doctor's period of sojourn on shipboard may be divided into two portions: that in which he was pulling, or "fixin'," teeth, and that in which he was sea-sick. He was happy in the exercise of the former, and unhappy in that of the latter. When the doctor appears on deck with a particularly happy expression on his countenance, and polishing somebody's molar on the lapel of his coat, beware of him! The whole crew would then shudder with apprehension.

The doctor and I went on shore. We climbed the paved streets and descended again to the beautiful *Jardin des Plantes*. On our way the doctor indulged in a free flow of that happy humor peculiar to the Western Yankee (for we are all Yankees in those islands). We met boys and boys, boys by dozens and boys by scores, and some girls; but the very first group that drew our attention and provoked an outburst of the doctor's ever-ready wit, consisted of boys.

"I say, young man, pull down your vest!"

A Group of Gamins.

This was addressed to a ragged little darky with beaming face and bright eyes, the center of a bunch of the most ragged and dirty gamins we ever beheld. There was not a whole article of clothing furniture among them. If one had a shirt, he had no pantaloons; and the one that boasted the latter, had the least of the former. There was not even an apology for a single whole garment in the crowd, yet every member of it was as blissfully unconscious of the grotesque appearance he made as were the doctor and myself aware of it. But the most glaringly conspicuous feature of the collection was a huge vest worn by the brightest and sauciest of the five — a very grandfather among vests, which, descending to the urchin's thighs, left but a scanty drapery of shirt visible beneath.

We sailed away from Antigua one evening, the doctor's store increased by nearly eight hundred dollars; mine, by one new bird. This was in September, the very worst month of the year for travel. Nearly every craft that sailed these seas was drawn up on shore to await the close of the "hurricane season;" and this one in which we had taken passage was on her way to Barbados, hoping to escape a blow until she could make shelter there.

The "hurricane season" extends from the middle of July to the middle of October, and is at its height in the autumnal equinox. It is a season of calms; the sea is deceitfully quiet, and the wind variable. During the greater part of the year the wind blows from the east or north-east in the well-known "trades;" but at this season it dies away, coming in puffs from different quarters. The winds that precede the hurricanes usually commence blowing from the west or north-west, and increase in strength until they acquire that terrific force that devastates islands and destroys in a few hours the work of years. They shoot through the air in different directions, sometimes from above, perpendicular to the earth; and woe to the vessel caught abroad at such a time.

In this connection I may speak of the seasons of the year, which are not so distinctly marked as is commonly supposed. The first three months of the year are generally fine; they constitute the best portion of the hunting season, when the woods are driest and coolest, and the birds in perfect plumage. In April commence light showers, which sometimes extend through June, and are of daily occurrence. The heat increases, and the months of August and September are the hottest, as they are the sickliest, of the year. August ushers in the season of storms and hurricanes, when the calm intervals are almost insupportable on account of the heat. The last three months of the year constitute the season of the great rains, when for days together the rain falls heavily. These are the months for endemic fevers. Though the storms are frequently accompanied by thunder and lightning, I did not see, during my stay of nearly two years, such furious displays as I have witnessed in the North.

We drifted south of Antigua without a breeze. The morning and the afternoon saw Antigua's hills not far away; and the long, hot day was spent upon a motionless sea, without a breath of wind to fan our flapping sails. At sunset Guadeloupe's windward island was in sight — a low, flat land, with misty mountains far to westward. The triple peak of Montserrat showed black against a glowing sky; the sun in its descent drew a pathway of gold along the silvery sea and darted into our faces its fiery beams.

> "The western wave was all aflame ; ·
> The day was well-nigh done."

In heat and discomfort the day went out; but darkness had scarcely enveloped us when the sea began to dimple with little wavelets, that increased and lapped with refreshing sound against our vessel's sides; then the sails felt the coming of the evening breeze, and lay well over to leeward, and we moved slowly on our course. To avoid being becalmed under the lee of Guadeloupe, our captain had taken the longer route to windward, and we were now crossing the pathway of Columbus when he first approached these islands of the Caribbees. Next morning, when we went "about" for Marie Galante, the only island in sight was that lone rock of Désirade — the "desired island" of Columbus, when he was expecting to discover land.

Our captain was a negro, black as his African ancestor and without a brutish instinct the less. Plainly, he had missed his calling, which was to labor in the cane-fields beneath the lash of insolence-rebuking overseer. His provisions of yam and fish gave out on the evening of the second day, and my private store, also, failed me. The only meat on board was in living shape — a turkey and a jackass. That night the turkey died, welcoming death as a relief from sore disease. The jackass, patient for a day, waxed wroth as time passed on without food or drink, and broke the stillness of the second night with discordant brays.

The deck was crowded with sable passengers; the "cabin" was filled high with bags of coffee and guano and sundry boxes, and at the farther end was a stifled room in which was a berth allotted by the captain to me as a first-class passenger. Late in the evening I worked my way with difficulty to the room to retire. It was very dark and very evil-smelling, and I reached my hand up to open a little slide above the bunk, for air and light. It came in contact with something foreign, which, upon being shaken, gave signs of life and alarm, and a woman's voice demanded what I wanted. Retreating hastily, I inquired of the captain if there were not some mistake, and he replied that the berth was mine, and he would have the woman removed. She was one of several, who, having only deck passage, had been allowed to lie down in the cabin on the bags of coffee, as the deck was damp. Waiting a little while, I again went down; and my anger and dismay may be imagined when I found another colored female in the place of the first. Again I sought counsel of the captain; again was the cabin boy dispatched to warn these interlopers out. Allowing another interval to elapse, I again descended, removed shoes and coat, and sprang lightly into the bunk, ready to fall asleep in an instant. As I alighted, a cry of pain saluted me; I became conscious that another of those detestable women had usurped my place, and fled quickly to the deck. The cabin boy rescued my shoes and coat, and I sat down upon a coil of rope, resolved to brave the dangers of the night-damp rather than those of that vile hole below.

The third morning brought with it hunger, and a drink of black coffee. Later, the turkey, having had the feathers duly plucked from his bones, was placed before us; but my regard for the turkey was too great to allow me to eat, and I drew my belt the tighter, and looked wistfully toward the purple clouds that I knew were mountains, south of us. The day passed, and in the afternoon the sailors caught a shark. Hunger had now overcome all scruples, and I ate with relish of the coarse flesh that at any other time would have been disgusting. Another night came, and, warned by the experience of the previous one, I spread my blanket on deck and slept soundly, though we had several heavy squalls that careened our vessel alarmingly.

At daylight I awoke, dreaming of coffee and lime groves, for I recognized in the land-breeze that came to us the odor of spices and the freshness of earth, and knew that we were under the lee of Dominica. We were off Prince Rupert's Bay — a secure harbor for a fleet — with the town of Prince Rupert's, hidden in cocoa palms, lying in a fever-stricken valley. We were again becalmed, and night found us just entering the bay of Roseau, with a sea dashing over the sea-wall and jetty too violently to allow us to land.

"We expect you at your old quarters," wrote my good friend William Stedman; and one of his domestics shouldered my trunk and conveyed it to his hospitable mansion.

What a delight it was to be back among these generous people! Whatever the characteristics of English or Scotch at home, they soon acquire, in the West Indies, a feeling for a stranger fellow-man that is wondrous kind. It seemed like getting home again, this return to Dominica after a few months' absence, and I would gladly have remained among my friends of the coast; I was soon in the mountains, however, searching for some birds of which I had heard, and was rewarded by the discovery of several new varieties.

Returning to the coast after ten days' absence, I was caught in a thunder-gust, the rain coming from three ways at once, out of three converging gorges; the path was flooded in a few minutes, and the river roaring loudly and seething like a caldron. The storm passed and hurried on over the town, drenching it, and swept out over the sea, where it remained visible a long time as a heavy cloud. I found my friend putting up the "hurricane shutters" to his windows, which overlooked the bay directly above the sea-wall. The sea was agitated, and a dense cloud of mist came hurrying up from the south-west with a muffled roar. For a long time we were in suspense; the sun went down red and blinking behind a wall of vapor. The storm passed us without doing damage, though later intelligence reached us that it had struck the island of Grenada and toppled over three hundred houses.

Immediately preceding the hurricanes, there arrive off the Caribbean coast vast numbers of birds called, from their cries, "Twa-oo." They are said to be the harbingers of hurricanes, and only appear during the calms, immediately before a storm. They cover the water in large flocks, and come in from the desolate sandy islands where they breed. They are the sooty tern (the *Sterna fuliginosa*), but are known to the natives as "Hurricane-birds." When I arrived in Dominica the sea was black with them, but on the morning after the storm they had disappeared, to a bird, as completely as though blown into another sphere.

Steaming south, past Martinique, and by the way of Barbados, I found myself, one morning early in October, under the Pitons of St. Lucia, two pointed mountains rising out of the sea, the most beautiful and curious of any in these islands. They are about six hundred feet in height, wooded to their summits, and dark green. St. Lucia is famous as being the home of the infamous snake known as the "Iron Lance,"— of which I speak more at length in my description of

Martinique. Poisonous and venomous, it has yearly many victims, and is more feared than the fever, for which Castries, St. Lucia's principal town, is celebrated.

Crossing the channel south of St. Lucia, we arrived in the afternoon off the northern end of St. Vincent, which, from the steamer's deck, five miles off shore, appeared a dream of an island, suspended between sky and sea, yet solid and compact. As we glided through the blue waters, and the afternoon sun fell upon the island, we could view it from northern to southern end, one block of hazy, purple cloud, an immense amethyst, with shades and depths that varied as the sun lighted up the yellow plains and dark mountain-tops, and sought to penetrate the sombre valleys and ravines. Behind a curving beach a little town showed out, with red-tiled roofs gleaming from beneath thick groves of palms, through which a church pointed its spire skyward. There were no outlying rocks or islands, no jagged cliffs or jutting promontories, but, springing at once from the sea, every angle sharp and clear-cut, the island presented the appearance of a huge, opaque crystal. Though twenty-five miles in length, it appeared so small that one might fancy he could row around it in an hour or two.

At five in the afternoon we entered Kingston harbor, a bay open to the west and south-west, deep and spacious enough to float a navy. A sandy beach curves from headland to headland, and upon the northern promontory, six hundred feet above the bay, is perched a fort with massive walls, now used as a light-house and signal station. A jetty affords a landing-place from the steamer, fronting which and the sea is the police station, a fine, large building of stone, the best public building in the smaller English islands. A broad street borders the bay, and two more run parallel to it farther back, until the bordering amphitheatre of hills prevents further building. Streets intersect these at right angles and end at the base line of the hills, save three or four which traverse the valleys to estates among the mountains, and two that ascend the hills and extend around either shore to windward and leeward. Valleys run up from the bay far into the mountains, and the various spurs of hills increase in height as they recede from shore, so that Kingston and its bay are half encircled by a range of hills and mountains, above and around whose summits the clouds continually play.

The highest peak is Morne St. Andrews; rising to the east of it, and commanding the town, is a high, steep hill known as Dorsetshire Height, crested by a ruined fort. When the Caribs, in the last century, had overrun the island to windward, they swarmed upon this hill, attacked the fort, made prisoners the garrison, and were dislodged by soldiers from the town only after a desperate fight. There are a few old cannon remaining on the heights, but dismounted and imbedded in the earth. Most of them were bought by an enterprising speculator, during the late war between North and South, and sold to one party or the other.

The sunset view from here is superb. Conspicuous are the palmistes, or cabbage palms; one house is encircled by them, a white house with bright red roof; they raise themselves erect in clumps of a score or more, in rows like white pillars with dark green caps, and stand in relief upon all the hills. A mile from town is an avenue of seventy, which, though its symmetry is marred by the loss of some by hurricanes, is still a beautiful sight.

Three miles from town, one mile from the palm avenue in Arno's Vale, is a noted spa; from a hole six inches in diameter gushes out a volume of water impregnated with salts that give it value as a medicinal drink. It is equal in strength and beneficial effects to any water from the spas of Europe. It is averred that the water is more strongly impregnated, and that the flow is stronger, on the coming full of the moon. Water bottled at that time will sometimes break the strongest case.

When it became known that I was to visit the farther coast, I was furnished with letters by proprietors to the managers of their estates in different portions of the island. These were given me mainly by Mr. Porter, part-owner of a great number of sugar-estates; for the pleasure of whose acquaintance I was indebted to the U. S. consul, Mr. Hughes. So efficient were these letters, and so hospitable were the managers of the many estates traversed, that I made the complete circuit of the island on borrowed horses. When it is considered that sometimes my excursions were into the mountains over trails so rough that no one but a West Indian or South American would think of crossing them, and that I sometimes had a horse several days, the extent of their kindness may be appreciated.

The coast along the entire western shore is picturesque in the extreme, with volcanic rocks worn into caves, beautiful bays and broad valleys. Near Cumberland is an arched rock which bears the appellation of "Hafey's Breeches;" and in the valley is a huge cliff of columnar basalt, both of which are interesting to view. The manager of Richmond estate, Mr. Evelyn, received me kindly, and through his solicitations, and by the rain which fell in torrents every day, I was detained beneath his hospitable roof for nearly a week.

In a small boat I visited, one day, the Falls of Balleine, which are secluded in a deep gorge, about sixty feet high, and interesting. On this trip I was favored with a spectacle rarely seen even in this land of storms. It was a waterspout which formed over against the Pitons of St. Lucia, — a bulk of black clouds like an inverted funnel, sailing beneath denser masses above. It swept along with its tip trailing just above the waves, an elongated, spiral-pointed sack, until it met the sea; then the water was drawn up to it, forming a mighty pillar, spreading at base and summit, and joining black sea with inky clouds. A few moments it remained thus, then melted away, leaving only great banks of clouds, out of which came wind and rain. Seen across an angry sea, those cloud-pillars, with the picturesque Pitons as a background, were most impressive. They appeared at one time as if about to sweep down upon and ingulf us.

CHAPTER XII.

A CAMP IN A CRATER.

THE LAST OF THE VOLCANOES. — THE SOUFRIÈRE OF ST. VINCENT. — THE "INVISIBLE BIRD." — ASCENDING THE VOLCANO. — THE "DRY RIVER." — BIRD'S-EYE VIEW OF ST. VINCENT. — THE OLD CRATER. — THE NEW CRATER. — THE LAKE IN THE BOWELS OF THE EARTH. — IN THE CAVE. — SUNSET. — PREPARING FOR THE NIGHT. — TOBY. — FIVE DAYS AND NIGHTS OF MISERY. — FAUNA OF A MOUNTAIN-TOP. — EXPLORING THE CRATER-BRIM. — YUCCAS AND WILD PINES. — TOBY IN THE CAVE'S MOUTH. — A TERROR-STRICKEN AFRICAN. — JACOB'S WELL. — SNAKES AND PITFALLS. — TOBY'S "STOCK." — THE SOUFRIERE-BIRD. — A MYSTERIOUS SONGSTER. — UNAVAILING ATTEMPTS TO PROCURE IT. — SOUGHT FOR A CENTURY. — A DREAM. — NASAL BLASTS. — SEARCHING FOR THE BIRD. — THE CARIB BIRD-CALL. — THE CAPTURE. — A NEW BIRD. — A PLUNGE INTO DARKNESS. — SCARED BY A SNAKE. — TOBY DESPERATE. — DEPARTURE FOR CARIB COUNTRY.

ST. VINCENT contains the last of the West Indian volcanoes from which the present century has witnessed destructive eruptions; the Soufrière, that towered above and overlooked the Richmond plantation, having, in 1812, burst upon the island with terrible force. This eruption, which seemed to relieve a pressure upon the earth's crust, extending from Caracas to the Mississippi Valley, was most disastrous in its effects, having covered the whole island with ashes, cinders, pumice, and scoriæ, destroyed many

VOLCANO AND LAVA RIVER OF ST. VINCENT.

lives and ruined several estates. It lasted three days, commencing on or near that fatal day, in 1812, when Caracas was destroyed, and ten thousand souls perished in a moment of time.

Ashes from this volcano descended upon Barbados, ninety-five miles to *windward;* and this fact is cited by Elisé Reclus, in "The Ocean," to show the force of different aerial currents : "On the first day of May, 1812, when the north-east trade-wind was in all its force, enormous quantities of ashes obscured the atmosphere above the island of Barbados, and covered the ground with a thick layer. One would have supposed that they came from the volcanoes of the Azores, which were to the north-east; nevertheless they were cast up by the crater in St. Vincent, one hundred miles to the *west.* It is therefore certain that the debris had been hurled, by the force of the eruption, above the moving sheet of the trade-winds into an aerial river proceeding in a contrary direction."

Since that terrible outburst the volcano has remained inactive; having done its allotted work, it rested.

An eye-witness thus describes its appearance previous to the eruption : "About three thousand feet above sea-level, on the south side of the mountain, opened a circular chasm exceeding half a mile in diameter, and between four hundred and five hundred feet in depth. Exactly in the center rose a conical hill nearly three hundred feet in height, and about two hundred in diameter, richly covered and variegated with shrubs, brushwood, and vines about half-way up, and the remainder covered over with virgin sulphur to the top. From the fissures of the cone a thin white smoke was constantly emitted, occasionally tinged with a slight, bluish flame. The precipitous sides of this magnificent amphitheatre were fringed with various evergreens and aromatic shrubs, flowers, and Alpine plants. On the north and south sides of the base of the cone were two pieces of water, one perfectly pure and tasteless, the other strongly impregnated with sulphur and alum. This lonely and beautiful spot was rendered more enchanting by the singularly melodious notes of a bird, an inhabitant of these upper solitudes, and altogether unknown to the other parts of the island — hence called, or supposed to be, *invisible*, as it had never been seen.

"A century had now elapsed since the last convulsion of the mountain, or since any other elements had disturbed the serenity of this wilderness, besides those which are common to the tropical tempest. It apparently slumbered in primitive solitude and tranquillity; and from the luxuriant vegetation and growth of the forest, which covered its sides from base to summit, seemed to discountenance the fact and falsify the record of the ancient volcano."

To ascend the volcano was the object of my visit to Richmond, and also to procure that famous bird called "invisible." For a century, the people crossing the mountains had heard this bird, for a century no one had looked upon it. No one could affirm that he had seen it. Its weird music, ascending from the frightful ravines on either side the narrow mountain trail, seemed to float near them, but the bird ever remained undiscovered. By a preliminary ascent I found that it would be necessary, in order to procure the bird, to spend several days on the mountain-top, as it dwelt in deep gorges and ravines, requiring courage and patience to penetrate.

At last came the perfect day, when the Soufrière emerged from the mist that had enveloped it for two weeks, and stood out clear against a sky of blue and clouds of silver gray. A glorious day was that last day in October, with its bright sun illumining the mountain, over whose crest were flitting shadows cast by fleeing clouds. The good people with whom I had rested for a week and more, added to my provisions luxuries I could not purchase, such as guava jelly, Java-plum wine, limes and oranges, and Mr. Evelyn and his son rode with me a little way on my journey.

At first the road was along the shore, beneath cliffs and groo-groo palms; we crossed a turbulent river, with wide, rocky bed, and soon came to the bed of the famous " dry river," — the channel worn by that resistless flood of lava when on its way to the sea. It is two hundred yards in width, barren of vegetation for a mile from the sea, inclosed between high cliffs, clothed in verdure, hung with vines, spiny palms, tree-ferns — a wonderful hanging garden. There are three of these "dry rivers," where the lava filled up the bed of some flowing stream, or excavated an immense furrow for itself in its descent; nothing will grow in them near the sea, though their banks are rank with vegetation.

We went through a cane-field, and then over an attractive pasture land, leaving which I commenced the ascent. Here, at the foot-hills of the Soufrière, my friends left me, and here my friend's mule ("Betsey," the best mule on the estate) manifested a desire to return also. Vigorously I applied the spur, and she slowly ascended the winding path, over ridges covered with calumet grass, and through forest-like groups of tree-ferns and wild plantains. Having given Betsey a taste of the grass, while she was resting beneath a shade, she was prone to stop and loath to go ahead, and it was late when I reached the "maroon tree," half-way up the mountain-side.

Over and through the broad-leaved plants darted the humming-birds — crested, violet-breast, and crimson-throat. Most conspicuous and numerous was the latter, with back of purple-black and throat of crimson-gold; I found him oftenest in the upper forests, in the dark recesses of untrodden glens and along the borders of the mountain path. If you hear a sharp chirp in these silent woods, or are startled by a sudden whir, be sure it is he. Sparrows, finches, and humming-birds were in profusion; they flew hurriedly across the space in front of the tree, and darted at once into a thicket, as though afraid in the open, but reassured in the shade.

Finally my men appeared, loudly complaining of their loads; though I knew they had loitered and were at that moment chuckling to themselves over the manner in which they had "fool Massa Buckra." A wood-pigeon had been all the while feeding in the trees above, and parrots had proclaimed their presence by loud cries below, but both disappeared at the arrival of the men. After a biscuit and sup of beer, we went on; the trail, increasing rapidly in steepness, left the tall trees behind, and led through smaller ones scarcely fifteen feet in height. Soon even these altogether ceased, and we climbed the backbone of the long hill leading to the summit, which is destitute of anything like trees, and densely covered with a fern with flat, branching head, and giant lycopodiums. One would fancy he could walk over this hill in any direction, so dense and solid appears this leafy carpet, but a step outside the trail almost anywhere would plunge him waist-deep in ferns, and probably neck-deep into a hole. The view of the grand, rugged, dark-green mountains near at hand, and of the constantly unfolding shore, green with sugar-cane, is superb. Here St. Vincent seems but two or three miles across, and one sees what a little island it is; but, upon reflection, how grand are the works of nature contained herein!

Half a mile from the summit I heard the weird notes of the "Soufrière-bird," that songster about which hung the mystery I hoped to penetrate. Slowly climbing the winding path, I at length reached a cave, hollowed out of the bank, hung with ferns dripping with moisture. My cave, however, was a mile farther, and without halting I passed on; a sudden turn revealed the crater, deep and vast, on the very brink of which I stood. As my mule refused to go farther, and kicked and reared in a manner not desirable on the brink of a crater half a mile deep, I was forced to return to the cave and tie this mutinous mule; then I returned to the contemplation of the great work before me. The vapors wafted on the trade-wind, vapors in odor sulphureous, had, by their strength, warned me of its proximity.

It was a vast amphitheatre, a mile in diameter, as nearly circular as it is possible to be, three miles in circumference; the walls ran straight down from my feet to a lake at the bottom. The lip, or top, is irregular, of a wavy outline, rising into pointed peaks, sinking into hollows; but from any point in this vast circumference the wall descends rapidly, and almost perpendicularly, to the water beneath. The sides are covered with a stunted vegetation, forming a smooth, sloping surface, which might deceive the spectator into the belief that he could walk down to the bottom. On the southern and south-western sides it assumes more the amphitheatre shape, perpendicular ranges of rock being piled one above another, circling around the south-eastern side in columns that call to mind the ruins of the Coliseum.

The eastern wall divides the two craters — the "old" and the "new"; the latter blown out in the eruption of 1812, where before was solid mountain. It is a mere jagged escarpment, along which no one now dares climb. Before the rain and force of the violent winds had crumbled it so much, it was once scaled. It is said that Prince Alfred attempted it in 1861, on the occasion of his ascent of this volcano, but failed to accomplish it. It is so narrow that one can stride it, and so steep down either side that it makes the head swim to measure it from above. The northern brim is the lowest, and it is here that the lava poured out towards the Caribbean Sea at Morne Ronde; and beyond is the higher peak, against which was forced the fiery flood, as seen by the wondering inhabitants of the coast. On the southern side the trees and shrubs seem blasted and blackened by sulphur fumes. The southern wall rises high, and in its dome-shaped summit is excavated the cave, my home for nearly a week; its dark portal can be distinctly seen, though a mile away.

The whole shore of the lake at the bottom of the crater is incrusted with sulphur, a gray and yellow rim lining the base of the cliffs that dip down, no one knows how deep, into the water of the basin. Around the shore are little caves, grottoes, and black openings to the many ravines that seam the side of the bowl. A little islet is formed on the eastern side — the "new-crater" side — by a detached rock, or water-worn pinnacle from a submerged rocky base. In some of the ravines are scattered tree-ferns, stunted, to be sure, yet possessing grace and beauty that the fern, especially the tree-fern, never loses.

But how shall I describe that sheet of water slumbering in the bowels of the crater? It lies in the bottom of the bowl at least twelve hundred feet beneath the brim, serene, unmoved, a lake beneath the power of the elements to ruffle. Clouds of mist sail over it, and are blown into the crater from the eastward, but the fiercest gusts, and they are strong and frequent, cannot disturb that silent lake reposing in its bosom. Its hue is almost indescribable: pearl-green, creamy in hue yet with a decided greenish tint, opalescent with a tinge of the faintest aqua marine. Against gray cliffs, dark gorges and green moss, as it lies with its circling rim of golden sulphur, it resembles a huge opal in setting of gold and emerald.

In the apex of the southern hill bordering the crater, some one, long ago, hollowed out a place for shelter. It is only about ten feet across and in depth, and it is open on the northern side overlooking the lake, and, excepting a slight hollow, at the top, also; but it gives shelter from the keen, mist-laden winds of the Atlantic, and by crouching in one corner, one can avoid the rains from any quarter but the north-west. As the winds and rains, and all storms save the hurricanes and heavy gales — which latter are generally from the westward when at their worst — come from eastward, this cave gives protection in a majority of cases. It is cut out of gray rock, probably part of the mountain-side before the eruption, and the sides and fragment of roof are fringed with ferns and wild pines. I chose this cave as being more protected, nearer the windward coast, my ultimate destination, and as being near the only spring of fresh water on the mountain.

It was five o'clock before the men came up. Paying three of them, I dispatched them back to Richmond with the mule, and my compliments to its owner, and hurried on Toby to the work of preparing a camp.

Here, it is dark before six; on the western shore there is little or no twilight, for the sun drops into the Caribbean Sea with a celerity that surprises a Northerner, draws a nightcap of crimson and golden clouds over his head, which soon turn lead-color then black, and the day is done, finished at once without any dallying, and the stars come out ready for business. The blue vault is studded with silver stars and golden planets gleaming like lamps; and if there is a moon, mountain and valley are at once flooded with pale light. Forcibly such a scene brings to mind those lines in "The Ancient Mariner" —

> "The Sun's rim dips; the stars rush out;
> *At one stride* comes the dark."

Toby cut wood for a fire, and soon had a good one roaring in the little fireplace hollowed out of the eastern wall of the cave. By my direction, he cut four small trees having crotches at the tops, and planted them in the ground with their crotched parts meeting, where I lashed them together, one pair at either side of the cave. Across these I laid a pole the length of the cave, and secured it firmly with lines, thus forming a secure framework, to which I swung my hammock. Over the pole, sheltering the hammock, was stretched a square of canvas eight feet across, with each corner fastened to pegs in the ground. Thus was I provided with bed and shelter within half an hour from the time we reached the cave. A pair of army blankets to cover me, and a coat for a pillow, made a bed so soft and tempting that I could scarcely wait for the water to boil for the coffee; and after a lunch of sardines and crackers we turned into our respective quarters.

Toby, my only companion, deserves especial notice, for, though he did not conduct himself throughout our stay on the mountain-top with that courage and equanimity so desirable in an explorer, or the companion of one, still he was the only human being who accompanied me through it all. To begin with, he was black: if a bottle of ink had been emptied over him he could not have been blacker, it would have been only a waste of ink. And his eyes were white — that is, the whites of them; and whether the contrast between them and his skin was owing to the whiteness of one and the blackness of the other, or to the sootiness of the other and the chalkiness of the one, I could not determine. His nose was broad; to say that it was as broad as it was long would be confusion to one's ideas of length and breadth; and the end, or what was intended for the end, turned up, revealing such cavernous nostrils, that I often wondered why he did not utilize them in rainy weather and crawl into them out of the wet. Beneath these wide, dilated nostrils protruded a pair of lips without an equal this side of Toby; the upper one formed a protecting ledge, a threshold to the nasal caverns, and met the lower in a line that looked like a cut in a beefsteak. Between eyes and nose and mouth, there was little of Toby left, except wool and ears and a narrow strip of forehead, to constitute his head. The wool was of the kinkiest; and the ears, they might have been small for a large elephant, but they were certainly large for even a good-sized negro. The general make-up of Toby was in keeping with his features: large was he from his crown to his feet. As for those useful members of locomotion, I can only affirm as my belief that if my hammock had hung lower than it did — two feet from the ground — it would have brushed Toby's toes as he lay prostrate on his back.

In the night it commenced to rain, and during the succeeding days and nights that we stayed in the cave, five in all, rain fell with little intermission. I awoke at daybreak, my watch indicating five o'clock. A mist covered the mountains, a dense cloud filled the crater. It had rained all night, and everything was saturated; a most comfortless morning; yet, up from the trees beneath the cave, from ravine and hidden glen, from the crater's very heart, came the melodious notes of the soufrière-bird. A little later, I heard the whistle of a bird new to me, and the notes of the "wall bird," the house wren, and the chirping of sparrows. It evidently was not a comfortless morning to them.

It required considerable time for Toby to get the fire under way and coffee boiled; but when we had drunk the coffee and munched a biscuit, and I had cleaned and oiled my breech-loader, and inspected my photographic chemicals, we left the cave for the opposite rim of the crater. Down the rather steep hill, along the winding, rocky path, we walked rapidly; I once in a while halted to have a shot at some bird, but not one showed itself, except a wren, that I shot from a mossy stump only a couple of rods from the path; yet Toby could not find it; indeed, as his first step plunged him over head in a gulch that had been concealed by ferns, disturbing several black snakes that writhed around his legs, he was so terror-stricken that he would not look, and ever after he would only follow in my footsteps. Then we mounted the near peak, where no trail led, and skirted the crater-brim to the northern side. We went scarcely three quarters of a mile, yet it took us over an hour to reach the farthest practicable point.

Just there I heard the notes of the soufrière-bird, in a deep gorge back of the crater-rim. There were some pigeon-berry trees growing there, thick and black in the shelter of a hill, and I distinctly saw a black-backed bird giving utterance to wild notes. This was the first time I had seen the soufrière-bird; indeed, I had almost come to consider it *invisible*, as it was popularly supposed to be, for this was the third time I had hunted for it. In a previous ascent, for the purpose of reconnoissance, I had sought it vainly, heard it singing, apparently near me, but could not discover it: around, below, above, the mysterious music floated on the air, but the bird remained unseen. The notes, I am certain, are ventriloquial, for they never indicate the place in which the bird is at rest while uttering them; a bird may seem at a distance, while in reality he is close at hand.

Cautiously I plunged into the dense thicket of wild pines and yuccas that grew on a quaking bed of sphagnum, waded into a growth of calumet grass higher than my head, and so, plunging deeply and holding by rotten trees, I got within shot. At the report, the bird flew wildly and fell at a distance from where I stood; a few steps farther, and I found myself on the edge of a deep gulch over which hung a tangled mass of dead bushes and grass. Toby came to my assistance with his cutlass, but we only succeeded in getting a foot or two farther. I was obliged to leave my first soufrière-bird, Toby remarking, "No use, make um too much bad." We retraced our steps, and when within sight of our cave, discovered some people there; a nearer approach revealed a party of ladies and gentlemen from the windward sugar-estates, who had come up to the mountain marooning. At my request, they made their headquarters in the cave, and then we all started for the "new crater," reaching it after some tough walking, and plucky riding on the part of the ladies.

The "new crater" lies east of the "old," and is reached by a narrow trail half circling the huge basin of the latter. The climb from the regular trail to windward is steep and fatiguing, and made worse by over-trailing grass and filamentous yucca, which will get entangled in one's legs spite of endeavors to prevent it. You come upon it as abruptly as upon the first, and the bank is steep, even shelving in, so that you are obliged to lie down and peer over the brink to see to the bottom of the abyss. Unlike the first, it has no water, save a small pool, dark and gloomy enough to be an opening into the great infernal regions below, as it undoubtedly is. This pool is in the eastern side of the crater-floor, which is here comparatively level, with a dip in the direction of the water. The walls arise from this floor, jagged and rent, torn and water-worn, for nearly a thousand feet, precipitous, seamed in places with ravines and covered with ferns.

There is not much of interest here outside the fact that it had its origin in that terrible explosion in 1812, before which the space occupied by this great crater was solid mountain. At the same time also that conical island which rose from the center of the other crater was blown into space. It has been entered and the bottom reached, but all attempts to fathom that black pool have been unavailing. From a little distance can be seen the bulging wall that arises from the slope eastward, which gives this mountain summit a cone-like character. Beyond is an enclosing ring of mountains, and in a narrow valley between crater-cone and mountains are deep, very deep, ravines and gorges, where flowed that fiery tide of lava when it swept down upon the windward coast.

We returned to the cave, and soon the party left us, with offers of assistance when I should arrive at their plantations. Toby sat in the cave's mouth, nor would he stir from it during the ensuing three days and nights, except to get water and wood. His experience with the snakes had satisfied him. The attendants of the party had related to him the idle tale current among the negroes of the coast, namely, that the first individual who saw the soufrière-bird would surely die. Much more was the danger increased when the bird should be killed; and with what vengeance dire the evil spirits would visit the author of its death, they hesitated, shuddered even, to think. Consequently Toby was in trepidation; his spirit was perturbed. Sullenly he performed his daily work. He even hesitated to go for water to the spring on the mountain-side — to "Jacob's well" — which gushed from under a huge bowlder, forming a little pool, half a mile from the cave. He was completely demoralized, and the incessant rain made him disconsolate; he sat in his corner resting his chin on his hand, his nose on his lips, nodding assent to his inward cogitations in a manner that boded no good to my enterprise.

He had constructed a little shelter of sticks and leaves in a corner of the cave, where he slept by night on a scanty layer of leaves, and drowsed by day. The second day he informed me that he felt it imperative to go down to see his "stock;" that he had left his "stock" with no one to "care fur dem," — a "pig high like dat" — measuring a distance of about a foot above the ground, — "one high like dis, an' one high so, sah." After this, I noticed that his anxiety for his stock increased with the inclemency of the weather. Altogether, I do not think Toby enjoyed his residence on the mountain-top, especially as he looked forward to the death of the bird with fear, while I could only think of it with feelings of lively joy. Hence, he not only refused to accompany me on my excursions, but exercised his little wit to throw obstacles in my way.

The local name of the "Soufrière-bird," from the French word *soufrière*, a sulphur mountain, an inhabitant of the volcano, has been obtained from the Caribs and the negroes, as the bird is rarely heard outside a gunshot limit from the crater. Its habitat is strictly mountainous, and I do not think it is ever found at a lesser height than one thousand feet above the sea, and in the dark ravines and gorges seaming the sides of the cone it finds a congenial retreat. It resembles a closely-allied bird of Dominica, the "Mountain whistler," in many particulars, especially in its habits of seclusion, shyness, and melody of song. It is, however, much shyer than even the Dominica bird; and while the latter seems to prefer the solitude of dark gorges more from a love of retirement than fear of man, the soufrière-bird is timid, even suspiciously watchful of man's presence, and flies from his approach. In its wild, sweet, melancholy music it strikingly resembles the "mountain whistler," but the notes are different.

From the dense thicket of trees bordering the trail around the crater this bird sends forth its mystic music, and darts away at the slightest indication of human proximity to its haunts. As the earth supporting the trees it inhabits is cut into every conceivable shape of hole, rut, and ravine, and as, moreover, the place swarms with monster snakes, the terror of the negroes, almost the only people crossing the mountain, it has been connected with the superstitions of the negro, and has ever remained the "invisible, mysterious bird with the heavenly song." Naturalists have sought for it, and residents of the island have tried to capture it, but without success. Misled by its ventriloquial music and deterred by the character of its rough retreats, they have returned bootless to the coast, almost believing, with the negro, that it was indeed invisible. The Indians avoided its haunts, and regarded with veneration this bird that filled the air with unearthly melody; for generations they have preserved the tradition of its existence, and vaguely associated it with the tutelar deity of the volcano.

The third night passed wearily. My blankets, hammock, and garments were saturated by the mist, and the air was so charged with sulphur fumes that it seemed difficult to breathe. Toby rested uneasily; his uncomfortable couch and his anxiety regarding his "stock" interfered with perfect repose. By the aid of a line fastened to a stake, I managed to keep my hammock moving, and thus rocked myself to sleep; but my naps were short and fitful, and frequently interrupted. Toward the small hours I was asleep and dreaming. The events of the preceding days, and the constant reminder before me of that catastrophe of sixty years before, when this mountain was shaken and rent and the fire in its bosom let loose, gave shape to my dreams. I was living through that terrible week in April, when the volcano vomited forth the volume of ashes and fire that desolated the island; nay, more, I was camped upon its very summit. I felt the heaving of the earth beneath, but could not move; I heard the gathering of those internal forces preparatory to the bursting forth of flame and steam; the rumbling roar that came up from that subterranean

furnace grew louder and increased to the howling of
the hurricane, and seemed to approach the very crust
of earth upon which I lay; the thin shell vibrated,
cracked, fire leaped forth, and, amid the most terrific
explosions, I descended—to the bottom of my cave.

Confused and astonished, I gathered my blanket
about me, and looked around. The hammock was
oscillating gently, small stones and particles of loosened earth were falling from above in a gentle shower;
and Toby was snoring earnestly. Returning to my
hammock, I lay there cogitating, with the rain pattering on my canvas roof, and watched Toby as he
emitted those nasal blasts. An idea struck me—
ideas often strike me. Why could not this wasted
power be utilized? Snoring causes vibration; vibration communicated causes motion; motion was what
I wanted to swing my hammock, to rock me to sleep.
Instantly I had conceived a device for utilizing this
force; and such was my faith in its merits, that, if
I had been on American instead of English soil, I
should have hastened at once to get the invention protected by patent. This boon to people who sleep in
couples, this invention that will do away with midnight rising to rock the cradle, is not yet patented;
hence it would not be policy in me to give the details
of its construction to the world.

The morning of the fourth day dawned dimly.
Toby prepared coffee, and I took my gun and game-
basket and went down the mountain a short way,
where I had heard the song of the bird the day before. It was a sort of shoulder in the hill, where a
curve in the crater-brim and a hollow in the hill gave
shelter from the vapor-charged wind from the "wind-

ward." I entered the thicket of stunted trees with dense tops, and sat down. As I did so, the whistle of a soufrière-bird, that had emanated from it, suddenly ceased, and I knew he had seen me and had flown. I waited a long time in silence, but they seemed to have been made aware of my presence, and only the distant murmur of their music came to me from different parts of the slope. Tired of this solitude, I started down the steep declivity. The first step taken beyond the range of my vision as I sat, plunged me into a hole to my neck; it had been concealed by ferns and mosses, and I slowly crawled out through them with painful exertion.

I found that the surface was cut up into ravines and gullies, starting from the crater-rim. Probably the deepest of them were gouged out by the flood of lava that poured over the crater's edge in that terrible outflow of volcanic wealth. Rain flowing through the loose volcanic ash may have cut the more recent, but it could not have descended with sufficient impetuosity to have hollowed out the deep well-holes and cut those deep ravines with perpendicular walls. Starting from the narrow edge of the crater, they spread out like a fan, furrowing the outer surface of the cone, growing deeper, broader, and gloomier, until lost in the dark recesses below. Over all grew the small trees, densely crowded; ferns, filamentous yuccas, moss and wild pines covered the earth and rocks in impenetrable confusion, so concealing the openings to the narrower gullies that it was impossible to ascertain their whereabouts without a very careful examination. It was into this wilderness that I plunged, floundering through tangled masses of branching fern and through dense clusters of ground-orchids. But I found few birds save a sparrow or two and a sucrier, and the prospect was most discouraging.

A death-like stillness pervaded that gloomy slope, disturbed only by the *swirr* of the volumes of mist as they swept over the eastern spur, and the faint notes of the soufrière-bird down below. Suddenly I bethought myself of a bird-call taught me by the Caribs of Dominica; and with such success did I use it, that, in ten minutes, the hitherto silent trees were alive with stirring feathered forms, hurrying forward in anxious flight. The first to respond — and I afterwards found it always in advance of the others — was a flycatcher; it flew precipitately to the very tree beneath which I stood, and hopped about the branches, peering anxiously beneath; closely following him was his mate. Then the sparrows (two species) took up the cry, and close behind them came the certhiolas; but these latter satisfied themselves with a glance and then went about their business. The little humming-bird, the crested, was the most attracted and the most audacious, and flew directly for my face, halting on buzzing wings before me, darting from side to side, finally alighting on a branch close by, crest erected, every feather of this pigmy beauty seemingly electrified, darting glances in every direction. Then the rapid whirring of wings gave token of the coming of the great crimson-throated hummer, and he seemed as anxious, and circled as closely about me, as his little cousin; he likewise perched himself upon a near twig, his back and throat resplendent in the fugitive sunbeams that stole through the branches.

But, gratified as I was with this stir of animated life that my seductive call had evoked, I still awaited anxiously the appearance of that rara avis of these solitudes. Soon I heard a low call-note, such as I had heard that bird give utterance to, and imitating it closely as possible, I was gratified to hear it repeated nearer at hand, and then caught a glimpse of a dusky body flitting on rapid wing through the farther shades. Its flight was very rapid and noiseless. It suddenly came into view a good gun-shot off, evidently excited, twitching its tail, jerking its wings, and uttering a low whistle. In a thought it saw me, just as I caught a snap-shot as it darted through the closely-woven branches. Through the thin veil of smoke I caught sight of a few floating feathers, and hurried forward without reloading, breaking my way through matted masses of ferns, leaping gullies, and swinging myself finally beneath the tree upon which he had for a moment rested. There was nothing in sight. Disappointed, I yet trusted those floating feathers had not misled me, and renewed the search, carefully displacing the ferns and fallen branches one by one. It was only upon searching lower down, where a steep incline had given it impetus, that I found it, lodged in a wild pine on the verge of a ravine.

Exultant was I then, as that soft-plumaged bird lay in view before me; forgotten was the toil and previous exertion, forgotten the rain and discomfort of the night. I had triumphed over all obstacles in my path, and was about to hold in my hand the first soufrière-bird known to have been shot within the memory of any one now living. In my anxiety, in my headlong eagerness to possess the bird, I neglected to examine the ground beneath my feet; I saw only the bird, and darted forward. The loose earth gave way, the mass of orchids and roots, loosened by the rains, fell without warning, and I, wildly grasping at overhanging roots which broke in my grip, was thrown into the ravine. It was not more than fifteen feet in depth, and so narrow that my fall was broken by the adjacent walls, and I landed on my feet, bruised and a little torn, but without serious injury.

Joy at escape from immediate danger was quickly turned to apprehension regarding escape from the gulch, for the walls were as smooth as water could wear them, and the lower portion of the ravine disappeared suddenly in the direction of the lake. The head of the ravine was a hole like a well, and into this I had fallen. Through the crevice below me I could see the shimmering waters of the lake, a thousand feet beneath, and a few steps farther would have precipitated me into its unfathomed abyss.

A shower heavier than the others came down fiercely, setting rivulets running down the crater and washing the earth from beneath my feet, warning me to be out of the hole if possible. Clinging to some projections in the rock, I worked my way slowly up until near the top; when about to thrust my arm through the vines that darkened my chamber, I was startled by the appearance of a black, shining head with glittering eyes, thrust right into my face. But for the nearness of the opposite wall, I should have fallen, this apparition took me so by surprise, for it was none other than an immense black snake. Fortunately, I could secure myself in position by bracing my legs against each opposing cliff, and was near enough to the top to clutch some roots, otherwise I could not have maintained the ground I had gained. The snake crawled out of a crevice in the rock, and though he may not have intended to harm me, I will confess to a feeling of fear at that time, and remembered with regret how thoughtlessly I had laughed at poor Toby, the day before, when he fled in terror from a snake I had caught by the tail. My gun, which had not been injured in my fall, was slung at my back, and by loosening it I managed to strike the snake a smart blow, which, though it angered him, caused him to glide down the cliff instead of up. Thus relieved, I scrambled through the dank vegetation, and stood once more above the ground.

TOBY.

From the lake came up a strange hissing sound, as though the water was boiling, caused by the many streams set in flow by the rain running into it. Its usually placid surface was agitated, and I could detect a perceptible change in its color.

My precious bird had landed safely at the bottom of the gulch, though somewhat soiled, and he now reposed in my game-basket, wrapped in a paper cone. This was the first soufrière-bird I secured; the next day I shot three others; they proved to be a *new* species and were named the *Myiadestes sibilans*. Another species, shot in the same locality, proved to be also new, and was afterwards named the *Leucopeza Bishopi*.

The day following, Toby's patience gave out entirely, and I was obliged to descend the mountain to the Carib country, which, as the cloud of fog lifted, I could see from my cave as a lovely green slope, lying between dark mountains and blue, white-rimmed ocean.

CHAPTER XIII.

TRADITIONAL LORE. A MISADVENTURE.

CARIB COUNTRY. — SANDY BAY. — CAPTAIN GEORGE. — CAPTAIN GEORGE'S FAMILY. — HIS SUPERSTITIONS. — A CARIB ROMANCE. — A LOVE TEST. — COURTSHIP AND MARRIAGE. — PREPARING CASSAVA. — FARINE. — AN INDIAN INVENTION. — THE OBEAH CHARM. — THE CARIB WARS. — A BRAVE COWARD. — THE CARIBS CAPTURED. — SENT TO COAST OF HONDURAS. — THE SURVIVORS. — THE SEMINOLES. — A PARALLEL. — CARIB SONG. — CAPTAIN GEORGE'S TREASURE. — A MISADVENTURE. — BALLICEAUX. — A SEARCH FOR SKULLS. — BATTOWIA. — THE "MOSES BOAT." — THE MONSTER IGUANA. — THE CAVE. — THE TORTOISE. — A RELIC OF A PAST AGE. — TROPIC BIRDS. — OUR BOAT SMASHED. — A NIGHT ON THE BEACH. — THE SOUTHERN CROSS. — PAUL AND VIRGINIA. — CHURCH ISLAND.

CARIB COUNTRY is that portion of the island of St. Vincent lying between the central ridge of mountains and the Atlantic coast. It is the most fertile and level, spreading from the foot of the hills in gentle slopes and undulating plains. Formerly in possession of the Caribs, it early attracted the English by its fertility, and, by processes well known to the white man when he desires his red brother's land, it soon changed hands. Though one may lament this usurpation of the Indian's territory, and deprecate such deeds on general principles, one is soon reconciled to the change after he has been domiciled among the people in present possession.

It has never been my fortune to meet a Scotchman on his native heath, and whether he is improved by being transplanted to another clime, I cannot tell. One thing is indisputable, he could not be more generous, more hospitable, more companionable than are those rare Scotchmen in the West Indies, with especial reference to the managers of those estates in Carib country. As all the estates were owned by one firm, and that firm held that there were no managers so skillful and faithful as their own countrymen, this part of the island was often alluded to as New Caledonia.

From " Happy Hill," accompanied by its manager and those of adjoining estates, I cantered, on a borrowed pony, down the coast to the Carib settlement. At Rabaca is the celebrated " Dry River " of the eastern coast, which is very broad, and often swept by torrents from the mountains. My friends rode with me as far as Overland, a most interesting negro village of wattled huts, built in a thick wood of cocoa-palms and bread-fruits. Here they left me with friendly adieus, and I went on alone. The Soufrière rose grandly from out its surrounding forests, and the great rock, shaped like a lion couchant, near which my cave opened, was sharply cut against the bluest of skies.

The Carib settlement of Sandy Bay is the most secluded in the island; it is also the most picturesque; but, as rocks and wooded hills are the principal elements of a picturesque landscape, I fancy the Caribs isolated here would gladly exchange their portion for the more fertile fields near Rabaca.

An Indian named Rabaca, a pure Carib, one

descended from an ancient family, met me and aided me in my search for a house, and I was comfortably fixed before night in a little house of reeds, wattled and thatched. It contained two rooms eight feet square, separated by a matting of tied wild-plantain ribs. The result of my observations here is incorporated in chapter nine, but there are some incidents of Indian life that have not been alluded to in that narrative.

My nearest neighbor was "Captain George," an Indian descended from the "Black Caribs." That is, his father, or grandfather, was a negro, while his mother, or grandmother, was a Carib. From either paternal or maternal ancestor he had inherited a kinky wool and rather thick lips, but the Indian blood showed itself strongly. Captain George was intelligent beyond the average Carib, and possessed a good knowledge of the ancient language, which his grandmother, who had "brung him up," had taught him; and as he was always ready to impart to me the words and idioms of the Indian tongue, I was a frequent visitor to his cabin, where I would sit for hours listening to the tales and traditions handed down from his ancestors. He had an interesting family; and, as he had married a "Yellow Carib," a woman of uncontaminated Indian blood, his children did not resemble in complexion either him or his wife. Nothing can better show this difference than the photograph I took of the group one afternoon, as we returned from hunting in the hills. The children were blessed with abundant, black, straight hair, which was worn by the girls in long braids; it was a trifle coarser than that of the mother, but yet beautiful.

CAPTAIN GEORGE AND HIS FAMILY.

Sandy Bay takes its name from a beach of gray sand guarded by volcanic rocks, lined with tropical vegetation; at its northern end was a single cocoa palm leaning over a thatched hut used as a boat-house. Beneath this hut I encountered some of my Indian neighbors, dividing their spoils from the sea; there were fish of every color: "parrot fish," "butter fish," and "silver fish," radiant with all the hues of the rainbow. To each man Captain George laid aside his portion, and from each little heap took a fish for the stranger sojourning among them. This done, he retired with me to a log beneath the thatch, and over-hauled his store of traditional Indian lore. The seas came up with white crests, reaching far up the strand; the sun was down behind the volcano, leaving a long, cool twilight, to which the leeward shore is a stranger.

Our conversation turned upon ghosts and those evil spirits called by the negroes, and by the Indians, jumbies, or jombies. "I have saw jumbie not more than three times," said the old Indian. "Once time, I runned away from Rabaca, an' when I reach de dry ribah, walkin' along, swingin' my bundle, I see man, high so, as a hoss, an' he point me back; but I keep on. When I come to cross de ribah I see big bull-calf to come down de bank; he tail up, an' he come fo' me an' swing roun' an' roun' an' bawl, an' then he run back. It to make my har stan' up, so; an' when I make to meet him at nex' ribah I was want to cross, an' he came fo' me an' bawl, I say, 'Oh, good Massa, keep jumbie away;' an' he no come no mo'.

"A young man, he courtin' he sweetheart; he say, 'You lub me?' He sweetheart say, 'Yes.' He say,

'Like you life you lub me?' 'Yes.' Well, he say, 'I try you: Ef you lub me, so; ef you no lub me an' no mine me, I kill you dead to-day.' So he go to ketch some mouse—how he was to do dat I do' know; but he ketch um mice an' put him under calbash on de groun'. Den he call um sweetheart an' say, 'I go to leabe you now. You see dat calbash! Under dat calbash is my life, my lub. Ef you lif' um up he make um go; ef you lub me, you no lif' um up.' So he go 'way. When he gone, she walk all 'bout, she cannot to stay still; she mus' to see under de calbash; so she lif' um up. Shi! out pop de mice an' runned away with heself.

"When time come fo' dinnah, her lubah come back 'gin. She set down sad, sad, sad; no tell him howdy. He say, 'What de mattah?' She no speak. He say, '*Kaima, myiga*' (go and eat). She no go. He say, '*Kaima, goora*' (go and drink). She no go. She no make talk, but take de big calbash, and go to de ribah fo' watah. He say, 'Ah, my lub is out ob de calbash.' He lif' um up; no mice no pop out agin. Den he go to de ribah—bam! when she lif' up de watah, he mash he head with stone.

"When Carib court he sweetheart he must not to see her too often, only but once a month; an' den when he courtin' he must to sweep all de yard clean, clean, clean, by first cockcrow; ef he to be see after dat he cannot court dat girl no mo'. Ef he ketch fish he must to bring um to her father's house; an' he no see he sweetheart, only hes father; and he no see hes mother-law 'tall, [great deprivation.] When he to get married, he must go to de wood an' cut down tall gommier an' make six-oar boat."

The ancient marriage ceremony was very simple; the man and woman dug and washed some cassava, boiled it, and baked very thick cakes. From the liquor, boiled down, they made a drink which they mixed with rum and resinous leaves. These things were placed on a table around which were seated the man and woman, her father and mother, and two witnesses. The father cut the cassava into six pieces, and handed one to the groom, who dipped it in the liquor and gave it to his bride. She in turn dipped another piece, given her by her mother, and gave it to the groom. After this solemn ceremony came feasting and drinking to the extent the groom's purse would allow.

The inhabitants of the village were preparing cassava, or rather they were making "farine" from the cassava root, and Captain George and I went over to the river where the women were at work. The juice of the cassava (*Jatropha manihot*) is very poisonous. Cattle and children often die from eating the raw tubers, or drinking water containing the juice. To prepare it for use, the natives scrape off the dark outer cuticle, wash the tuber thoroughly and grate it; it is then again washed, and a small portion at a time wrung out dry in a cloth, leaving it in dry cakes which crumble. It is then sifted, rubbed through a sieve of reeds split and woven, and afterwards baked in very thin cakes on a large iron plate, over a hot fire. These cakes will keep a long time; they are hung up over a pole or line, and used as wanted. In some islands the people make more of the farine, the grated root dried on a large copper or iron plate, being well stirred the while. It is sometimes put up in barrels, and always commands a ready sale. During the baking process the poisonous quality, which is volatile, escapes, and the people eat with impunity these roots that in a raw state would prove poisonous. The juice itself is made into a drink by being boiled, which is palatable to a native.

I noticed here a curious method in use to press the cassava dry after it was grated; it was a cone of woven reeds, so constructed that, when filled with cassava and hung up with a weight attached to its lower end, a continuous and equable pressure was applied to the whole mass. This cone was about four feet long, and perhaps six inches across at the mouth, or larger end, and is an invention of the Caribs, having been found in use by them by the earliest voyagers.

This farine supplies the place of bread to a great extent, the natives preferring it to that article, and eating it dry by the handful. There are two varieties, the "sweet" and the "bitter" cassava; but the latter, though so dangerous, is more extensively cultivated than the former, which is harmless.

After inspecting the preparation of the farine, we adjourned to Captain George's cabin, where he regaled me with numerous stories of the achievements of the Caribs during the war with the English in the last century. He firmly believed that his grandfather and other Caribs owed the preservation of their lives to certain charms obtained from an obeah man in Martinique.

"One time, six Carib kill um white gen'leman, but dey not see he serbant hide in de bush. When serbant get 'way he tell soldier, 'Carib kill one buckra, my massa.' Well, soldier go dah; bam! bam! de ball fall all 'bout; hit um leg, hit um heel, but drop right off, and no hurt Carib 'tall, 'tall, fo' dey hab obeah charm to keep um from make to dead."

This allusion to the strife once carried on between Carib and English drew out the entire story of the war in which the Carib power was forever destroyed. In 1772, the best part of the Carib lands having been seized, the Indians commenced hostilities, but soon came to terms. By treaty, they were then secured in the best portion of their lands, and kept the peace until, six years later, instigated and aided by the French from Martinique, they revolted. Soon the entire island was in French possession, without much, if any, bloodshed. In 1784, the island was restored to Great Britain by the treaty of Versailles. Incited by the French republicans, in 1795, the Caribs again revolted, defeated the troops sent against them, and swarmed upon the heights above the town. By the opportune arrival of soldiers and marines from Barbados, they were driven back, but again assembled, and a great fight ensued, in which the English were at first beaten; but finally, by aid of large reinforcements, the Caribs were defeated.

Thus the war went on with varying fortune for a year and a half. The negroes were assembled, appraised at their full value, their owners to be reimbursed for any killed, and sent against the Caribs; but these "forest rangers," as they were called, though they proved very active and useful in destroying the canoes of the enemy, and in bringing in women and children from the mountains after the warriors had surrendered, did little good service. Doubtless they were animated with the high resolve of saving the colony the expense of paying their owners.

At one time, having been driven from Owia, a point on the north-east side of the island, the Caribs executed a masterly retreat over the volcano, to the Caribbean coast, and committed great ravages; a party sent against them there was defeated. In all their battles they showed consummate skill and great bravery, seizing upon the most advantageous positions, fortifying them and holding them to the last. The English were at first unfortunate in their generals. One of them, "Sir Paulus Æmilius Irving, Bart.," who was pursuing the Caribs with a large body of troops, became frightened by a six-pounder ball passing near him, and ordered a retreat. Subsequently the English were nearly cut off, and lost several hundred men under this gallant general.

The Indians understood and practiced the trick of posting their best shots in the tall trees, for the purpose of picking off the officers. At last there arrived the famous General Abercrombie, fresh from his capture of St. Lucia, who pushed the French and Caribs so hard, with his army of four thousand men, that they were obliged to surrender. The French and colored, officers and soldiers, were released on parole, with the privilege of returning to their own island; but the poor Caribs, thus abandoned, were allowed only unconditional surrender. Refusing these terms, most of them fled to the mountains, and in the dense forests found shelter for a long time, defeating several detachments of troops sent against them.

Deprived of crops, and all provisions such as a successful foray could obtain, they were gradually gathered in, by use of force and by the necessities of their situation, until, of men, women, and children, nearly five thousand were captured. These were removed to the small island of Balliceaux, off the coast of St. Vincent, deprived of canoes and arms, and kept there for months. Captain George declared that the English government aimed to destroy as many of them as possible, and caused lime to be mixed in their bread; but of course this was false, and probably arose from the fact that the water, being impregnated with lime, caused much sickness and death.

In February, 1797, they were all carried to the island of Ruatan, off the Honduras coast. When the vessels arrived there, it was found necessary to dislodge a party of Spaniards in possession, who had built a fort. After a hard fight it was taken, and the Caribs left to the mercy of whomsoever should appear against them. The Carib lands were thus left desolate; they were declared forfeited, surveyed and sold. In 1805, the few remaining Caribs were pardoned, and a tract of two hundred and fifty acres, near Morne Ronde, was granted them, this territory not being considered fertile nor available for sugar-land. Here the majority of the Indians have lived in peace ever since.

It appeared strange to me that this settlement at Morne Ronde was composed almost wholly of Black Caribs, the few families of pure Yellow Caribs living on the eastern shore and paying rent for land once in full possession of their ancestors. It may have been that the innate cowardice of the Black Caribs, born of their negro blood, prevented them from taking an active part in the war, and may have induced them to seek the protection of the English. The "Rangers," also, who scoured the woods after the Caribs were subdued and scattered, and committed many murders, may have been moved to spare people so much resembling themselves.

How similar has been the fate of the Caribs to that of the Seminoles of the Southern States! At the beginning of the present century, the latter were peaceful and happy, cultivating their gardens with an intelligence that shows them to have been superior people. They, too, were driven to war, stripped of their property, and hunted by white troops. Their resistance lasted for seven years, but in the end, nearly all were captured and transported far from their homes. Of them a remnant lingers in the hunting-grounds of their fathers, engaged, like the present Carib, in agricultural pursuits. With them, too, the negro found a home, married with them, and to them communicated the curse of his race.

The memory of the war of his ancestors stirred Captain George to wild song, and his daughters danced in the moonlight while he made music on a drum hollowed from a log and covered with cow-skin, chanting the while a song, of which I can remember but two lines:

"*Neech-i-goo, bah-li, boó ni,*
Leh-bi chi, wei-i-ga-mah, ah'-wah-si."

He attended me to my cabin, late in the evening, and as he had imbibed freely of distilled cane-juice (vulgarly known as rum) he was very confidential, and communicated to me the important secret that, in a cave on one of the islands to which the Caribs were transported, there was a treasure. Of the exact nature of this "treasure" he did not inform me, but left me to infer that it might be gold, or might be of value only to the archæologist. To this latter opinion I was inclined when told that it belonged to the oldest Indian of the nation, who, rather than allow it to be taken by the English, buried it in the cave. I inferred from this that it must be of the nature of a charm or token, such as the Indians, when living in primitive simplicity, carried about them.

Nearly three months later I visited the island where the Caribs had been incarcerated previous to their transportation, and as my discovery there strongly verifies my Indian friend's story, it may be as well in this connection to relate my adventures during that short trip.

The island of Balliceaux, the scene of Carib captivity, is about twelve miles from St. Vincent, and is one of the northernmost of the chain of islands and islets known as the Grenadines. It is about a mile in length and perhaps an eighth in breadth, rocky and dry, covered for the most part with a sparse growth of trees. It is owned entirely by one of the largest land proprietors in St. Vincent, Mr. Cheesman, who has stocked it with goats, guinea-fowl, and deer, intending it as a preserve, to which he occasionally resorts for sport with some friends.

As his guest, in company with a dozen more valiant Scotchmen and Creoles, I left the blue hills of St. Vincent, one morning in February, for Balliceaux. We landed from the drogher on a sandy beach, above which drooped a solitary palm, and wended our way to the comfortable house, where we were met by the manager, and to which, later, our store of provender was transported. Our generous host understood well the art of entertaining guests, though it is almost superfluous to say this of any West Indian, either adopted or to the manor born, and as soon as our feet touched the soil of his preserve we felt the truth of his assurance, that all was ours as well as his.

I searched the shore for traces of the Caribs, but was unrewarded save by a few shards of pottery; however, I was promised a guide for the morrow, who could pilot me to a sepulchre of skulls. Alas! that morrow did not bring its promised pleasure, and those skulls may yet linger for some other explorer, for aught I know to the contrary.

Close in sight, about two miles distant, rose the islet of Battowia. It was little more than a huge rock several hundred feet in height, and clad with vegetation on its western slope. In the eastern cliffs was the cave which some of the Indians had occupied, and which we desired to explore. After early coffee the morning succeeding our arrival at Balliceaux, three of us embarked in a "Moses-boat" for Battowia.

The Moses-boat is a peculiarly strong boat built for transporting sugar and other heavy freight through the heavy surf of the eastern shore. In shape it is something like the famous craft in which those "three wise men of Gotham" departed on their sea-voyage. It is very buoyant, and owes its great strength to numerous knees and thick planking. Regarding its name, whether it was named for Moses the great "lawgiver," or for the man who built the first of the kind, will forever remain a mystery.

In the Moses-boat we embarked: the sea was smooth, and we made the passage without mishap. There were four of us "buckras," or white men, and an equal number of negroes. The negroes pulled the boat, and the whites encouraged the negroes, and withal we made a very satisfactory voyage. Having secured the boat a little way from shore, we marched up the slope toward the summit. Our host had provided a substantial breakfast, to be eaten at the cave, and the men staggered under divers kinds of nourishment contained in bottles with wired corks, a tub of ice and other necessaries.

Soon the bushes grew so thickly that we were obliged to "cutlass" our way, and took turns in cutting out a path with the great, sword-like knives of the blacks. It was hot, weary work, and we made slow progress. C. started up a great iguana, quite five feet in length, which was basking on the rocks. Part of our party got lost in the thick growth, and this delayed us so that it was well toward noon when we arrived at the ridge and felt the cool breezes from the east.

After a light lunch, we scattered down the cliffs in search of the cave. A whoop from one of our attendants drew us half-way down the precipice, where we were introduced to a deep fissure-like hole in the rock, hidden by trees. Crawling carefully over the loose rock, three hundred feet above the surf beating at the base of the cliff, we entered the cave and prepared to explore it. A glance showed that it was not large nor deep, and we soon found that it led in only a hundred feet before the crevice grew so narrow that it could not be followed; but we were satisfied that it led down to the sea as we could distinctly hear the booming of the waves.

Along each side of the cavern were hollows, evidently artificial, begrimed with smoke, as though they had been used as fireplaces. We found no living things but bats and tarantulas; the former flew about in great numbers. While my companions were engaged in the farther end of the cave, I groped among the loose fragments of stone near the mouth, where, one of the men told me, an Indian chair had been found some fifteen years before. Carefully displacing the stone chippings, I at last found what seemed to be an image of stone; but scraping with a knife revealed that it was of wood. It was a tortoise, four inches long and two and one-half broad, curiously carved. Two holes, a quarter of an inch in diameter, are bored through back and breast; the back, upper part of the head, and the throat, are covered with incised figures, and the eyes carefully carved hollows, as if for the reception of some foreign substance.

There is little doubt that this image once belonged to an Indian living many years ago. I choose to consider it a *zemi*, having as my authority the account given in Irving's "Columbus," of the finding of similar objects by the Spaniards, among the natives of Haiti. Speaking of their religion, he says: "They believed in one Supreme Being, who inhabited the sky, who was immortal, omnipotent, and invisible. They never addressed their worship directly to him, but to inferior deities, called *zemes*, a kind of messengers or mediators. Each cacique, each family and each individual, had a particular *zemi* as a tutelary deity, whose image, generally of a hideous form, was, placed about their houses, carved on their furniture, and sometimes bound to their foreheads when they went to battle. They believed their zemes to be transferable with all their beneficial powers; they therefore often stole them from each other, and, when the Spaniards arrived, hid them away lest they should be taken by the strangers. They believed that these zemes presided over every object in nature. Some had sway over the elements, causing sterile or abundant years; some governed the seas and forests, the springs and fountains, like the nereids, the dryads, and satyrs of antiquity. Once a year each cacique held a feast in honor of his zemi, when his subjects

An Indian Zemi.

formed a procession to the temple; the married men and women decorated with their most precious ornaments, the young females entirely naked, carrying baskets of flowers and cakes, and singing as they advanced."

In the "Smithsonian Report" for 1876 is an elaborate article describing, with many engravings, a collection of antiquities from Porto Rico, containing several Indian "stools" of stone and wood. These stools are ornamented with a head-piece resembling this tortoise, and even the eye-sockets have the appearance of having been hollowed out for the reception of jewels or bright metal; as the author of the article mentioned above remarks: "In the wooden objects, as in the stone one, the eyes excavated for precious stones are plainly visible, but the stones are wanting."

The same author quotes Herrera's account of the visit of Columbus to Cuba, when a party, having penetrated to the interior, returned with glowing accounts of their reception by the Indians. They found a village where each house contained a whole generation. "The prime men came out to meet them, led them by the arms, and lodged them in one of the new houses, causing them to sit down on seats made of a solid piece of wood in the shape of a beast with very short legs and the tail held up, the head before, with eyes and ears of gold."

This relic of antiquity was undoubtedly taken by the Caribs from their enemies of Haiti, and brought here by the captor, or it may have belonged to a captive Arowak living among the Caribs. The same old negro who found the "stool" was of our party, but he could not afford any further light except to say, "Me tink him b'long to Injun seat."

Beneath the cave, a hundred feet farther down the cliff, was a grotto sparkling with lime crystals. In descending to this, we found some great birds, which are seldom seen except high in air, sailing above the ocean, the Tropic-birds (*Phaethon æthereus*); and they sat so quietly upon the shelves of the cliff, permitting us to approach, that at first we took them for young birds. We soon were convinced that they were adult birds by finding some eggs beneath them, and by the strength of their powerful beaks as they pecked at us when we inserted our hands into their retreats to pull them out. Dotting the cliff here and there, and floating above our heads, with their long tails, of but two cylindrical feathers each, fluttering in the wind, they formed a graceful element in the picture spread before us from the ridge.

At the summit, where we had left our lunch, we exerted ourselves to finish the contents of baskets and bottles, and so successful were we that nothing was left to burden our men down the slope but a few chicken-bones and a little water. Then we hastened down to the shore, anxious to join our friends on the other island, and rejoicing in our good luck.

As we turned the great rock which hid the little cove in which the boat had been left, we were greeted by a loud cry: "De boat done mash, sah!" A fact we verified a few minutes later; for there floated the boat, its rail just above water, thumping on the rocks.

It was growing late, and there was no time to be lost. Our men stripped and plunged into the water and commenced bailing the boat, but it was labor thrown away; then, by direction of Mr. C., they hauled the boat up upon the pebbles of the narrow beach at the base of the cliff, and turned her over — no easy work — and we were all obliged to assist. As the heavy boat came down, bottom up, it caught the ankle of the manager and wedged it fast against a rock. In releasing him, and hauling the boat into position, we all got wet; but this did not dampen our spirits. Pieces of board were nailed on with nails extracted from fragments of a wreck, pants and shirts were torn up and calked into the seams, together with such moss as we could find, and then we launched the boat again, with four men at the oars and two men bailing, and started.

We had not gone a gun-shot from shore before the water was up to the thwarts, and the boat fast sinking. The seas met and howled, running up to the rocks in huge, white-crested breakers, and it became evident that we could not possibly survive the passage across. Reluctantly, our captain gave the order to go back; we reached the little beach just as the water touched the rail, jumped out and waded ashore. Some sharks, whose triangular fins we could see cutting the water outside the rocks, were evidently disappointed, and manifested their disapprobation by darting in close to the boat, much alarming the negroes.

All hope of escape by means of the boat was abandoned, and we turned our attention to the prospect of obtaining help from our friends on the other island. A portion of a sail was attached to an oar and held aloft on a high point, as a signal of distress. It was nearly dark by this time and the hour for dinner, for the preparation of which Mr. C.'s cook had been all day busy. We turned to our stores and discovered nothing but the chicken-bones and a tin of sardines. There was not a drink of water apiece, and we reverted regretfully to those bottles we had emptied so lavishly a few hours before.

Darkness inclosed us, and we sought a couch on the bank; my game-basket served me for a pillow, as it had often done before, and a heap of grass for a bed. Fortunately the night was warm and dewless, and had it not been for the groans of Frazer, whose ankle was badly crushed, we should have slept soundly; as it was, we lay awake most of the time and counted the stars.

Very late in the evening we were aroused by a shouting, and became aware that our friends had sought us. They had all embarked on the drogher, after becoming satisfied that some accident had befallen us, and, after anchoring off our island, had sent a boat to seek for us. The night was pitchy dark, and the heavy seas clashed so fearfully that to attempt a landing would have been certain disaster; so we warned our friends back, to wait for us till morning.

Our voices seemed drowned in the roar of the breakers, but the regular click of the oars, growing fainter and fainter, told us that we had been heard. Frazer told us, between his moanings, that sometimes it is impossible to land for weeks, just about this season of the year, and we fell to calculating upon the chances of subsisting upon iguanas and wild goats for a few days, notwithstanding the proximity of our friends. On the morrow, however, we safely embarked, though hungry, weary, and exceeding thirsty. Our more fortunate companions had indeed devoured the dinner, while we were fasting on that desert rock, but there yet remained sufficient to stay our needs; and they coaxed us with toddies and punches and brisk champagne, until we forgot our trials and remembered only our triumphs.

Ever memorable will be that night on the beach — the second time in a twelvemonth I had fallen a victim to Neptune's rage — as that in which I for the first time saw the Southern Cross. As the night waned, and the cross assumed an upright position upon the horizon, there came to mind that passage from one of the saddest of romances, in which the old servant warns *Paul* and *Virginia* of the approach of midnight, as indicated by the position of the cross.*

That glorious constellation, watched by the hapless lovers in the far-off Mauritius, I saw gleaming above the Caribbean Sea, north of and nearer the equator, as I lay upon the beach. By a rare coincidence, it hung in the sky above a cathedral-shaped rock known to the natives as Church Island.

* "*Ill est tard, il est minuit ; la Croix du Sud est droite sur l'horizon.*" — PAUL ET VIRGINIE.

CHAPTER XIV.

A MONTH ON A SUGAR ESTATE.

OUT OF THE FOREST. — INTO A SICK-BED. — MY GOOD ANGEL. — CONVALESCENCE. — RUTLAND VALE. — THE HAPPY VALLEY. — NOCTURNAL NEIGHBORS. — THE LABOR QUESTION. — A PLANTER'S TRIALS. — COOLIE IMMIGRATION. — THE NEGRO, RETURNING TO SAVAGERY. — A SELF-APPOINTED PHYSICIAN. — GOVERNMENT HOUSE. — TREES OF THE TROPICS. — BREAD-FRUIT AND COCOA-PALM. — FIRST EXPERIENCE WITH BREAD-FRUIT. — ITS APPEARANCE. — TASTE. — HISTORY OF ITS INTRODUCTION. — ABUNDANCE IN ST. VINCENT. — THE PALMS, THEIR GREAT BEAUTY AND UTILITY. — COCOA-PALM, PALMISTE, GROO-GROO AND GRIS-GRIS, ARECA AND MOUNTAIN PALMS. — THE VINE WITH PERFORATED LEAVES. — THE INDIAN MAIDEN.

ON the morning of the twentieth of December I cantered into town from Carib Country; at night I lay stretched out with fever, having galloped, as it were, from the woods to my bed. For ten days I had been suffering from the effects of a severe cold, caught in the cave on the volcano. In two weeks there remained but a wretched apology of my former self, and the doctor ordered that I remove what little there was left of me to the country as soon as I could walk, or mount a horse.

The days passed wearily. I had exhausted all the resources of the room; had watched my favorite lizard as he caught flies on the window-pane, and the great, naked-limbed spider, that every morning caught a cockroach and dragged it to my headboard, where he spent the rest of the day in absorbing its juices. The question of convalescence seemed a doubtful one, until, one day, I was startled by the sound of a cheery voice, and my good angel burst into the room like a mountain breeze.

"What! down with fever? This won't do; can't get well here; must go down to my estate." And he literally dragged me forth, assisted me to dress, packed up some clothes and my gun-case, and carried me on board the little steamer at the landing. At his beach a horse was waiting, and he placed me in the saddle and led the way on his own bay mare. Clinging to the saddle, I rode slowly up the cane-covered slopes to the house, perched on a spur commanding the valley, surrounded by bread-fruit and almond trees. There I was taken in charge by my friend's good wife, and established at the house until fully recovered.

"Rutland Vale," to which my friend had carried me, is a long, narrow valley, extending from the Caribbean Sea to the mountains, nearly two miles. The estate occupies the whole of this valley, and is the best cultivated of any on the Leeward coast, being, in the season at which I visited it, one waving mass of cane, filling the valley and covering the billowy ridges.

The memory of those sunny days, in which my strength came back to me, is the pleasantest, the brightest, of the many delightful reminiscences of that lovely island. My good host, James Milne, a native of Bamff, in Scotland (celebrated as the home of Tam Edward, the "Scottish naturalist"), had resided on this estate, as manager, for twenty years. In all that time he had been sick but once, though exposed to the morning mists and mid-day sun, and, in the season of crops, sometimes engaged in the millhouse whole nights at a time, without rest. Surrounded by a large family of healthy children, who enjoyed without stint the blessings of the delightful climate, my friend reposed in this valley with his flocks and herds in almost patriarchal simplicity. He was a man of educated tastes, and had gathered about him a large and well-selected library, which proved a blessing in the heat of the day, when it was not possible to stir out of doors.

At that season, January, the sun sinks behind the low ridge that barely hides the sea before six o'clock. Hardly has it given its last wink, and left the valley in cool shade, when the bats come out in large numbers, taking the place of the swifts of the day-time, who, morning and evening, and after every shower, are skimming the cane-fields and circling swiftly about the trees and buildings. Thus the aerial insect world is left without rest from incessant pursuit; scarcely has one class of enemies departed than another comes forward, waging a nocturnal and diurnal warfare that must be very destructive, when carried on with so much vigor and by so many foes.

One evening my attention was called to some bats, or birds, which appeared only when every trace of twilight had faded, and circled rapidly around an almond tree, either after insects or nuts. After one or two turns, perhaps poising themselves on a twig a few seconds, they would dart off, returning in ten minutes or so to make their circuits about the tree.

They increased in number and frequency of visits as darkness deepened. After waiting several evenings on the veranda, I secured a quick shot at one, just as it hovered above the top of the tree. Long had I waited; the wind had died away, leaving the trees rigid as stone, every leaf motionless; the depths among the leaves were impenetrable, but against the sky I could discern a dark object. Directly I had fired, down dropped a large, dark body; but though we searched a long time with a lantern we could not find it in the long guinea-grass; and the hogs had been through the place in the morning long before I was up. Three months later I obtained the same animals in Tobago, and found that they were frugivorous bats; in the latter island they were robbing a spadillo tree of its soft fruit.

With a bread-fruit and a strip of salt fish, the Ethiopian is happy, is contented; so long as bread-fruits grow and fishes swim the sea, so long will the labor question remain a perplexing one to the planter. In the time of slavery the planters of the West Indies set out a great many bread-fruit trees, so that at the present time they may be found wild in the forest. That their introduction has been a questionable benefit to the islands, nearly every one viewing the subject with unprejudiced eye is inclined to believe. The negro will not work while he can obtain his bread so easily. He will endure hunger and inferior food in preference to plenty and work.

To aid the planters in their difficulty, natives of the East Indies were imported as laborers. These came out indentured for a term of years, generally five, to work at a stated price per day. The planter is obliged to provide a physician and to keep a large stock of drugs constantly at hand. The Coolie is protected by government to such an extent that the planter is really the slave of the "laborer." Upon the slightest pretext the Coolie can call his manager before a magistrate. If he does not choose to work, he can remain in his house on plea of sickness; if the manager or overseer uses force in trying to make the laborer perform his task, he is at once summoned before the governor, imprisoned or fined. For a few years the Coolies worked well; they are sprightly intelligent people; and if the anti-slavery party, in power in England, had not hedged the planters about with so many restrictions, prosperity might have attended their efforts, ruined estates might have been reclaimed, and these fertile islands once more have blessed the world with their products. But the result has shown how a party of fanatics can pervert power that, used judiciously, might have brought about a new era of prosperity.

The Coolie, though naturally docile, was intelligent, and saw his opportunity; and the planter now is not much better off than when he was wholly dependent upon negro labor. Wages, to be sure, are ridiculously low, though the profits of cane culture do not seem to warrant the payment of much higher rates. Twenty cents per day; for women sixteen cents; for children four cents and six cents per day. Some male laborers, by extra work, can earn thirty-six cents, and those who have "tasks" assigned them as a day's work can finish by noon, and prefer lying idle the rest of the day to increasing their wages.

Even upon this small pay the negroes live comfortably; two cents per day, I have heard it stated, will keep them in fish — the only article the poorest of them buy. In the mountains they have their provision-grounds, where they cultivate yams, plantains, sweet potatoes, cassava, and bananas, and to which they devote every Saturday. Sunday, with them, is a day of recreation. Thus the estates get from their laborers but five half-worked days in a week. To the staple article of salt fish there should be added another which they purchase when impossible to be obtained otherwise — the native rum of the island, which is their stay and strength.

The Coolies are even more frugal than the negroes, and soon acquire money enough to purchase goats and cattle, which they pasture in some obscure corner of the estate. Upon the expiration of their indentures, they flock at once to the towns, where, like the Portuguese, they set up small shops — proving in the end rather a detriment to the island than a benefit. Though by the terms of their contracts they are obliged to work six days in the week, none of them do, appropriating to themselves Saturday as a holiday.

The labor question does not fall within the scope of this book, and I fear I have trenched upon ground I should not; but these remarks were suggested by seeing my friend of Rutland Vale trying to persuade his own hired laborers to go into the field. Even after himself and his overseer had led the refractory Indian to the field and placed a hoe in his hand, he refused to work. It is between such fires as these that the planter is placed; and it is time some champion of their interests should appear, to place them in a proper light before the world.

From the delightful retreat at Rutland Vale I returned to town recuperated, though still shaky and very thin. My first visit was to the treasurer of the island. "Bless my soul," said he, "you haven't any blood; it is blood you want. Come with me; I'll show you what you must do now, if you would build yourself up." Saying which, he led me by the hand to the sideboard, poured out a glass of ripe old Madeira and handed it to me. "Isn't that going to restore your vigor?" said he, as I set down the glass with a sigh of satisfaction.

Then I was suddenly converted to that man's belief. Since my first skirmish with doctors, many years agone, I had never met a physician who prescribed and administered so sensibly as this one.

I looked at the old man with admiration; I thrilled through with hope and the effects of the potent wine. It was blood I wanted, was most urgently in need of, and I waxed blood-thirsty; not all the Indians on all the plains could be fiercer for blood than I. My physician smiled — a complacent smile; said he, "I knew it, hit the nail on the head that time. Bless your soul, take some more, you don't get such wine every day; bottled myself, imported direct; take some more blood!" It danced along every vein, and every pulse beat responsive gratulation.

"Now," continued my friend, "you can't get that medicine anywhere else, at present; I have thought of that, and as we are, I think, agreed as to its efficacy, you must accept a few bottles, which I shall send down by Thomas, to-morrow. You know the dose: a wineglassful every three hours, and oftener if you feel it necessary."

A mile from Kingston, at the base of the hills, is Government House, the residence of the lieutenant-governor of St. Vincent. It is in the center of grounds formerly used as a garden of acclimatization for tropical plants and trees not indigenous to the West Indies. The garden was opened in 1763, but given up in 1828, and many of the plants removed to Trinidad. Here are still found the teak, mahogany, almond, screw-pine, Malacca-apple, nutmeg, clove, cinnamon, pimento and areca palm, a grove of palmistes, bread-fruit, bread-nut and cannon-ball trees. The latter is very interesting, growing to a great height, with large bole and branches, along which grow twigs and shoots so thickly that they resemble a vine entwining them; on these grow great flowers which look like the sarracenias of northern climes; stamens and pistils are packed away inside half a dozen protecting petals. The petals are of a delicate rose-color, recurved upon themselves; when the blossom bursts it looks as rough as the bristling burr of a chestnut. The fruit is as large as a six-pounder cannon-ball; it is spherical, russet brown in color, and very heavy. They are continually growing and dropping; and are of no apparent use except to stir idle people into activity, by falling on their heads — people who might otherwise be tempted to recline beneath the tree.

Mango and cinnamon, introduced into Jamaica by Lord Rodney, were sent here also; nutmeg from Cayenne, in 1809; clove from Martinique, in 1787, where it was introduced from the East Indies. It was thought that these species would become abundant and profitable, but such seems not to have been the case. The nutmeg has best repaid the efforts made for its introduction and preservation, and has grown into trees of great size, appearing at a distance like well-trimmed orange trees. The male trees, in February, were just flowering, while the female trees hung thick with nuts resembling our walnuts before they burst their husk. Some of these nuts had burst their outer covering, disclosing the mace lying between the outer shell and an inner one inclosing the nut, of a rich vermilion hue, and possessing

COCOA PALM, BREAD-FRUIT.

a warm, spicy taste. There are several nutmeg groves throughout the island, though but little attention is paid to their cultivation. The income from each nutmeg tree in bearing is estimated at five dollars per year — a pound sterling per season.

The clove did not prove so successful as the nutmeg, though its cultivation is attended with little labor and the profits sure. A very instructive account of experiments in clove culture is that of a gentleman in Dominica, who wrote in 1796. For several years he persevered on his estate, Montpelier, in the hills of Dominica. From the first two trees in bearing he gathered seven pounds of cloves; he then had, six years after commencing to plant, fifteen hundred growing trees. Probably, even if this attempt was successful, nothing farther was ever done by the other planters, so wrapped up were they in cane culture, and cane only. Montpelier is to-day gone to decay, difficult of access, with fields of waste land, and without inhabitants. A tradition only remains of clove and cinnamon-trees being found in the wild growth that covers the abandoned fields.

A broad walk leads under the nutmeg-trees, from a little stream beneath the teak and mahogany, to Government House, the residence of the lieutenant-governor, — a long, low building, surrounded by a veranda, having in front a flower-garden in perpetual blossom, such a garden as only this climate is capable of producing, with a row of lovely areca palms, and vines in profusion adorning pillars and balustrades.

We are constantly reminded of the East Indies and the South Seas by the numerous trees brought from those far-off regions. Not the least curious is the screw-pine, growing to the height of a tree, and bearing fruit that closely resembles the edible pine-apple.

In the society of the governor, George Dundas, Esquire, C. M. G., I enjoyed many delightful hours. Like many another cultivated Englishman and Scotchman, he was a zealous votary of Daguerre — an excellent amateur photographer. To wealthy English amateurs, who have pursued the study of photography as a pastime, that science owes its greatest advancement, especially in recent times. In the "dry-plate" process — the process of the future — they have made

Gambetta flavipes	Lesser Yellow-shanks, Lesser Telltale. Western hemisphere. Breeds from northern States northwards.
Cypseloides niger	Black Swift, Martinet de Saint-Domingue. West Indies, Jamaica, Cuba, Porto Rica, Guadeloupe.
Glaucus hirsutus ?	—
Porzana	a Rail a Crake. cosmopolitan in distribution.
Æstrelata	a Petrel. (typo hesitata, Capped Petrel) Southern hemisphere

Siurus nævius, Water Thrush. New York Warbler, & Spotted Yellow Warbler.
The whole of N. America, ranging in Winter through Central America, Guiana, Colombia & Ecuador, as well as throughout the Antilles.

Phaëthon flavirostris = americanus, Tropic Bird,
East coast N America from Bermuda to the West Indies.

Herodias egretta, White Heron, Great White Egret.
Temperate portions of N. America, southward throughout the whole of Central & S. America, with the West Indian Islands to Chili & Patagonia.

Garzetta candidissima } = Leucoprymna. Snowy Heron, Little White Egret.
Temperate & Tropical America from the northern United States throughout Central & S. America, to Argentina & Chili.
This bird is slaughtered on account of its plumes.

the greatest number of, and most valuable, discoveries. Governor Dundas was an enthusiast, and exhibited to me many pictures, taken by himself, of the scenery of St. Vincent and Barbados.

Of the many trees which were introduced into the West Indies none have proved so great a boon to the laboring classes, and bane to the planter, as the bread-fruit. It was at once a success, and from this garden of acclimatization many hundred plants were distributed over the island. The tree would attract attention from the arrangement of its deeply-lobed leaves; but the great balls of fruit, varying from five to eight inches in diameter, make it a conspicuous object even amongst tropical vegetation. Inside the shell, which when baked is hard, though thin, is a thick flesh like that of a melon. Though I cannot recall any substance that tastes exactly like it, it is certainly very good, and so nutritious that the natives of the islands in which it was discovered subsist upon it almost solely the year through. It is their "daily bread," indeed, and takes the place of the manufactured article entirely. It more than fills that place, for those who are dependent upon its bountiful harvests need scarcely any animal food. The people in the favored country of its growth do not need to labor; a score of trees planted by each man will furnish a supply of food for a lifetime, and he need concern himself about nothing else than sleeping and eating. In its fruitfulness it exceeds even the generous plantain, upon which the natives of the tropics subsist almost solely where the bread-fruit is not grown. It dispenses entirely with the labor of the agriculturist, the miller, the baker; there need be no care for seed-time or harvest; there is no threshing, no grinding, no kneading; in fact, the islanders of the South Seas have their bread ready prepared, and have only to place it on the coals as they need it.

In its native islands the tree bears for about eight months in the year. Toward the close of the fruitful period the natives lay the fruit in heaps and cover it with leaves, where it ferments; the core attached to the stem is then pulled out, and the fruit, placed in a hole, changes from sweet to sour, after which it will keep until another season of fruitage.

This allusion to the home of the bread-fruit very naturally recalls the story of its introduction into the West Indies — a story romantic, and worthy of frequent repetition. In 1797, in answer to a petition from the planters of the West Indies, the armed transport, the "Bounty," was fitted out for Otaheite, commanded by Lieutenant Bligh, who had been around the world with Cook. Her cabin was fitted with a false floor cut full of holes, sufficient to receive one thousand garden-pots. She was victualled for fifteen months, and carried trinkets for trade in the South Sea Islands. After many difficulties, being obliged to abandon the route intended and seek a new one, Lieutenant Bligh reached Otaheite. A tent was erected on shore to receive the trees, some thirty of which were potted every day.

On the 4th of April, 1789, the "Bounty" set sail, with one thousand roots in pots, tubs, and boxes. On the 27th broke out the mutiny which has become a matter of history. Lieutenant Bligh, with eighteen others, was placed in the launch, which was cut loose with one hundred and fifty pounds of bread, twenty-eight gallons of water, a little rum and wine, a quadrant and a compass. A few pieces of pork, some cocoa-nuts, and four cutlasses, were thrown to them as they were cast adrift. The nearest civilized land was the Dutch colony of Timoor, distant three thousand five hundred miles. This they reached in forty-one days, after incredible hardships and the loss of one man; here they received hospitable treatment, and eventually reached England. Ten of the mutineers were afterwards found and executed; the others removed to another island, where most of them led dissolute lives and miserably died. The history of Adams and his companions has been told in missionary tales so often that every one is familiar with its minutest details. After sailing to Pitcairn's Island, in the Bounty, they burned her, extirpated the male inhabitants in three years, and laid the foundation of a colony upon which England looked with interest, even with favor.

At a subsequent period Lieutenant Bligh was furnished with another vessel, in which he accomplished the object for which he was sent, and the bread-fruit was introduced into St. Vincent in 1793. In this island it flourished in greater abundance than in any other of the Caribbean chain, and aside from forming small groves on many of the plantations, it has extended its range into the forest-borders, and may be found in some of the deeper valleys in a wild state, a companion of the "trumpet tree," which somewhat resembles it in appearance.

There was a hollow, near my Carib cabin in St. Vincent, between two high hills, the center deepening to a gutter where generally ran a little brook. Up the bed of this gutter I climbed one day, at noon, first

GROO-GROO PALM.

past a clump of cacaos, shaded by tall trees, and then past a group of groo-groo and gris-gris palms. These palms are erect and straight, but aside from their own graceful beauty, they are enriched and encircled by a clustering vine, throwing out a mass of large, perforated leaves. This vine climbs up the trunk by clinging closely — a slender thread of a vine, which throws out, when it has attained a certain height, a cluster of leaves. As there are numberless climbers, and as each sends out its leaves in a group, the tree is sometimes inclosed in a pyramidal column from top to bottom, most beautiful to see.

The groo-groo is most abundant on the coast and plentifully besprinkles the woods of the hillsides; it can be seen anywhere in long ranks on the ridges, and in clumps and groups by the roadside. It is not as tall as either the cocoa or the palmiste, is stouter than the mountain palm, and with a denser head than either of them. Its leaves are curled laterally from the mid-rib, and droop feathery and plume-like. It covers all the hills and upper valleys along the sea-coast, and seems to take the place the tree-fern occupies in similar localities in other islands.

All the palms are beautiful: the mighty palmiste, towering to a height of one hundred and fifty feet, with its column-like trunk and spreading head of long leaves, is unsurpassed in grandeur. The cocoa palm, perhaps, is the most picturesque, as its stem is so slender, and its loose leaves droop so gracefully, waving with every breeze, ever and anon disclosing its wealth of fruit. Nothing can be more picturesque than a cocoa bending above a thatched hut; than a group of cocoas on the bank of a stream reflecting back their beauty. If utility were considered, then certainly the cocoa would bear away the *palm*, as it assuredly is the palm of this tropic zone. The mountain palm, found only in the high woods and on elevated ridges, has a slenderer stem, and its long leaves give it a resemblance to the cocoa. The areca palm, the seeds of which are used with the famous betel nut, with small straight stem and a single tuft of plumes, is a very ornamental tree. No matter which species of palm I look upon, I am tempted to say, this is the most beautiful!

But to return to the groo-groo and gris-gris. The former rises straight up, with a gray trunk, scarred all the way up with little circles left by former leaves, fusiform, swelling out in the middle like the main-boom of a ship, supporting a solid head of leaves, which are curled like the heated feathers of an ostrich plume, and form a dense ball almost circular in shape. At the base of these leaves springs out a branching stem covered with the seeds which, when ripe, are black, like small grape-shot, and sheltered by a spathe shaped like a shield. Both trunk and leaf-stalks are covered, especially in young trees, with black spines; which detract from its beauty somewhat in the estimation of one who has stepped upon them. The seeds are made into a variety of chatelaine ornaments, as they are black and hollow, and take a fine polish. The wood is black as ebony, and is also susceptible of a high degree of polish.

Scarcely had these observations on the palms been written down when my retreat was invaded by a buxom Indian girl of fourteen or fifteen, carrying a cutlass. She stood by the stream for some time, wondering, perhaps, what "buckra" was doing there: comely features, black braids of hair, shapely limbs, short and ragged dress. She was even more picturesque than all the palms. And if there could be a more attractive picture, it was when she returned, an hour later, bearing on her head an immense bunch of plantains, and stood poised upon a rock, where she lingered for some time gazing at her image in the stream.

CHAPTER XV.

GRENADA AND THE GRENADINES.

BEQUIA. — CONTENTED ISLANDERS. — THE "BEQUIA SWEET." — CARIB ANECDOTE. — UNION ISLAND. — CANOUAN. — AN ENERGETIC PATRIARCH. — CARIACOU. — ON THE ANCIENT CONTIGUITY OF THE LESSER ANTILLES. — THE LOST ATLANTIS. — "WHAT IF THESE REEFS WERE HER MONUMENT?" — A GLANCE AT THE MAP. — AN ISOLATED GEOGRAPHICAL AND ZOOLOGICAL PROVINCE. — GRENADA. — ST. GEORGE'S. — MORE CRATERS. — THE CARENAGE. — THE FORTS. — THE LAGOON. — THE "EURYDICE." — IGUANAS. — THEIR HABITS. — IGUANA-SHOOTING. — OYSTERS GROWING ON TREES. — COLUMBUS AND HIS PEARLS. — LIZARDS. — A MISSIONARY'S GRIEF. — FOOD OF THE IGUANA. — THE MANGROVE. — CACAO. — ITS DISCOVERY. — PRESENT RANGE. — ITS CULTIVATION. — CACAO RIVER. — COCOA AND CACAO. — THE TREE. — THE FRUIT. — THE FLOWER. — IDLE NEGROES. — CHOCOLATE. — FOREST RATS. — MONKEYS. — THEIR DEPREDATIONS. — AN INSULT.

THE GRENADINES, a great number of islets forming a connecting chain between the islands of St. Vincent and Grenada, extend over a degree of latitude. They are small and low-lying, many of them being merely rocks protruding from the water, without rivers, little cultivated, with no communication with the larger islands except by small boats, and yet some of them densely populated. The largest of these is Bequia, nearest to St. Vincent, which is six miles in length and above a mile in breadth, with a range of hills eight hundred feet in height. The character of soil and people of every island of the Grenadines may be summed up in the following paragraph from the "West India Pilot":

"Bequia has no running streams, and there is no watering-place. There are some wells at the head of the bay, but the water is not very good. Wood is plentiful, and may be obtained by permission from the owners, but it is doubtful if the natives would cut it. Poultry may be had occasionally in small quantities, and sometimes fish, but vegetables never."

The people are apathetic. The sea yields them sufficient for the day; of cotton and sugar their lands produce sufficient to supply them with commodities not obtainable from the sea. The contrast between these silent, sleepy islands, whose people are content to exist and will not work, and an island like Barbados, where the negroes all must work or starve, and where they harass a visitor nearly to the verge of insanity, is refreshing. Some of the islets, like Balliceaux and Battowia, are owned by single individuals, or firms, who raise there cattle and sheep; all are well stocked with wild doves, plover and ducks in their season, and their rocky shores are surrounded by myriads of sea-fowl.

In Bequia, and extending throughout the chain, is a blackbird — a new species named the *Quiscalus luminosus* — which makes the air resound with its joyous cry: "Bequia sweet, sweet, Bequia sweet." The Caribs told me of this bird several months before I obtained it, as its peculiar cry had caused it to be marked by them. They had preserved a touching story of its connection with Carib captivity, when the

Indians were confined in the small island of Balliceaux.

The island in which they were prisoners was low and dry, without a tree large enough to shelter them from the sun; a few miles distant, full in sight, was the island of Bequia, six times theirs in size, with high hills covered with green forests. To them it was as Paradise; they longed for its breezy hills, sighed for the cool shade of its trees, but sighed in vain. Deprived of their canoes, of houses, of material for constructing more than slight shelter, these poor people lay gasping beneath a tropic sun, gazing at the misty mountains of their native island and the green slopes of Bequia, without a possibility of reaching either. All about them the blackbirds sang praises of the distant island: "Bequia sweet, sweet, Bequia sweet." Though St. Vincent is but ten miles distant, the blackbird is never seen there, affording but one of many peculiarities in the distribution of animals throughout these islands.

The natives of the Grenadines display a love for their islands not easily understood by a resident of more fertile and more attractive lands. I can understand this, but can hardly explain it. There is a feeling born of the isolation, of the very barrenness of the land, of the loneliness of an island, that attracts one to it, especially if one there had his birth and passed his earlier years.

We steamed out of Kingston Bay and down along the lovely Grenadines. Their appearance is that of a nearly submerged line of mountains. Sometimes a whole ridge is exposed; again, a conical peak or a mound of green just appears above the water.

Union Island and Cariacou, seemingly near together, with a few water-surrounded peaks between them, are whole chines of ridges. The latter has a well-cultivated appearance, and on some hillsides are houses thickly clustering. Grenada appears a cloud-line when we are off Union Island, and gradually emerges from the haze as we draw nearer, purple in hue, of course, long, but not so high as St. Vincent and the islands north. Canouan, half-way down the Grenadines, appears small and dry, but the white houses gleaming from a hill-top give it a cheerful look. Canouan is principally inhabited by one family, the descendants of one man, who has successfully emulated the patriarchs of old in the extent of his family, if not in his domain.

Many years ago — I don't know just how many — he came to Canouan, bringing slaves, it is said by some, finding there a colony of blacks, it is said by others. At all events, he set himself up as a patriarch, and commenced a church. So successful was this good man, whose name was Snagg, so successful were his efforts in ameliorating the color and condition of those around him, that the entire chain has felt his influence. This zealous missionary had a brother, an English baronet; and it is related by those who cruise the Grenadines, that one cannot visit any isle in this archipelago without encountering some brown-skinned descendant of the missionary, who boasts offensively of "my uncle, Sir William Snagg."

Union Island is black and gloomy from the east, as we coast along, indicating a virgin vegetation and little cultivation. Its sharp, serrated outline, reminding one of a line of snow-drifts after a heavy midwinter storm when a fierce wind has swept along, leaving them combed or sharply cut, suggests either immense denuding, eroding floods, or upheaval.

Were these islands once connected with the main land of either continent? How often this question arises in one's mind as he gazes on these mountains peering above the sea! Did they, in the language of Humboldt, "belong to the Southern continent, and form a part of its littoral chain," or have they been upheaved from the depths of the sea? The great naturalist thus refers to these islands and the various theories regarding their origin : "The supposition of an oceanic irruption has been the source of two other hypotheses on the origin of the smaller West India islands. Some geologists admit that the uninterrupted chain of islands from Trinidad to Florida exhibits the remains of an ancient chain of mountains. They connect this chain sometimes with the granite of French Guiana, sometimes with the calcareous mountains of Paria. Others, struck with the difference of geological constitution between the primitive mountains of the Greater and the volcanic cones of the Lesser Antilles, consider the latter as having risen from the bottom of the sea. In opposing the objections of some celebrated naturalists, I am far from maintaining the ancient contiguity of all these smaller West India islands. I am rather inclined to consider them as islands heaved up by fire, and ranged in that regular line of which we find striking examples in so many volcanic hills in Mexico and in Peru. The geological constitution of the archipelago appears, from the little we know respecting it, to be very similar to that of the Azores and the Canary Islands. Primitive formations are nowhere seen above ground; we find only what belongs unquestionably to volcanoes."

We would fain connect these mountain-peaks with a submerged continent, a continent that extended over the vast space now occupied by the Caribbean Sea, and into the Atlantic far over toward the coast of Africa. We are ready to believe that the "lost Atlantis" of the ancients is not a myth, that it is not a "fabled island," but had a real existence, and that the land discovered by those Tyrian navigators who sailed beyond the Pillars of Hercules and were driven by a storm many days westward, was part of a continent now beneath the waves — the eastern shore of a region which these mountains once traversed; for —

> "Who knows the spot where Atlantis sank?
> Myths of a lovely drowned continent
> Homeless drift over waters blank;
> What if these reefs were her monument?
> Isthmus and cavernous cape may be
> Her mountain summits escaped from the sea."

The early geological history of the area occupied by the Caribbean Sea, its coasts and its islands, has excited the attention of many eminent scientific men, and much light has been afforded by the study of the land and marine faunas and of the geological formation of the islands and adjacent coasts. The conclusions reached by the later scientists are, that the West Indian islands present the remains of a sunken continent. Says that eminent naturalist, Wallace: "The West Indian islands have been long isolated and have varied much in extent. Originally, they probably formed part of Central America, and may have been united with Yucatan and Honduras in one extensive tropical land." These remarks apply to the Greater Antilles, probably, and do not preclude Humboldt's hypothesis that the Lesser Antilles are islands "heaved up by fire."

At a meeting of the National Academy, held in Washington, in April, 1879, Professor Agassiz read a report of his dredging operations during the previous winter, expressing the opinion that he had brought to light the outlines of old continents, of which the islands enclosing the Caribbean Sea are the remnants. Mr. Bland, of New York, the well-known conchologist, who has especially studied the land-shell distribution of the West Indies for many years, adds his testimony as to the continental character of the faunas of the different West Indian islands.

And these few general remarks upon the Lesser Antilles as a whole lead me to call the reader's attention to their regularity of position, as shown upon the map. It will be seen that the distance between any two adjacent islands lying between St. Vincent and Barbuda, is about thirty miles: from Barbuda to Antigua, from Antigua to Montserrat, Montserrat to Guadeloupe, from the latter to Dominica, from Dominica to Martinique, Martinique to St. Lucia, St. Lucia to St. Vincent. A sixty-mile circuit, with Grenada as a center, touches St. Vincent, Tobago, and Trinidad, and includes all of the Grenadines.

The almost semicircular line they describe cannot but be noticed; nor will it fail to be suggested to the most casual observer that, if not vestiges of a continent, these islands once formed a continuous barrier between the Caribbean Sea and the Atlantic Ocean; though facts may prove the contrary. I may also remark, in passing, that the *avi-fauna*, the bird-life, of this cluster of islands is as distinct and isolated from that of Tobago, Trinidad, and South America, as is the geographical position of the group.

Grenada is the southernmost of these volcanic islands and terminates in latitude twelve, north, the Caribbee chain. It is a little over eighteen miles in length and seven in breadth, and is very rugged, the interior of the island being one mountain ridge with its offsets, and there is a lesser comparative area of fertile land than in St. Vincent. The mountains are volcanic; there are several extinct craters, in the largest of which there is an attractive lake two and one-half miles in circumference, two thousand feet above the sea.

St. George's, the only port of any size, lies on the south-western coast, its walled fort, St. George, occupying a bold promontory commanding the town, along and over the ridge of which it is built. With its deep, fissure-like harbor, its sandy "carenage," its white-walled houses of stone, its encircling, battlemented hills seven hundred feet in height, St. George's, harbor and town, is highly picturesque.

We reached the harbor at night, but our captain dared not enter, and stood off and on till morning. The sky was ablaze with stars, and the Southern Cross appeared when the clouds passed. Two planets glowed in the sky till sunrise, streaming fire from out the murky clouds and casting bright reflections on the water.

The harbor of St. George's seems to have been formed by volcanic forces, as it is hardly more than a narrow fissure, and the hundred-fathom line of sound-

SAINT GEORGE'S

ings is only a little over a mile from the fort. Veins of deep water extend in from the sea, on both sides of which the water is quite shallow.

Making out from the harbor proper is a bay or lagoon, about a mile in depth, where are sandy beaches bordered by mangrove swamps. Behind this bay, ascending the hills, is the estate of Belmont, where resided a gentleman to whom I had letters of introduction, Chief Justice Gresham, who, like the good governor of St. Vincent, was an amateur photographer of great ability. Very naturally, I gravitated toward Belmont soon after landing, and passed a pleasant week on and about the estate. Among some excellent photographs which his Honor gave me, was one of the unfortunate "Eurydice," taken by the judge as she lay under the walls of Fort St. George, just prior to her departure for England on the voyage that had such a terrible ending.

Skirting the belt of mangroves bordering the lagoon, one morning in March, I anxiously searched the intertwined branches for iguanas. Grenada is celebrated as being the home of great numbers of these reptiles, which may often be found basking on old walls within the limits of the town. My boatman was a negro, who, accustomed to the appearance of the iguana in the trees, discovered one long before I could distinguish the difference between green reptile and green leaves. Even after it had been pointed out, I had difficulty in recognizing it, so nearly did its colors harmonize with those of the tree in which it was feeding.

It lay quite still, stretched flat upon a branch, its tail hanging down like that of a snake. Though it was evidently suspicious of our intentions, its quiet was not due to that alone, for it is naturally a sluggish animal. Yet, when once thoroughly aroused, it will dash over the ground at great speed. I fired, yet it still clung tenaciously to the bough, and a second shot did not kill it, for it would have escaped had not my boatman pinned it with an oar, after it had fallen into the mud. From one that we captured that morning, the man with me procured a dozen large, white eggs, which he saved to eat.

As we rowed along, the breaking of overhanging branches was accompanied by the crackling of shells, as the oysters, clinging to the roots and branches, closed their shells at the disturbance. Some of these oysters were more than a foot above water, where they had been left by the tide. The sight of them, hanging there with gaping mouths, brought to mind the cruise of Columbus in the bay of Paria, only one hundred miles south of this island of Grenada. He was in search of pearls, and " he had read in Pliny, that pearls were generated from drops of dew which fell into the mouths of oysters. There were great numbers of mangroves growing within the water, with oysters clinging to their branches, their mouths open — as he supposed — to receive the dew which was afterwards to be transformed into pearls."

The order *Sauria*, the lizard order, is well represented in the West Indies, though in none of the smaller islands between Porto Rico and Trinidad is to be found that greatest of the *saurians*, the alligator. The Indians of Dominica, to whom I described the alligator, were greatly amazed to hear of a "lizard" twelve feet in length, as they had never seen one larger than the iguana, which seldom attains a greater length than five feet, and is as mild in disposition as the alligator is sanguinary. The islands, especially the shores, are teeming with lizards of every color, of every variety of marking, and of all sizes.

Especially do they love the cliffs, and if you are walking through the bushes at the base of any sunny precipice, or over any rocky tract, you will be startled by the frequent dashes made by these reptiles across your path. In a country where you must keep every sense on the alert, to guard against sudden surprise by serpents or poisonous insects, it is very annoying, often startling, to be so frequently disturbed by these active creatures. In the mountains are fewer species, and they are more sluggish, but in the warm lowlands you must be very active to capture one. The little negro and Indian boys are very expert at it and catch them by means of slip-nooses of grass, attached to the ends of sticks, which they pass over the heads of the lizards as they lie asleep in the sun. They are not poisonous, though repulsive to many, and though some of them will bite severely, they do not inflict dangerous wounds.

There are many hideous forms, especially among those of South America, like the Basilisk and the Flying Dragon; but in the West Indies there is none of more hideous appearance than the iguana. Never was more harmless creature invested with more frightful aspect. Clothed with scales, like the alligator, but finer and more flexible, with a long, slender and powerful tail, a gular pouch, hanging like a dew-lap beneath its throat, and having along its back from head to tail a crest of spines, it would not be attractive were it not for its beautiful colors of varying green and yellow, and its brightly glancing eye. In the islands where it exists it is eagerly sought as food, and its flesh is palatable and delicate, as I can testify from experience, being white, tender, and nutritious.

The good father Père Labat (worthy missionary and *bon vivant* withal) compares fricasseed guana to chicken for the whiteness of its flesh and delicacy of its flavor. He gives a delightful account of catching one, two hundred years ago :

"We were attended by a negro who carried a long rod, at one end of which was a piece of whip-cord with a running knot. After beating about the bushes for some time, the negro discovered our game basking in the sun on the dry limb of a tree. Hereupon he began whistling with all his might, to which the guana was wonderfully attentive, stretching out his neck and turning his head as if to enjoy it more fully. The negro now approached, still whistling, and advancing his rod gently, began tickling with the end of it the sides and throat of the guana, who seemed mightily pleased with the operation, for he turned on his back and stretched himself out like a cat before the fire, and at length fell asleep, which the negro perceiving, dexterously slipped the noose over his head, and with a jerk brought him to the ground. And good sport it afforded, to see the creature swell like a turkey-cock at finding himself entrapped. We caught more in the same way, and kept one alive seven or eight days; but it grieved me to the heart to find that he thereby lost much delicious fat."

The iguana eats only vegetable food, and passes most of its time in the trees, though it has holes to which it can retire. The mangrove is its favorite resort, and many have I seen lying along the branches feeding upon the leaves. This tree, though not majestic, nor really beautiful, is extremely interesting from the aerial character of its roots. Growing on the border of the ocean, so near that the waves lap against its stem, and in salt-water lagoons, where the water is shallow and the mud very deep, it sends forth numberless roots from above the water, which strike out in all directions, and finally seem to lift it up as though upon a trestle-work. It is thus a curious sight; and as these mangroves grow in masses, their roots form an intricate and impenetrable network, beneath which all sorts of marine and sea-side shell-fish and vegetation abound.

Though cacao grows in all the islands of the Caribbean Sea, I found it most abundant in Grenada, where it shares with sugar exclusive cultivation, finding a soil and climate most suitable for its perfect growth. This plant was discovered in Mexico by the Spaniards, who invaded that country in 1519; we read, in the "True History of the Conquest of Mexico," by Captain Bernal Diaz, "one of the conquerors," that fruit of all the kinds the country produced was laid before Montezuma; "he eat very little, but from time to time a liquor prepared from *cocoa*, and of a stimulative or corroborative quality, as we were told, was presented to him in golden cups. We could not at that time see if he drank it or not, but I observed a number of jars, above fifty, brought in filled with foaming chocolate."

Its adoption and introduction was rapid, and now it flourishes nearly all over the tropical world, and in the Lesser Antilles and along the northern coast of South America it grows in perfection.

Much confusion exists regarding the names of two totally distinct vegetable productions: the cocoa, the palm which bears the nut, and the cacao, from which chocolate is made — words so nearly alike that even great men have used them interchangeably, much to the bewilderment of the student of tropical flora. The cocoa palm is the *Cocos nucifera*, and by some the generic name of *cocos* has been abbreviated into *coco*, which is the French and Spanish name also. Grand old Linnæus gave to the cacao the beautiful name, *Theobroma* — food for gods — and *Theobroma cacao* is the name by which it is known to botanists.

Unlike the towering cocoa, with smooth shaft,

crowned with waving branches, a notable object in surrounding vegetation, the cacao seldom reaches a height of over thirty feet, and would be passed by without notice, were it not for its peculiar fruit. It flourishes only in damp valleys, on the sides of shady hills, and embosomed among mountain forests, where the surrounding scenery is eminently interesting.

So little care does it need, and growing, as it does, in soil so rocky that it will produce nothing else, nearly every negro in the island has a few trees around his hut, which yield him sufficient for his simple wants. I found this to operate greatly to my disadvantage, where, among the mountains, all luggage must be transported on the heads of the people, as I could get no one to carry my camping equipments. By the aid of a half crazy mulatto, named Maunie, I was able to reach a valley on the eastern side of the mountain range; but once there he left me, and for several days I was obliged to remain among the cacao groves, unable to return. My stay was made delightful by the attentions of the physician of the district, Doctor Lang, and the parish priest, Canon Bond, both genial and cultivated gentlemen. Through the valley ran the largest river in the island, Cacao River, which in the rainy season overflowed its banks and committed great havoc among the trees of the cacaotière, or cacao grove. The trees grow to the height of twenty feet, some to thirty, with a leaf something like that of the chestnut. The tops of the trees are intergrown, forming dense shade, beneath which, among the smooth stems, one can walk in comfort even at noon. Dead and fallen leaves strew the ground thickly, even as the chestnut leaves in autumn, and all around are little heaps of opened pods, from which the pulp has been taken and the seeds extracted.

The tree is about as long in attaining its growth as the orange tree; it may produce in the third year from the seed, but does not reach its full bearing period until at the age of seven or eight. It is a tender plant during the first stages of its growth, and, like the coffee, must be shaded by some broad-leaved plant like the plantain or banana, which, of quicker growth, are set out near the seed at time of planting. Heat and moisture are indispensable to its existence, but one without the other proves fatal to its growth.

We may consider it as a blessing or a curse to the islands, according to the light in which we view it. As the bread-fruit is reckoned by the planters as a curse, because it enables the negro to live without work, and deprives the plantations of his labor, so the cacao, by giving its cultivators a certain income without toil, after the first few years of its growth, induces the production of an idle, and consequently insolent, population. Once started in life with an acre or so of cacao trees, the negro asks for nothing more, his wife and children gather the harvest, and he enjoys an idle existence as only a negro knows how.

The fruit of the cacao resembles somewhat an overripe cucumber about six inches in length, oval and pointed. Many of the pods grow right out of the trunk of the tree, hanging by short stems, and remind one of tailless rats. They are beautifully colored, varying according to the specimen and the progress towards maturity; some are green, some yellow, crimson or purple, some variegated by veins of different colors. Each pod is divided into five longitudinal cells, containing a sweetish, agreeable pulp, in which are enveloped the seeds, from twenty to thirty in number, a white, pulpy substance in a thin shell. When the fruit is mature it is gathered, and the seeds removed and dried; sometimes they are buried in sand or dry earth for the purpose of absorbing the moisture and pulp adhering to them.

Great care is necessary in curing them, as they mold easily, and the planters generally provide large platforms on wheels, upon which the seeds are spread, which they run out from under a shelter, on sunshiny days, and keep an old negro on the watch for rain. When perfectly dry, the seeds are put in bags for shipment to England. The native method of preparing chocolate from the seeds, is to roast them, and grind finely on a warm, smooth stone. When well kneaded it forms a tenacious paste, which, with the addition of a little sugar, is made into small rolls, or sticks. This, in its pure state, is made into a delightful drink; but, as prepared in places foreign to the country of its production, is largely adulterated. It is generally flavored with vanilla, or some other agreeable extract, this being the favorite.

Happy and contented as the negro may be in his wealth of cacao trees, he is sometimes enraged at the depredations committed by the forest quadrupeds, for the rats, not content with the succulent sugar cane, eagerly seek out the sweet pulp of the cacao. Where monkeys are abundant, as in Grenada, they commit great havoc, not only gnawing holes in the pods as they hang on the trees, but carrying away all they can hold in their arms. In one of my monkey-hunting excursions I stopped at the house of a very agreeable planter, in the mountains. He declared that one year the monkeys nearly destroyed his crop; and not only ate the cacao seeds, but brought the empty pods and placed them on his doorstep, thus adding insult to injury.

CHAPTER XVI.

A MONKEY HUNT IN THE MOUNTAINS.

ZONES OF VEGETATION. — NAKED NEGROES. — THE ROAD TO THE MOUNTAINS. — THE GRAND ETANG. — QUADRUPEDS OF THE LESSER ANTILLES, EXTINCT AND LIVING. — THE ALCO. — PECCARY. — AGOUTI. — MANACOU. — ARMADILLO. — RACCOON. — A VISIT TO THE "TATOUAY TRAPS." — THE FOREST SURROUNDING THE MOUNTAIN LAKE. — "HAGINAMAH": IS IT A CARIB WORD? — "HOG-IN-ARMOR," NOT A CARIB WORD. — "LE MORNE DES SAUTEURS." — THE PLANTAIN SWAMP. — SIGNS OF MONKEYS. — THE MONKEYS' LADDER. — HABITS OF WILD MONKEYS. — THE MAMMIE APPLE. — IN AMBUSH. — FEATHERED COMPANIONS. — THE BETE ROUGE. — AN AGED MONKEY. — HIS CAUTION. — DESCENDING THE LADDER. — MONKEYS, GIDDY AND GRAVE. — COUNTING HIS FLOCK. — THE MONKEY RECOGNIZES A BROTHER. — "SHOOT! SHOOT!" — A FREE CIRCUS. — A MAN, AND A BROTHER. — THE MONKEY-MAMMA. — HER TERROR. — AN IMPOLITIC IMP.

THERE are monkeys in Grenada; many a poor cultivator knows this to his cost. There are troops of monkeys, who thread the mazes of the mountain forest, living in the trees, scarce ever descending to earth. To get them, one must go to the mountains, must penetrate the great interior forests, and hunt patiently the dark woods encircling the mountain lake, the lake in the crater. He must camp by the lake in the crater to get the "crayters" by the lake.

In this island there are two zones of vegetation and of animal life, that of the coast and that of the mountains. The shore lines are broken; precipitous cliffs shoot up out of the sea and huge rocks stand out gray and bare, alternated by lovely bays. A vegetation of low growth covers the hills along the shore, affording shelter for few birds; where a dense growth of vines, or a flowering shrub occurs, a cactus, or a frangipanni, there may be found the humming-birds. The second zone, or belt, comprises that portion containing the most luxuriant vegetation and the greatest variety of tropical forms. It may be roughly estimated as lying between one thousand and twenty-five hundred feet above the sea. Here are nearly all the birds of the lowland in profusion and many species not found below. To the mountains, then, I must go, if I would secure new birds or seek to slay a monkey.

Leaving the hot road that wound along the shore, I took another, beneath volcanic cliffs, rode beneath rustling palm-trees and out upon a river bank, where were congregated the washerwomen of the town. Cool were they in attire and in effrontery, as they waded knee-deep the shallows of the stream, reclined upon the rocks, or sat chatting upon the banks, with no raiment save a handkerchief wrapped about the loins. Old women, young women, girls and boys, and little "pick'nees" waded the stream, most of them naked as the rocks the river laved. Black were they as those traditional crows, and no raven's wing could be glossier than their shining skins.

Half-way to the mountain lake is the little hamlet of Constantine, where, on a narrow ridge between two deep valleys, a little chapel overlooks other valleys of palms to the sea. Above, the road is narrow and steep, but flagged with rough stones; it leads through diminutive forests of cacao, each with a little thatched hut as its center, and then houses and groves are left, and the high woods entered, cutting through banks of clay over which vines and trees lean, ready to fall. On the crest of the mountain-ridge, three miles from any neighbor, is a house surrounded by a cleared space; flowers bloom in a little garden, and

GRAND ETANG.

bananas wave tattered pennons in the wind. A veranda looks to the south, and a negro policeman looks at me as I ride to the door. This was the police station, the "Grand-Etang House;" and to the man in charge I gave a letter from his chief in town, directing him to aid, by all lawful means, my attempts to secure a monkey.

From the elevated character of the region, the Grand Etang House was most unpleasantly cold at night; rude blasts assailed it, and fierce tempests wrestled with it. In town, seven miles distant, the temperature was ten degrees hotter than here on the mountain-top, ranging from eighty to ninety. The sudden change in temperature chilled me; the elevation depressed me. There were hooks for hammocks, and an iron bedstead, but no mattresses; the hooks were high up, and my hammock (a netted "Ashantee") from long use now bulged like a pudding-bag, consequently I was doubled up all night, neck to heels.

The lake, elliptical in outline, two thousand feet above the sea, is in full view from the house. A range of mountains encloses all — two craters, and the dividing ridge on which the house is built. An inner circle of hills, clothed in tropical trees, rises around the lake, forming the basin.

The man in charge of the house, its sole occupant, had a number of traps, or dead-falls, set in the forest beyond the lake, for the agouti and armadillo. These two animals, with the monkeys, are about the only forest quadrupeds larger than an opossum remaining in these islands. At the time of their discovery, the Lesser Antilles possessed several species now exterminated. The most interesting was a small animal like a dog, found by the Spaniards among the Indians of Haiti, a native of the New World, called by them the "alco." In St. Domingo there were no other dogs. It was a shy, gentle creature, and perfectly *mute*, and was as much beloved by the Indians as their children, being carried by them in their arms wherever they went. It is now extinct. The peccary, or "Mexican musk-hog," once abundant in these islands, has been exterminated from all but Tobago; the hogs of Dominica and St. Vincent being the domestic species run wild. The agouti (*Dasyprocta agouti*), a rodent, native to the West Indies and South America, is the most abundant of any quadruped in the Antilles, being found in most of them at the present day. An opossum, said to have been introduced from South America, called by the negroes the manicou, or manitou, is very numerous, and is a terror to the negroes' chickens. In Guadeloupe, alone of the chain, may yet be found the raccoon, though the present species is not considered an indigenous one. The armadillo, once common in every island, is now found only in Grenada and Tobago; it is the nine-banded armadillo, called by the natives the "tatou," or "tatouay," and is nocturnal in its habits.

To visit his "tatou traps," my new friend the black policeman, and myself, sallied forth early in the morning. In a few minutes we were out of sight of the house and in as deep a forest as any in these wilds. All forests of the "high-woods" resemble each other so much that my description of those of Dominica and Guadeloupe will answer for this. They are composed of giant trees, woven together by masses of vines, through which a path must sometimes be hewn with the cutlass; trees and vines are hidden beneath thousands upon thousands of air-plants and parasites, which are the most conspicuous vegetation of these forests.

> "Like restless serpents clothed
> In rainbow and in fire, the parasites,
> Starred with ten thousand blossoms, flow around
> The gray trunks."

We passed through groves of the mountain palm, and here put to flight a mountain dove or two, and found a nest containing two coffee-colored eggs. It was built right in the center of a great parasite, a plant with broad leaves resembling those of the symplocarpus, attached to the stem of a tree, about four feet from the ground. A humming-bird or two dashed past us, and falling seeds, as we entered a tract of high trees, warned us that there were wood-pigeons in the leafy tops above us. All around was strewn a sweet fruit, like a yellow plum, called "penny-apiece," which is much enjoyed by the negroes and by the birds and agoutis.

My friend stooped, pointed to some impressions of feet in the moist earth, and whispered, "Haginamah." They were tracks of the armadillo, though the black had designated them by a name unknown to me; it had a Carib flavor to it. So I asked him if "haginamah" was a name for the armadillo, and he replied that it was; "Haginamah and tatou same with arm'-dilla, sah." Here was a discovery — an animal that retained its original Carib appellation.

In Grenada the Caribs once maintained supreme control; they were fierce, and a terror to the inhabitants of the continent, upon whose coasts they often descended. At the northern end of Grenada is a high bluff, descending to the sea in a precipice, over which, tradition relates, the last of the Caribs leaped in despair when pursued by their enemies. The cliff is yet known as the Hill of the Leapers — *Le Morne des Sauteurs*.

It rejoiced me to find, as I thought, a pure Carib name, handed down among the people of an island from which the Caribs themselves had been extinct a century; but my pleasure was suddenly checked;

"Haginamah, sah, because him have *amah,* an' look like hog." Then I saw my mistake — *hog-in-armor* — an applicable name.

We inspected several traps, but found no armadillos. When two-thirds around the lake, we came to the borders of a swamp containing acres of plantains and bananas in a semi-wild state. What a tropical forest — those huge plants rising fifteen feet above the ground, with their broad leaves flapping in the breeze! It seemed as though I had been transported to a world directly beneath the equator.

My companion enjoined caution now, for, the plantains being heavy with fruit, it was possible we might meet with monkeys, or at least such traces of them as might lead to the capture of one on the morrow. We floundered through the dark forest, the negro cutting a path with his cutlass through the fallen leaves which made a deposit sometimes waist-deep. In about the center of the swamp he stopped me, and pointed to the ground beneath an immense clump of plantains, where I saw some scattered fruit, torn from the depending stems above and thrown upon the ground, half eaten by those wasteful creatures, the monkeys. The bunches of plantains were some of them a load sufficient for a man to carry, and now and then there was a banana-plant, with a bunch of a hundred or more. These plants, all of them, must have originated from some runaway negro's provision-ground, abandoned many years ago.

Following a broken and interrupted trail, as indicated by fragments of banana and plantain, we finally traced the monkeys to the base of a high cliff forming part of the enclosing wall of the ancient crater.

Here we found the tree by which they descended from the heights above when they visited the banana swamp — an immense *figuier*, which had grown out of a cleft in the rock, and had established itself on the face of the cliff by a hundred roots and rootlets, aerial and terrestrial, covering the rock with a mesh-work; from the upper branches hung long lianas, like twisted cordage, down which monkeys would take delight in swinging themselves. Down this great natural ladder — the monkeys' highway — they always came, whence they scattered through the plantain groves. Often have they been hunted while there; but upon the approach of any one, no matter how silently, their noise ceased at once, though they were grunting and barking noisily before; and in a few minutes they could be heard hundreds of yards away.

It is difficult to find them if wounded, as they hide, and cling tenaciously to bush and tree. While traveling (always among the tops of the highest trees) they grunt and bark like dogs, and while feeding they have a peculiar, low, murmuring chatter. They are invariably led by the oldest monkey, who is exceeding sly.

The negro examined the ground where the monkeys seemed to have held a last sitting over their harvest of plantains, and declared they had been gone several hours. He thought they would return in the morning, as they have regular circuits of travel, appearing in one section in the morning, and in another miles away in the afternoon; among the wild plantains and nut-trees of the mountains in the evening, and carrying destruction to the cacao and nutmeg groves at dawn. I have seen heaps of cacao-pods, each with a small hole in it, an inch or so in diameter, where the monkey had thrust in his hand to scoop out the pulp. They gather the nutmegs also, but after biting the shell throw them away, not liking them. Yet they repeat this every time they visit a grove.

The man decided it was better to leave the place till morning, and I yielded to his superior knowledge of monkeys, though I could not refrain asking why it was not as well to wait for them then. He turned upon me with: "You know *macaque, oui!* He heah now, and den he no heah; umph!" Throughout Grenada the natives speak French patois, and even those who claim to speak English cannot avoid giving utterance to a French word now and then.

We returned to the house, where I passed another wearisome night. People from St. George's passed in the evening on their way to La Bay, a distance of fourteen miles, carrying loads on their heads sufficient to stagger an Irish laborer. From a woman who came up from the negro village of Delphi I bought a Carib basket; this art of basket-weaving having survived the Indians who practiced and taught it. The plant from which the baskets are made grows in the deep woods — a slender, reed-like shaft, with a coronal of leaves about a foot in length.

A man shouted out to us at dark, as he passed, that a whole troop of monkeys came down to his grounds near his cacao, where he might have shot one had he tried; and a woman also stopped and told us that another troop had been feasting on the "mammee trees" near her grounds, a few miles distant. Just before dark, our dog rushed out and barked furiously at something in a tall parrot-apple tree in the basin below the house. We could just see that it was alive with monkeys, before they were gone. Between monkeys and dogs there is a strong feeling of antipathy; the former take pleasure in annoying the latter, and will sometimes approach a house, when no one is in sight, and sit at a safe distance, "making faces" at the dog, who in turn nearly goes frantic with rage in vain attempts to reach them.

At daylight, guided by a little black boy, I revisited the plantain swamp. It was full of gloom, and I sat down under a tree. Soon a black object descended the cliff, and I was about to fire, when my little guide whispered that it was only a wild-cat. Light appeared, the birds awoke, and the forest was vocal with sounds. The tree beneath which I had seated myself was a "mammee-apple," whose huge bole swelled out above me, and gnarled limbs stretched out and up, supporting a dense canopy of leaves, among which hung clusters of fruit. This fruit is about as large as an orange, has a large stone, a thin rind of yellowish flesh, and tough, russet skin. The monkeys had left the ground strewn with fruit, which they had bitten in mere wantonness, and then thrown away. The many fresh leaves on the ground here also attested their recent visit. Behind me was the cliff, below me the waving plantains, surrounded by forest so dense as to hide the sky.

A large, brown humming-bird frequently dashed at me with a "whoof, whoof," of its wings, halting in air to look at me, then darting off to return for another look, regarding me with suspicious eyes. Humming-birds of the deep woods do not seem to be familiar with the presence of man, for repeatedly in the past two years I have been attacked, as it were, by them. Instantly they see me they will dart at my face, halting only a foot or so from it, or whirl in dizzy circles about me. The whir of their wings will often startle me, coming unexpectedly from some dark thicket in some walled-in river-bed, or from behind some great tree-trunk in the high woods. It is always in the mountain forest that this happens. I can call a few about me at any time, by imitating their excited cries; they dart at once to ascertain the cause, with sharp, nervous chirps of alarm. Even when they have flown right into my face they will not be satisfied, but must perch near, and regard me for a while intently. If I then move, they dart at me with a chirp of indignant defiance, and at once disappear.

The fragrance of the bitten fruit filled the air, and insects gathered on the broken skin, but no monkeys came to claim the remainder hanging on the tree. For nearly an hour a mountain dove had been "groaning" near me — the hollow moan they oft reiterate is aptly called a *groan* by the negroes. They have a soft, rapid flight, with a hollow *shirr* when startled or surprised in their flight by coming near you and suddenly altering their course.

Eleven o'clock. The sun had long since shone through the trees above the cliff, yet the coolness of this dense wood was little abated. Birds in the tree-tops were shaking down berries now and then, and the wind showered down leaves, but no monkeys yet disturbed the branches above. Lizards leaped from bough to bough, climbing up the tree and pattering over the leaves; they were pursuing one another everywhere, and caused many of the various movements in the trees that attracted my attention and made me look up anxiously, expecting monkeys.

A little carthiola was building its nest; he was actively at work and had nearly finished it, and was tearing strips from the dead and dry balisier with which to line it. It defended its nest with great spirit, and attacked any bird coming near. Now and then it robbed another nearly completed nest of material, making a squabble with its owner.

By an intolerable itching, which no amount of scratching could allay, I became aware that my legs were covered with that insect pest of the tropics, the *bête rouge* — an insect so small as to be scarcely visible to the naked eye, the bites of which cause great suffering. In the rainy season, especially, is this insect annoying; then one cannot walk in the grass without getting covered with it. It sometimes causes sores or ulcers, the result of scratching, and the only remedy is to cover the body with grease or oil. So intense became the pain that I could no longer remain quiet, and was dancing a frantic jig when my little darky pulled my coat and pointed to the cliff.

The vines hanging from the limbs of the great tree were shaking, and a low murmur of many monkey voices announced the coming of the troop. A round head peeped forth from the leaves, a hairy face, that was directly withdrawn, and its place supplied by another, older apparently, and having a look on its wrinkled visage of preternatural wisdom. This wrinkled face was followed by a grisly body, and soon an immense old fellow was clinging to the lianas and swinging himself downward. He was followed by a score or more of others, tumbling promiscuously one over each other, clutching at the vines and at one another's tails. There were old monkeys, fathers of families, with serious countenances, cautiously feeling their way, and sniffing the air; matronly monkeys, with young ones clinging about their necks, a world of care and responsibility expressed in their faces; young and frisky monkeys, who came trooping down, hand under hand, snatching at a tail here and there, or tweaking an ear, as they tumbled over the slow-going fathers and mothers, stopping a second now and then to bite the tail of some unfortunate baby-monkey, who would instantly set up a howl of anguish.

Ah! how those young sports enjoyed themselves. They had not a care in the world; the gray old patriarch who had reconnoitred the situation had pronounced "all safe," and upon him rested the responsibility; they would not burden themselves with care. They ogled the maiden monkeys — shy and coy were those virgin monkeys — and they snapped spitefully at any gallant who seemed disposed to take unwarrantable liberties. They pressed upon the patriarch, who at once resented such unseemly haste and familiarity by seizing the nearest by the scruff of his neck, shaking him violently, and then, without moving a muscle of his solemn countenance, dropping him into a clump of parasites.

This episode threw the foremost monkeys back upon the column, so that they were so densely crowded together as to hide the cables; they looked like a huge, braided string of onions. Then they stretched out again, over the hundred or so feet of lianas, a perfect chain, like an immense link of living sausages, and — though I do not claim to have discovered more than

Darwin — in my monkey chain there was not one missing link.

At last they disappeared below the plantain-tops, and I could hear the old chief marshalling them at the foot of the cliff. "Hark!" whispered the little negro by my side, "he old man counting him *macaque*." True enough, the old man was counting his flock; there was silence immediately after the descent, broken by grunts, as old gray-back tallied them off — "ump, ump, ump — go!"

It really seemed as though he gave the word; and there is no doubt he did, as, at the last grunt, there was a scampering, and the monkeys scattered themselves through the grove. Not so with the ancient; he duly felt the weight of responsibility, and did not join the rest in their sport or search for food, but ascended the ladder of vines, and perched himself in the fork of a limb overlooking the whole field.

During this time I was most assuredly excited. By darting forward, when that chain of monkeys was suspended in mid-air, I could have got two good shots into them before they dispersed. But at least two motives restrained me: first, I wished to observe their actions; second, I shrank from killing creatures so human-like. The temptation was so strong, however, that I could only withhold myself by great effort, and was trembling with excitement. Again, what if there was some remote relation in that throng? or — what was more probable — some descendant of an ancestor in common with the little negro crouching by my side? Such thoughts restrained me.

Meanwhile, the grove was alive with monkeys, tearing down bunches of bananas and plantains, scaling the mammee trees and twisting off the fruit. In a little while one of them reached the tree beneath which we sat; a young male, about half grown, rejoicing in his strength. The black monkey by my side could not rest, and urged me, in excited whispers, to shoot! He at least had no misgivings on the score of relationship, even though the resemblance between the two — the monkey in the tree, and the African, the monkey on the ground — was strong enough to excite a smile.

I think the monkey in the tree must have noticed this resemblance, for he saw us just then and stopped. The more he contemplated my companion, the stronger seemed to become his convictions that he had found a long-lost brother. He let himself down by his tail, and beckoned for the negro to come up; and then commenced a series of evolutions that would have shamed an acrobat; all, evidently, with a desire of impressing his brother on the ground with the advantages of an arboreal over a terrestrial mode of life. And the little sinner near me was all this time urging me to shoot that innocent animal in the tree, whose only fault consisted in being a monkey. But I could not. I would as soon have thought of shooting the clown who performed for my amusement in the circus, as of killing that little harlequin in the tree. I now regarded the whole thing as the "biggest show on earth," — as Barnum has it, — and would not sully the pure enjoyment of it by what, I could not help thinking, would be murder in the first degree.

The little man in the tree swung himself into space and disappeared; in a few minutes he came skipping gleefully along, followed by a monkey of maturer years, evidently his mother, about whose neck was dangling an infant a few months old. To her the delighted reprobate pointed us out; inquiring, in monkey language, probably, if those objects below were not " a man, and a brother."

What a look of horror convulsed the old lady's face when she saw herself in such proximity to a dreaded man, an enemy to her race! She turned about with such violence as to jerk loose the infant that clung about her neck, who fell to the ground. Maternal solicitude, even, could not arrest her flight, as she fled chattering to the vine-ladder, and hurriedly ascended it, followed by her wondering son.

A bark from the patriarch summoned the rest of the gang so quickly, that they slid over those lianas and out of sight behind the cliff, in less time than I can write it in. Not one remained, save that infant monkey on the ground, which was just recovering its scattered senses as little Jim darted forward to secure it. Quickly as Jim rushed out, the monkey was yet more agile, and gathered himself up and leaped into a clump of razor-grass. Into this the little negro dashed, regardless of the cuts of the cruel blades.

The razor-grass is a terrible pest in these woods, climbing into trees and overhanging trails; every leaf of it which touches you clings to you and cuts like a jagged-edged razor. Spite of his burning desire to capture a monkey, Jim was obliged to stop and disentangle himself, and before I had gained the scene, the monkey was in the lianas. Slowly and feebly it ascended, but I could not shake it down, and to shoot it was out of the question.

As it reached the tree, its mother sprang to seize it, and glided with it into the forest, and I awoke to the fact that I had missed my opportunity, and had been spared the pain of slaying a monkey.

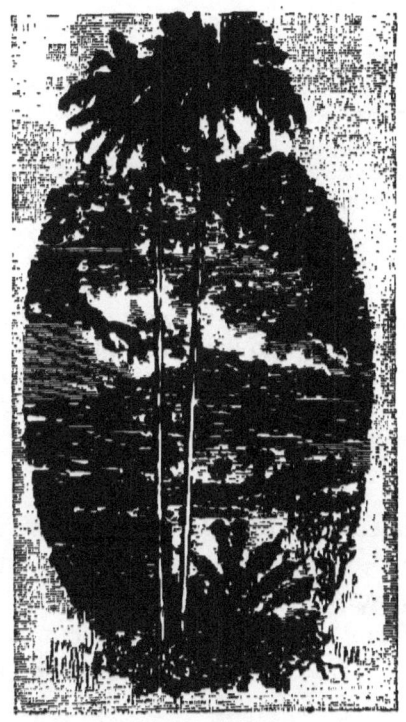

Palmiste.

CHAPTER XVII.

SOME SUMMER DAYS IN MARTINIQUE.

FROM CRUSOE'S ISLAND, NORTH. — FROWNING CLIFFS. — GOLDEN SANDS. — BIRTH OF A RAINBOW. — ST. PIERRE. — THE VOLCANO. — OUR CONSUL. — "OLD FARMER'S ALMANACK," GOOD FOR ANY LATITUDE. — FRENCH BREAKFASTS. — "LONG TOMS." — THE WIDOW AND HER WEED. — PATOIS. — COSTUMES. — GOOD CLARET. — POOR CALICO. — MARKET-WOMEN AND WASHER-WOMEN. — GAUDY GARMENTS. — PROFUSION OF ORNAMENTS. — JARDIN DES PLANTES. — THE SHRINE AND THE TRAVELER'S TREE. — CREOLE DUELING-GROUND. — PALM AVENUES. — THE CASCADE. — SAGO AND ARECA PALMS. — THE LAKE. — LAND-SNAILS. — LIZARDS. — TARANTULAS. — THE LANCE-HEAD SNAKE. — VENOMOUS AND VENGEFUL. — THE MOUNTAIN REGION. — HOT SPRINGS. — AN EXTINCT VOLCANO. — A HOLY CITY. — SABBATH IN THE COUNTRY. — WARNED OF SNAKES. — HAVE ALLIGATOR BOOTS. — THE HUMBLE SHRINE. — A SHRIEK. — NARROW ESCAPE. — THE CRAFTY SERPENT.

UP from Tobago, the island of Crusoe's adventures, I sailed, one week in June, for Barbados. Ten weeks of camp-life in that historic island had brought me rich returns, in rare birds and pictures of interesting scenes. The captain of a Nova Scotia schooner gave me passage from Barbados to the Isle of Martinique, good captain Rudolph, who navigated his vessel so skillfully that we sighted the mountains of Martinique on the morning of the second day; the same mountains I had first looked upon eighteen months previously coming down from the north.

The wind was light; flying-fish darted in all directions; little sharp-prowed canoes came sailing in out of the distance, hailed us with cheerful *bon jours*, and disappeared again in the spray and mist. We sailed in under high, frowning cliffs, down which fell silver streams into the sea; past broad fields of cane, smiling in the sunshine; past long stretches of yellow sand, overtopped by silent palms; beneath a towering gloomy mountain hiding its crest in cloud. A shower came down from those impending clouds and pattered over deck and sea, ending as suddenly as it had commenced; and a rainbow, born of the mist and the sunshine, spanned the bay of St. Pierre from headland to headland, dissolving at either end above a little fishing-village, bathing houses and boats, and nets, and beach, in glorious showers of light.

A second time I sailed into the bay of St. Pierre, a second time looked upon the volcano rising above it. The town is about a mile in length, straggling at the north away down the coast, ending in scattered villages; and at one place, where a river makes a break in the cliffs, creeping up toward the mountains. A narrow belt between high cliffs and the sea, built into and under them; the houses, of stone and brick, covered with brown earthen tiles, tier upon tier, climbing up to the hills. With the soft mellow tints of the tiles, the grays of the walls, the frequent clumps of tamarind and mango, and with the magnificent wall of living green behind it, St. Pierre strikes one as a beautiful town — until he comes to analyze it. Then, the windowless loopholes — there is hardly a square of glass in town, save in the stores — the flapping shutters, the conglomerate material used in its construction, combine to produce a feeling of revulsion. But viewed from a vessel lying in the harbor, sufficiently remote to hide its incongruous elements, St. Pierre again appears charming, picturesque.

Aside from the hills which embrace the town and come down to the sea in bold spurs, forming an arc with a chord three miles in length, there is the noble *Montagne Pelée*, above four thousand feet in height, a mass of dark green with jagged outline, cleft into ravines and black gorges, down which run rivers innumerable, gushing from the internal fountains of this great volcano.

The streets are narrow but well-flagged, and every few squares is a fountain; and adown the gutters through them all run swift streams, carrying to the sea the refuse of the city. St. Pierre is the commercial port of the island, and there are many stores filled with the wines and wares of France. There are a fine cathedral; a theatre of large capacity, to which for three months each winter a troupe from Paris draws crowded houses; a bishop's palace and governor's residence, with large and handsome barracks for the troops.

Landing, I went, as a matter of course, to the consulate, where a picture of an eagle, grasping the red man's arrows, and digging his claws into a prostrate shield, smiled serenely above an open doorway. The consul, a Massachusetts man, extended to me a warm welcome. He had been in the naval service, retiring wounded, and being connected with influential politicians, had secured this mission to Martinique. It is well known with what liberal hand our government rewards its wounded heroes, giving the more importunate, positions like this, where, with a salary of fifteen hundred dollars, each year calls upon the incumbent of the office for an expenditure of at least two thousand. The British consul had resided in Martinique fifteen years, and received a salary sufficient to maintain him in comfort. Within eighteen months the American consulate had had two representatives. As soon as one is prepared to execute his duties, he is kicked out and room made for another.

Knowing that the consul was from Boston, I was not surprised to see in his office an "Old Farmer's Almanack;" but I was greatly enlightened as to its uses when, one day, I saw him take it from its nail and gravely announce that, according to the tables for July, it was "time to take a drink." As the tables in that almanac are prepared for the latitude of Boston, I wondered at the genius that could adapt them to the latitude of Martinique; but it is probably owing to the fact that much latitude is allowed, and that there a drink is in order at any time.

Through the aid of the consul, I secured a room and board in a private family, whose delightful *déjeûners* and suppers will long be a pleasant remembrance; and may the good old mulattress who prepared them fulfil her mission for many years to come! She could originate savory stews and ragouts from as nearly nothing as any cook it has been my misfortune to meet; her "ros-bif" was excellent; and with a few potatoes and a little flour and fat she would produce "*pomme de terre a la Martinique*" — as she called it — that would make an exile from Erin howl with delight. With each plate a bottle of wine and a little twisted loaf of bread; and after the dessert, of bananas, oranges, and sapadillos, or sour-sops, came a decanter of rum, a little cup of black coffee with sugar, and cigarettes. My *vis-a-vis* at these delightful repasts was the Commissaire of Police, an ex-officer of the navy of France, and a Chevalier of the Legion of Honor. It need not be added that he was courteous and agreeable.

The creoles of Martinique, as well as the inhabitants coming from France, have but few vices, the chief of which is that they will smoke the vilest, rankest, most disgusting of cigars. These obnoxious fabrications are of American tobacco, twisted by the hand of the negress, or mulattress, into a long cigar, called by the sailors "long-toms," and sold at a sou apiece. The better classes smoke cigarettes of imported French tobacco, and are as expert in rolling them when wanted as any Cuban; but the negroes all, male and female, smoke the "long-toms." In enumerating the good qualities of my ancient cook, I overlooked the fact that from morn to night, while attending to her domestic duties, anxiously bending over the pots and kettles, she never once relinquished the comforting weed.

Through the kindness of the photographer of St. Pierre, Monsieur Hartmann, an amiable and accomplished gentleman, I was introduced into the *cercle*, or club, where French in its purity is spoken. The universal language, however, is that of the common people, the *patois*, or provincial dialect; and even the cultivated speak, colloquially, the French tongue in this rude form. The prejudice against everything not exclusively French is exceedingly bitter, though the increasing amount of foreign imports is bringing articles from the United States into favor. Clothing is higher than in the English islands, and tailors few and inexpert. The business dress is the loose-fitting, blue or black, blouse, and white pants. The hot and stiff panama is preferred to all other hats, though its closeness of texture, affording no chance for ventilation, makes it the very worst possible for a tropical climate. Some of the more sensible, however, are adopting the cool and well-ventilated Indian pith helmet, so much worn in the English islands. Panamas are the rage, and every street has its *magasin*, or store, with the conspicuous sign, " *Chapeaux de Panama veritable*," some of which sell as high as fifteen or twenty dollars. Silks and cottons are extremely dear. The only thing cheap and tolerably good is the claret, which comes direct from France duty free; and the vessel that brings the claret carries back as ballast the essential logwood.

Nothing can be said against the costumes of the ladies, which are really elegant and in good taste. As in these islands there are no teachers of the terpsichorean art, so there are no dressmakers — or, if any, very few — and the ladies cut and make their own garments. In this they take especial pride, and their toilettes, as seen on a Sunday at ten-o'clock mass, do credit to their hands and heads. There is nothing that attracts a stranger's attention so quickly as the costumes of the hucksters, the *demi monde*, and the market-women: a single flowing robe of bright-colored calico, or white muslin, sometimes of silk, loose at the throat, and with a waistband high up under the shoulder-blades. It is that of the past century. These women are mulattresses, quadroons, or octoroons; among them are many pleasant faces with regular features, and some are even handsome. The colored creole of French extraction is notably handsomer than those of Scotch or English, and more graceful and pleasing. The washerwomen and domestics sometimes wear their dress with one shoulder and arm exposed, and to such an extent was this carried but two years ago that a law was passed regulating the extent of exposure.

Passionately fond of jewelry, these ladies of the street carry their ornamentation to an exaggerated length. It is not uncommon to meet one of them with great coils of beads around the neck, with immense earrings, brooches at the throat, lockets and medallions suspended from massive chains, and the turban completely covered with pins and brooches, and the fingers with rings. The earrings of this class deserve especial mention, as they exceed in size anything worn elsewhere in the West Indies. The most gorgeous and most coveted are those composed of five gold cylinders, each as large as a lady's little finger, bound together, and suspended from the lobe of the ear by a large ring. All this jewelry is of pure gold, though thin and fragile, as not a woman among them but would scorn to be seen with an article of baser metal; and not a dealer in the colony can sell a spurious piece. The wise French law that provides that every thing sold for genuine shall be of eighteen carat gold, and stamped with the eagle, is here enforced, even to the confiscation of the stock of a dishonest dealer. One of these females was pointed out to me as having more than five hundred dollars' worth of this character of jewels. Nothing exercises their taste and patience more than the shape and fit of their turbans or head-dresses. These are made from a single bright-colored or black handkerchief, dexterously twisted into shape; and in this there are as many styles as the fancy of the wearer can invent.

Market Woman.

Contented and happy are these people, laughing and singing and smoking all the day long. Even the old woman who comes into market from the mountains, bearing upon her head the vegetables and fruits of her garden, carries herself with an air that betokens independence, and would sooner lose your patronage than dispense with her pipe.

Through the *Grande Rue*, past the *Gendarmerie*, up a narrow street to the rear of the theatre, I followed a little gamin, one cool morning, to seek birds in the *Jardin des Plantes*. A shower dropped suddenly now and then, but the summit of the volcano stood out cool and purple against a sky of untroubled blue. Gaining a level road at the base of high cliffs, I walked beneath almond and tamarind trees, looking down upon the *savane*, or level field, beneath, where are held the reviews and occasional shows that visit this island, and across to the lower town, where a white dome thrust itself up from a sea of cocoa palms. The huge cone swept from cloud to foaming river — the Rivière Roxelane, which divides the town, and from which, even thus early, came the sound of blows, telling the listening ear that inoffensive linen was being maltreated by vengeful females. A broad stretch of cane-field climbed well up the mountain, meeting the forest, which sent out detachments of trees to greet the cane, then spread out all over the peak, vast and dark. Houses looked out from gardens of fruit-trees; everywhere was cultivation and growth.

Descending slightly, I passed a little shrine to the Virgin, built right beneath the vine-hung precipice, which sent down a wealth of trailing, clinging plants to cover it. Leaning above it, as in benediction, is the famous and beautiful *Arbre du Voyageur*, which, if pierced, will give forth a stream of pure water. Its long leaves, fan-like in their arrangement, de-

THE WAYSIDE SHRINE.

scribe a semicircle above its stem. Inside the shrine is the sorrowful mother, carved of wood, and having her heart, pierced with arrows, on the outside of her robe, showing that sculptors, like poets, have a license to do not as other mortals. "MATER DOLOROSA, ORA PRO NOBIS." Good Catholics are they who pass this shrine, for, one and all, they cross themselves devoutly.

At the entrance to the garden is a keeper's lodge, of stone. A foaming stream rushes under a wooden bridge, across which is a smaller garden, in which are roses and choice plants, and a small museum containing a good collection of birds, pictures of native types, and insects and reptiles of the island, which figured in the Exposition of 1867.

Near the main walk a grotto, in a bank covered with vines, overhung by a palm, spouts out a glistening shower. This broad path runs by the side of a stream, under tamarinds and screw-pines, ascending between a double row of tall palmistes. This, my guide tells me, was the old dueling-ground of the creoles, and the many holes with which the gray pillars are perforated were caused by bullets; the names carved there, in memory of those who fell. This may well be credited when I can state upon my own evidence that there were three duels on the tapis when I left the island. Though many of the affairs of honor are merely farcical, and the empty air gets the pistol-shot and sword-thrust, there are some in which the participators are in dead earnest, and blood is often shed.

Above the palms is a cascade sixty feet in height, which flows from a deep cut in solid rock, in a single sheet, into a broad basin below. From the cascade another path, broad and shaded, leads to a garden of acclimatization and a nursery, where are all kinds of tropical plants — groups of palmistes, treeferns, fan-palms, broken-leaved African palms, and forms of plants strange even to these tropic isles. Near the basin of a fountain, containing the Egyptian papyrus, are the tallest sago-palms ever seen out of their native isles of the Indian Archipelago, for they are twenty feet in height, have stout trunks and dense crowns. Candelabra çacti, night-blooming cereus, roses, honeysuckles, and a hundred other plants, may here be found.

The gem of the garden is the lake in its center, surrounded by great trees; tall palms pierce the leaves above it; a broken stream, tumbling down from the hill, half screening some fern-covered grotto as it falls, plunges into it. It is a small pond, but contains vegetable wonders on its three small islets that at home would be priceless. One island is completely covered with a mound of vines wound about a screw-pine and frangipanni — a tangled mass of jessamine and wild vines of the tropics, spangled with white, red, and yellow flowers. Another, a mere foothold for the tree, contains a "traveler's tree," its magnificent leaves reflected in the lake. The other islet contains more rare plants, wild plantains with golden cups, ferns and flowers, and is further graced by two very slender areca-palms, exquisitely graceful, shooting upward with stems not larger than one's wrist, and forty feet in height. Their delicate leaves droop above dense clusters of nuts — the famous nuts with which the betel is mixed and chewed by the natives of the East.

The low bushes are covered with land-snails, and lizards dart out from every crevice, from under every rock and dead limb, and run up the trunks of trees by scores — lizards of all sorts, sizes, and colors; and they are sluggish, too, and it is easy to catch them. But in searching for snails, I encountered an insect not very agreeable, whose bite is certain fever, sometimes death. Horribly gay is this spider, the Tarantula, in the long hair that covers body and legs, which serves well to conceal it while waiting for its prey, in a dark crevice or under a drooping leaf. They like to conceal themselves beneath the leaves of such plants as the aloes, where one broad leaf underlaps the other, and where they can rest almost unseen. You see it also on the walks, its hairy legs outstretched, its ugly body flat to the earth, resembling a bunch of catkins from the trumpet-tree, which everywhere lie scattered about. Poke it with a stick, and, instead of trying to escape, it will climb up that stick so vigorously toward your hand, that, ten to one, you will drop it and run. Turn it over, and it discloses a pair of sharp, beak-like jaws, red within, which, with its gleaming eyes, have a cruel appearance. With its legs spread, this spider will sometimes cover the area of a saucer.

Centipedes and scorpions, also, abound here. Indeed, it seems that nature has bestowed upon this island of Martinique all the pests and scourges known to these islands; for only here and in the adjacent island of St. Lucia is found that most venomous and vengeful of all serpents, the Lance-head snake—*Craspedocephalus lanceolatus*. The isolation of this snake in these two islands, when its nearest habitat is Guiana, is one of the most vexing stumbling-blocks to one studying the distribution of animals. How came it here? Was it introduced, or is it indigenous? Was it wafted here upon some floating tree, or was its home here from the beginning? The correct solution of this problem would, doubtless, throw some light upon that more important and gigantic one, Were these islands once a part of the continents? Certain it is, the adjacent islands of Dominica and St. Vincent, separated from these by channels less than thirty miles in width, are free from this scourge. Nay, more; it is recorded that, during the wars between the English and Caribs, in the last century, the Lance-head was carried to the islands just named, but could not be made to live.

Annually, during the crop season, many laborers are killed in each island, for this snake has its hiding-places in the canes as well as in the forests. It has been so abundant in this garden that the pleasant walks and shady drives are nearly always deserted. A serpent over seven feet in length, killed in the garden, is shown in the Museum. There is, it is said, no antidote for its bite; though the ever-traditional old negro, living in some secluded spot, with herbs and antidotes, likewise exists here. He is never found when needed, however. The poison is quickly fatal, and decomposition rapidly follows. A gentleman, whose father was once a wealthy planter in St. Lucia, and had many slaves, told me that an antidote that generally proved efficacious if used immediately, was forty grains of quinine in the juice of two lemons; in extreme cases he administered a glass of olive oil and rum, and used the vapor bath. The remedy used in the South, when bitten by the rattlesnake — whiskey, all that the patient can drink — seems useless here. The dread of this serpent is universal. It seems to possess a hatred for man; and it is seriously avowed by the natives that it will lie in wait for an opportunity to inflict death. The country people live in continual trepidation, and very few of them will venture from their houses after dark, even in the suburbs of the city.

Martinique is the largest of the Lesser Antilles,

being about fifty miles in length, and containing, it is estimated, about three hundred and eighty square miles. The surface is very uneven, the interior being one grand region of hills and mountains. The highest of these is Mount Pelée, over four thousand feet in height, north-west of the principal town, St. Pierre. Though a volcano which has emitted smoke and ashes within thirty years, there are now no signs of an eruption. Late in July I was hunting in these mountains, making my headquarters at Morne Rouge, a little village occupying a central plateau near the volcano. From there I made excursions to Morne Calebasse, Morne Balisier, Mount Pelée, and Champ Flore. There are many mineral springs in the mountains, two of which — one reached from St. Pierre, and the other from Fort de France — are famous resorts for the inhabitants.

Morne Rouge is a holy city; to it every year the people of the coast, high and low, make pilgrimages on foot. The church here is beautifully decorated, the interior containing valuable paintings and frescoings. The Virgin is magnificently arrayed and enriched by the spoils of the faithful and credulous. All about are shrines and crosses and sacred mounts of Calvary; and near the town is a most charming grotto, containing an image of the Virgin, overhung by tree-ferns, hollowed from a rock dripping with water, with a clear pool and fountain at its base.

Sunday is a fête day, and the busiest of the week. Then the young ladies from the convent and the brothers from the monastery attend church in a body. Every one is dressed in the best he can afford. A ven-

der of cakes pitches a
small bench beneath
the shade of a ve-
randa and offers an
assortment not pro-
curable on week-
days. She drives a
good trade in the
morning, as the peo-
ple return from early
mass; but as the sun
gets around in the
afternoon she leaves
bench and cakes to
themselves, covers
them with a ragged
blanket that has seen
unwashed service for

years, and contentedly sucking a cigar, snoozes
quietly in the shade. She has on a white chemise,
a man's hat of straw, a black skirt, and a white handkerchief bound about her forehead. At three in the
afternoon, all go to church. The universal dress is
black coat and white pants. Here are a few costumes
of the blacks: Black turban, black dress, cut with
waist high up under the arms, and black shoes; another in bright colors and green shoes; again another,
sans shoes; one with a parasol; a diminutive darky
stalking gravely along with a *bush* for parasol and
feet thrust into yawning shoes. All wear high heels
when dressed. Men and women pass and repass with
huge bundles nicely balanced upon their heads.

When it was known that I intended shooting over

the fields and through the forests about Morne Rouge, all my acquaintances of a day gathered about me, frantically expostulating, and I with difficulty secured a boy to pilot me. To satisfy these good people, to some extent, I drew on a pair of boots of alligator skin, old and grievously rent, which had accompanied me through flood and forest for full five years. Seven years had passed since these boots were sporting in saurian shape in the warm waters of the "Land of Flowers." The skin composing them I had wrenched from the lifeless bodies of two alligators measuring respectively nine and ten feet. They had shown gallant fight, and it was to perpetuate their achievements, and to protect my feet, that I had caused their skins to be tanned and made into boots. Impervious were they once, and gallant service had they performed; for they were fashioned and constructed by no less a cordwainer than Shadrach Fisk, a worthy knight of St. Crispin, Shadrach, and as honest a man as ever trod or manipulated shoe-leather.

Much courage did these boots infuse into my heart, and I strode forth valiantly, trusting that any well-disposed snake would be magnanimous enough to strike at the hide and not at the holes. Not Roderick Dhu, with targe of "tough bull-hide," felt better protected than I felt then. Let the short sequel show how vain are man's pretences. We marched out into the fields, my little pilot trembling with fear, and so craven that he dared not retrieve my birds. We came to an immense tree, a silk-cotton, which covered a broad area with its shadow. In this tree was a little shrine, rudely made, and a plaster figure of the immaculate mother; at her feet a candle burning, and humble offerings. It was the tribute of some poor laborer, this shrine. It has often been forced upon my notice, this reverence of the ignorant for a giant tree. Here they will bring their offerings, and prefer these leafy temples to the more pretentious cathedrals.

Steps were cut out from the great roots up to the shrine, and I walked up to examine it. A shriek from my attendant halted me, and I saw him upon his knees, imploring me not to venture farther. Thinking it was a foolish superstition regarding the approach of an armed man to a place of veneration, I was about assuring my boy that his fears were groundless, when a movement above me drew my attention.

Coiled along a branch, with half the body hanging and the head drawn back awaiting my approach, was the dreaded serpent, venomous glances, that hardly lacked the power to slay, darting from its fiery eyes. Another step and I should have received the blow; and that it would have been a fatal one I have little doubt. Shot after shot rang out until the loathsome reptile fell; but even when he lay stretched upon the ground did I not dare to tread upon him, so completely had I lost faith in the protection of alligator boots. I recalled the facetious advice of our consul, given as I was preparing for my excursion to the mountains, that my only safety lay in encasing myself securely in iron armor. As a substitute for this, he advised me to procure a barrel, cut holes for my head and arms, and thrust my legs through sections of stove-pipe.

CHAPTER XVIII.

THE BIRTH-PLACE OF THE EMPRESS JOSEPHINE.

FORT DE FRANCE. — THE PARK. — TAMARINDS AND MANGOS. — STATUE OF JOSEPHINE. — THE TROIS PITONS. — HISTORIC HILLS. — CORONATION. — INSCRIPTION. — AN EARTHQUAKE. — TERROR. — PARENTS OF JOSEPHINE. — HER GRANDMOTHER. — ALEXANDER DE BEAUHARNAIS. — A VALUABLE DOCUMENT. — MARRIAGE REGISTER OF JOSEPHINE'S PARENTS. — BUNGLING BIOGRAPHERS. — MUSTY MEMOIRS. — FORT ROYAL BAY. — THE PASSAGE-BOAT "JOHN." — TROIS ILETS. — THE BOULANGER. — A FESTIVE FATHER. — A DINNER IN JEOPARDY. — A LOW COUCH. — A HIGH BILL. — CHURCH IN WHICH JOSEPHINE WAS BAPTIZED. — A TABLET TO HER MOTHER'S MEMORY. — LA PAGERIE, BIRTH-PLACE OF JOSEPHINE. — THE HURRICANE. — THE ROOF THAT SHELTERED AN EMPRESS. — GROUND HER FEET HAD PRESSED. — YOUTH OF JOSEPHINE. — ANOTHER SHOCK. — THE NEGRO BARRACKS. — THE EMPRESS' BATH. — ONE HUNDRED YEARS AGO! — THE SIBYL. — THE HUMMING-BIRD. — IN PERIL FROM A SERPENT. — A PEACEFUL SCENE. — A RUDE AWAKENING. — THE RIVER COMES DOWN. — EARTHQUAKE AGAIN. — RAGS AND MELANCHOLY.

A LITTLE steamer runs between St. Pierre and Fort de France, the seat of government of the island, coasting the shore, past a most interesting landscape twenty miles, the banks high and precipitous, exhibiting many different strata, and affording to a geologist a glimpse of the manner in which the island was formed. Huge rounded hills come down to the sea, where they are abruptly cut down, looking like the halves of Dutch cheeses, the slices smooth and straight. The summer rains had caused an accumulation of water in the hills above, and I counted eight streams pouring over the precipices, all of which a few days later would have disappeared. Half-way down, the surface slopes farther back from the shore, though there is but little cultivation until the bay of Fort Royal is reached. A large stone fortress, a large *usine*, or sugar refinery, an open park, a few government buildings, and a river, are all that particularly claim attention.

Fort de France was originally known as Fort Royal, but this was before the days of republican rule. It is situated between two rivers, the Rivière Madame and the Rivière Monsieur; the former, on the north, is very beautiful during its short length, especially near its embouchure; palms reflect themselves in the still water, and a church, on the bank, sees its image on the glassy surface. The hills, such as hem in St. Pierre, here recede a greater distance from the shore, and the town occupies a low and level plain, with wide streets crossing at right angles, lined with well-built wooden houses. There are few trees save in the park, which lies near the shore between fortress and town. Here there are long and thickly-planted rows of tamarinds and mangos overshading the broad level walks. Enclosed by this double row of trees is a large *savane*, or common, covered with a luxuriant carpet of grass, in the center of which stands the statue of her of whom I came to learn.

Majestic in poise, graceful in outline, carved of marble spotless as her own pure soul, JOSEPHINE stands calmly aloft, surrounded by a circle of magnificent palms; the *oreodoxas*, glories of the mountains, add their glorious crowns to that which adorns the head of the empress. For hours I have gazed upon that beautiful creation, as, seated beneath the spreading tamarinds, I have striven to impress upon my memory an ineffaceable image of its loveliness. There is one view that is inexpressibly beautiful, with the snow-white statue sharply outlined against a distant group of mountain-peaks, the *Trois Pitons*, which are sometimes deep blue, again light green, or partially obscured by drifting clouds. Against this background Josephine stands out white as an angel. Another view, at a little distance, gives a background of tamarinds; another that of the purple-green mango. From any position it appears a perfect composition; an inimitable grace pervades the sweep of the royal robes, and the whole suggests a master's hand.

The statue fronts the sea, but the face is turned a few points south, so that it looks toward a line of hills, five miles away, nestled among which is the valley in which Josephine was born. The sentiment conveyed in the look of wistful yearning in that sweet face, turned longingly to the scenes of her childhood, is as beautiful as truthful. In front is the Caribbean Sea; the great fort hides the hills from the view of one standing by the statue, but a few steps to the eastward brings them in sight.

Upon a medallion of Napoleon, Josephine rests her left hand. On the pedestal, a bas-relief in bronze represents the famous coronation scene, recalling that extraordinary pageant, when Bonaparte surpassed all preceding coronations in the magnificence of this, summoning the venerable Pius VII. from the Vatican to assist in his assumption of royalty: In the center, the Pope; Napoleon, in the act of placing the crown upon the head of Josephine, who kneels before him. The inscriptions upon the dies are as follows:

North: "*L'an* 1868. *Napoleon III Regnant, Les Habitants de la Martinique ont élevé ce monument a L'Impératrice Joséphine. Née dans cette Colonie.*"
East: "*Née Le XXIII Juin, MDCCLXIII.*" (Crown, shield, and eagle of France.)
South: The bas-relief, — Coronation scene.
West: "*Marié Le IX Mars, MDCCXCVI.*" (Draped shield, eagle, and crown.)

The statue is enclosed by a neat iron fence, and is further surrounded by a ring of palms, planted, I believe, at the time it was erected. In the distance, on a hill, is an old fort and a little chapel, where the Virgin Mother extends her hands in benediction, and where a candle burns, bright by night and dim by day.

As amateur photographer I sought a resident artist, Monsieur Fabre, who received and aided me cheerfully, especially when he learned that I bore a letter from our good friend Hartmann, of St. Pierre. In his capacious court-yard I was soon busily at work preparing my chemicals, wrapped in a vapor of collodion. I was suddenly awakened by a strange shock, as though some one had shaken me strongly and was about standing me upon my head. At that instant, in rushed my friend, the photographer, with loud cries: "*Ah, mon Dieu! Tremblement de terre! Tremblement de terre!*" "Earthquake! Earthquake!"

The ground shook, walls cracked, and, in common with every one else, I rushed into the street. There was the entire populace crowded together in terror, most of them wildly shrieking and gesticulating. The shocks lasted but a few minutes, and then all went calmly back to their houses. After this the sky was as serene and blue, and the trees as quiet, as before,

Birthplace of Josephine.

and I finished my photographs of beautiful Josephine, who had been an unmoved spectator of it all, without interruption.

The town of Fort de France is intimately connected with scenes in the early life of Josephine, and of her parents. In 1755, Joseph Gaspard de La Pagerie, father of Josephine, returned to Martinique from France, whither he had been sent to school. That year war was declared between England and France, and the young officer, first lieutenant of artillery, was actively engaged in erecting batteries at Fort de France, then, as now, the naval port of the island. He aided in the repulse of the English under General Moore in 1759, and took such active part in the second defence, in 1762, when the town was captured, that he was complimented by the general commanding the English forces and allowed to retire to his estate at Trois-Ilets.

In June, 1760, there was baptized in the church of Saint Louis, at Fort Royal, an infant, born the preceding May, and named ALEXANDRE DE BEAUHARNAIS, who was destined to be the husband of Josephine. An aunt of Josephine was godmother to this child. The Marquis de Beauharnais, father to Alexander, had been appointed governor of Martinique and the French colonies three years previously, with authority over all the respective governors of the other islands. Leaving Martinique for France in the following year, the Marquis left his infant son in charge of Madame de La Pagerie, grandmother to Josephine. This lady resided principally in Fort de France, and when Josephine attended school at the near convent, she was a frequent visitor at the house of her grandmother, if indeed she did not reside with her.

But the most interesting event in the history of the island was the marriage of the parents of Josephine, the register of which I found among the musty archives of the island, in Fort de France. The document is long, and though I have a fac-simile copy of that page in the ancient register containing it, I will give but the substance here. It states that "*Messire Joseph Gaspard de Tascher, chevalier, seigneur de La Pagerie*, native of the parish of *St. Jacque du Carbet*, — of said island of Martinique, lieutenant in the artillery, son in legitimate marriage of *Messire Joseph-Gaspard de Tascher, chevalier, seigneur de La Pagerie*, and of *Madame Marie-Françoise Boureau de La Chevalerie*, living in the town of Port Royal," was married to "*demoiselle Rose-Claire des Vergers de Sannois*, native of the parish of Trois-Ilets, daughter in legitimate marriage of *Messire Joseph des Vergers de Sannois* and of *dame Marie-Catherine Brown*, natives of and dwellers in the parish of Trois-Ilets," etc.

Thus we have in this register of marriage, dated November the ninth, 1761, the names and rank of the parents and grandparents of Josephine, and, what is of equal importance, their place of residence at that time, only eighteen months previous to her birth.

Let us turn for a moment to her biographers. One or two will suffice to show how inaccurate are their statements. Thus, in " Memoirs of the Empress Josephine," by John S. Memes, LL.D., I find that the parents of the Empress were — "both natives of France, though *married in St. Domingo*, about 1761." . . . "Of this parentage, the only child, the subject of these Memoirs, was born in St. Pierre, the capital of Martinico, on the 23d of June, 1763."

A French dictionary of biography also repeats that Josephine was born in St. Pierre; but this is refuted by the register of baptism at Trois-Ilets, which the author of the "*Histoire de l'Impératrice Joséphine*," M. Aubenas, (to whose volume I am indebted for the facts relating to the early life of Josephine,) quotes entire.

A deep bay nearly divides the island of Martinique near the southern end. On its northern side, Fort de France; at its bight, La Montagne and Rivière Salée; and directly south of Fort de France is the little town (*petit bourg*, it is called) of Trois-Ilets — the Three Islets — hidden from sight by a high cape. I was going to hire a boat and three men to carry me across the bay; but just as we were ready to go, early one morning, the rain came down in sheets, and we were obliged to wait. I then learned that a boat plied regularly between the town and the *petit bourg*, and that it was but a mile and a half to "*L'habitation de La Pagerie.*" Its usual hour of starting was at four, but the rain delayed it until five in the afternoon. John, my self-appointed domestic, — a negro with an ugly face and one white eye, — had safely stowed my apparatus, hunting gear, and himself, and I found with difficulty, between a couple of negresses, a place for myself. There were twenty-five of us, and I, as the only white man, duly felt my insignificance.

Amid a great deal of jabbering, we pushed off. The boat was a long, open, flat-bottomed one, with a large mast, to be shipped in the bow, with a leg-of-mutton sail, and a smaller one perched right in the peak. A small negro boy had charge of the latter. They pulled out a bit, then shipped the mast. The wind came in puffs, at times very strong, and the captain at the helm was repeatedly shouting: "*Gar-*

dez! Fort vent! Coup de vent!"—"Look out! Strong wind! A squall." And when the wind struck the boat, instead of luffing, they had three negroes swinging at the ends of three ropes attached a little more than half-way up the mast, who, with feet braced against the rail, would sway their bodies out over the water, and thus restore the equilibrium when she heeled. It was a novel and interesting sight, but one calculated to excite reflection, when wind should prove stronger than African, with the sheets made fast, a stubborn helmsman hanging to the tiller for dear life, and the water pouring in over the lee rail.

We rounded the point and opened up the view of Trois-Ilets just after dark. A low church, with straggling tile-covered houses about it, backed by purple hills, with a cane field stretching to the east, in its center the presbytery surrounded by trees. The stars were gleaming in the sky as we landed and walked up to the house of the owner of the boat, a *boulanger*, who also kept a shop. There was no other place likely to afford me shelter, so I went to the baker's shop; but the first square look I had at the owner convinced me that he was not a man prone to hospitable acts. Subsequent events, I am happy to say, proved conclusively that I was right. He said he could give me a dinner, but no bed, so I went out with a cobbler who could speak a little English, in search of the curé, the parish priest, to whom I had a letter.

We arrived at the presbytery at about half past seven, knocked, and after some delay were bidden to enter by the housekeeper, a comely woman. The curé entered the room; short, corpulent, with sensual face, black hair and evidences of an abundant beard in reserve. As he came in he cast an anxious glance at the neatly-spread table, where one plate, one bottle of wine, and bread and napkin for one, plainly indicated that the curé did not expect visitors, — and then at the sideboard, where was a dish heaped with fruit, and another bottle of wine; and then a smile spread over his countenance, and he advanced to meet me. After a few compliments — for I saw the worthy curé was unhappy about something — I handed him the letter, which stated substantially that I wished permission to photograph the church, and desired a glimpse of the ancient registers, and recommended me to his good offices. As he read, there appeared upon his face a multitudinous smile. He assured me that most certainly I could photograph the church, that it would give him actual pain if I did not, etc.; then ensued a painful pause. My friend had told him that I could find no place in which to sleep, which he had not apparently heard, or, rather, concluded that it mattered not to a naturalist, who could probably sleep anywhere, like a bat, hanging up by his toes.

Meanwhile, a savory odor came in from the kitchen. It was pretty evident that soup was ready and being kept in waiting over the coals; that the mutton even was ready to be served, and the fish swimming in its sauce. The curé's nostrils dilated, while a look of sadness stole over his face. My friend then suggested that I had ordered dinner at the baker's; after discussing which, my only thought was for a couch, a rug, a floor — anything, so I had shelter from the evening damp. The curé's face brightened, then clouded again, and he hastened to say that he was really distressed, but he had no room to spare. "He has three chambers," said my friend, in English. This was enough. I hastened away, leaving the curé with one eye on me and one on the table, uttering the most dismal of lamentations that he could not be of service to me. Well, thought I, here is a brace of generous men to welcome a stranger to the home of Josephine.

The clock in the church struck eight as we reached the baker's. There I found that John had arranged to sleep on the floor, where I was obliged, after a greasy dinner, to sleep likewise. Awaking in the night, thirsty, I was agreeably surprised to find some rum and water with sugar. I found them also, next morning, in the bill, which, unlike my bed, was not low. At daylight I hastened on, anxious to escape from such a place.

Later in the week I visited the little church hard by, and took the first picture ever made of the church in which the infant Josephine was baptized. Presuming that the exterior has been slightly altered since Josephine's time, the present spire constructed and the clock inserted, it is the same structure that existed a century ago. On either side the doorway is a "flambeau-tree," which at the time of my visit were scarlet with blossoms. Two bells, rung for Sabbath mass, are beneath a rough shed near by, the prevalent earthquakes forbidding they should be raised to the steeple. Above the clock is the image of the patron saint. Back of the church, stretching down to the seaside, is the cemetery. The interior is attractive, the altar, as in all Catholic churches, being particularly ornamented. The two most interesting objects to a visitor are, first, a picture on the right of the chancel, given by Napoleon, and on the left a *tombeau*, or tablet, to the memory of the mother of Josephine.

And here let me venture a remark upon the fallibility of certain biographers. In Meme's "Memoirs of the Empress Josephine," I find the following:

"The infancy and youth of Josephine were passed, not under the paternal roof, but with an aunt. Instead, therefore, of returning to *St. Domingo* with her parents, the infant remained in the island of Martinico. We can discover no cause for this save a family arrangement in the first instance, and the premature death of her mother. Without being aware of this circumstance, however, and perhaps not recollecting that her father died before she had become known, the reader might deem it remarkable, and even ungrateful, that Josephine so seldom mentioned, and consequently has left such slight and imperfect memorials of, her parents."

Headley[*] is careful not to commit himself upon this point, and truly says: "The data are imperfect from which to gather a complete biography of their gifted daughter." But J. S. C. Abbott, in his history of Josephine, launches forth the following remarkable statement, evidently culled from Meme's Memoirs:

"But little is known respecting Mlle. de Sannois, this young lady who was so soon married to M. Tascher. Josephine was the only child born of this

[*] Headley's "Life of the Empress Josephine" is the most complete, and comprises all data at that time published regarding her. It is an interesting and valuable book.

union. In consequence of the *early death of her mother*, she was, while an infant, intrusted to the care of her aunt. Her father soon after died, and the little orphan appears never to have known a father's or a mother's love." And this careless statement of a stay-at-home biographer has gone forth to the world.

Here is a literal translation of the inscription upon that tablet in the church at Trois-Ilets, in which the parents of Josephine were married, she was baptized, and in which her mother lies buried:

>HERE LIES
>
>THE VENERABLE
>
>MADAME ROSE CLAIRE DUVERGER DE SANNOIS,
>
>WIDOW OF MESSIRE J. G. TASCHER DE LA PAGERIE,
>
>MOTHER OF HER MAJESTY THE EMPRESS OF THE FRENCH,
>
>DIED THE SECOND DAY OF JUNE, MDCCCVII,
>
>AT THE AGE OF LXXI YEARS.
>
>PROVIDED WITH THE SACRAMENTS OF THE CHURCH.

It will thus be seen that the mother of Josephine died in 1807, when her daughter was *forty-four* years of age, having lived to see her married to Beauharnais at the age of sixteen; to welcome her back to her home when separated from her husband; to hear of the latter's death, in 1794, of her marriage to Napoleon, in 1796, and of her coronation as Empress of the French, in 1804. Fortunately, she passed away before the cruel act of divorce, and while Josephine was the happy wife of Napoleon, but did not leave her daughter at what is generally considered a tender age. And again, Josephine is spoken of as being an *only* daughter, when the records of the parish show the registers of the baptism of three and of the death of two.

From the bourg to La Pagerie the scenery is uninteresting, being only of cane-fields. About a mile out we reached a narrow valley running up from the sea for about three miles. In this valley once stood the house in which Josephine was born, in 1763. Jutting hills hide the site until you are close upon it, when a turn in the road discloses a secluded vale, and a few rods farther brings you to a low wooden house with roof of tiles, old and dilapidated, with a little "shingle" over the doorway, having upon it the common shop-sign of the country, "*Debit de la Ferme*," which means that you can buy there rum and salt fish in limited quantities.

I will confess to feelings of disappointment and disgust; and it was with a sinking heart that I drew my water-logged and mud-clogged feet toward the doorway. But I was at once reassured by a sight of the face of an honest man, a good-looking, intelligent one, with blue eyes, and a pleasant mouth shaded by a heavy gray moustache. He readily gave me permission, and assisted me so ably that in a short time I had secured four photographs of the two buildings coexistent with Josephine, and had explored the rooms where she resided in youth. I was made happy by learning that the house he occupied was not one of the original buildings, but had been constructed of materials from the house in which Josephine was born, which had been destroyed by a hurricane shortly after her birth.

We traced the walls of the ancient building, which gave evidence of one of ample dimensions — the walls once supporting the gallery and those enclosing the court. The only buildings now standing which were in existence at the time of Josephine's birth are two — the *ancienne cuisine*, the kitchen once attached to the dwelling, and the *sucrerie*, or sugar-house. Lowly and humble, with walls of stone and roof of earthen tiles, whose mellow tone and gray lichens suggested great age, was the old building which once had been the home for many years of the mother of Josephine. For tradition, as authentic as tradition can be, states that here lived Madame Tascher de la Pagerie after the death of her husband, and while her daughter was the wife of Napoleon. Those two small windows in the roof look into two chambers, now dilapidated and unused, chosen as the widow's abode when left solitary and alone. Not many years ago there died in Trois-Ilets a very old woman, once a domestic in the family, who attended Madame La Pagerie in her later years, and it is through her this tradition was preserved. Above the humble roof droops a stately mango, rich in golden fruit and dark-green leaves.

Lieutenant La Pagerie resided with his bride, in 1761, on the estate of his father-in-law, a portion of which was given him at the time of his marriage. A few years later he came into possession of it, and it is known at the present time as La Pagerie. The estate was a large one, employing one hundred and fifty slaves in the cultivation of cane and coffee, and yielding a large annual revenue.

Here, on the 23d of June, 1763, Josephine was

The Home of an Empress.

born. She had scarcely reached the age of three years when the island was visited by a terrible hurricane that destroyed an immense amount of property and many lives. The hurricane was accompanied by shocks of earthquake, thunder and lightning. None so serious had occurred in the memory of man. The mansion of La Pagerie was utterly ruined and the crops swept away. The walls of the sugar-house alone were left standing, and to this building M. La Pagerie fled for shelter with his wife and two children. Shortly after they had taken up their residence in the sugar-house, a third child, a daughter also, was born to Mme. La Pagerie. This child, with the other sister of Josephine, died young; and a mistake on the records of the burial of the youngest caused the erroneous statement subsequently that Josephine had an elder sister.

Down the hill, within a stone's-throw of the dwelling, is the sugar-house to which M. La Pagerie removed after the visit of the hurricane. It is of stone, its walls are very thick, at least two feet, and it is covered with the durable brown tiles so in harmony with the landscape. In the eastern half are, or were, two large chambers extending two-thirds the length of the building, which is above one hundred feet long and fifty wide. The roof is fallen in at one place, and you can look into the interior of one of the chambers in which Josephine and her parents lived during her youth.

Ah, if those massive walls could speak! Through these low windows how many times has the youthful empress looked out upon a landscape that once possessed all the beauties of the tropics! Through the wide doorway on the southern side how many times has she descended to indulge in the gambols which she loved so well!

I climbed to the great rafters, from which the flooring had been many years removed, and looked through those windows, and stood in the same doorway in which the happy Josephine had so often stood — a doorway bordered by blocks of granite, connecting the two chambers. But there was nothing there to recall her who had once illumined these walls by her presence, and who had now been absent a hundred years. Above, the roof was black with bats clustered in noisy groups, hanging from the tiles; beneath, the rafters; and below, the ground. The sun sank low behind the hills that ringed this lovely valley round, and fell with feeble glare through the rent in the roof that once had sheltered an empress. Nothing could be evoked from empty space; I could merely say that I had seen the home which once was hers, and had trodden ground her feet had pressed.

Of the first years of this illustrious child we know little. She resided here with her parents until ten years of age, when she was sent to the convent at Fort Royal, where she remained until fifteen. During the brief period which elapsed between her return from the convent and her marriage to Beauharnais, she dwelt with her family, engaged in domestic duties and in the education of her sisters. At the age of sixteen she was married to Alexander de Beauharnais, in France. In 1788, having separated from her husband, she returned to her birthplace, and passed three tranquil years. With her little daughter, the charming Hortense, then five years old, she rambled over the hills and valleys endeared to her by the memory of her childhood days.

With a loving mother and father, and in the company of her youngest sister, surrounded by sympathetic neighbors, she seems to have passed some of the happiest days of her existence. Thus she writes of her retreat, during the separation from Beauharnais:

"Nature, rich and sumptuous, has covered our fields with a carpeting which charms as well by the variety of its colors as of its objects. She has strewn the banks of our rivers with flowers, and planted the freshest forests around our fertile borders. I cannot resist the temptation to breathe the pure aromatic odors wafted on the zephyr's wings. I love to hide myself in the green woods that skirt our dwelling; there I tread on flowers which exhale a perfume as rich as that of the orange grove, and more grateful to the senses. How many charms has this retreat for one in my situation! . . . I find myself in the midst of my relations and the old friends who once loved and still love me tenderly."

On the day succeeding that on which I took my photographs, some of the tiles above the dormer windows were shaken down by an earthquake. Around the house are cocoa and mango trees, sapadillos and avocado pears; but none are left of the majestic palms that are said to have surrounded the dwelling. The quiet beauty of the place, the gentle manners of Monsieur Mareschal, the proprietor, and the historic associations of the valley, all combined to form an attraction not to be resisted, and I begged permission to stay a while. My new friend readily acceded, but hesitated to offer me the only accommodations the estate afforded, a room in the negro barracks; but I assured him that I had camped in worse places, and before nine o'clock that night I was established. My room was very small, but in it Madame Mareschal had placed an iron camp-bedstead and a chair, and to it my faithful John had removed my effects. It was in the center of a long, low structure, built against the garden wall, once used as quarters for the servants when the estate was in flourishing circumstances. Right and left of me were negro families; but of their dirt and noise, and kind attentions, I will not speak. For ten days I stayed there, having a seat at my friend's table, and sleeping at night in the barracks.

Over the hills which surrounded the valley on every side I rambled, with a little negro as guide, and explored many a nook, that, if it could speak, would tell delightful stories of the historic past. Of the many pleasant days passed there, let me give a description of one, the last. It was morning, the sun had not appeared above the hills, as, guided by a little negro, I took the footpath up the valley, south, reaching the narrow lane between the hills on the west and the river. Cool and grateful was the shady vale. Jessamine and frangipanni and acacia, bent low beneath the weight of last night's showers and sweetened the air: birds, few in species but many in number, burst into song as we passed. A little wren, that had its habitation beneath the eaves of the sugar-house — doubtless a descendant of those who sang carols to Josephine— delighted me with a trill of melody. We passed beneath a tall silk-cotton tree, hung with silken flowers, about which were buzzing bees and glancing humming-birds; across the stream on rude stepping-stones; a little farther, past groups of mangos, and across a rude bridge, till we reached a cliff, its face hidden behind a veil of vines. Then beneath a wide-spreading mango we halted, and I climbed a great rock and prepared for my morning bath.

There were places in the river better than this, deeper and wider; but there was an association here, clinging to water-rounded bowlders, to gray cliff and gravelly basin, that rendered this little nook doubly charming. It was the favorite resort of Josephine, where daily, at early morning, she came to bathe. This tradition has been handed down from parent to child among the negroes, whose ancestors were slaves here, on this very estate, and is better based than the tales of distant biographers. "*Le bain de l'Impératrice*," it is called to this day. Though time and flood and earthquake have changed it much since then, and its original proportions somewhat lessened, it still remains, with solid towering rocks on one side, and bowlders above and below, as in the days of her who once blessed it with her presence.

It must have been somewhere on this very path, if not within a gunshot of this same bathing-pool, that Josephine met the Sibyl who prophesied so truly her future fate: "You will be married soon; that union will not be happy; you will become a widow, and then — then you will be Queen of France!"

It is not difficult to imagine her here again, sporting, dancing, along the bank of this rocky stream. From her own pen we have a glimpse of her at that period, one hundred years ago: "I ran, I jumped, I danced, from morning to night. Why restrain the wild movements of my childhood?"

And this maiden, who graced in later life the *salons* of an emperor, who lives in the memory of the people as a creation of our own generation, this "lovely creole," passed the happiest days of her existence *here;* roamed over these very hills, danced along these self-same valleys; gazed perhaps upon this same silk-cotton that rears its towering crown above me now!

One hundred years ago!

Leaving the river, we climbed the hills to the west and began our search for birds. Above a tangled mass of thorny acacia hovered a tiny humming-bird, with slender beak and pointed helmet, darting at the spicy blossoms of an unknown vine; gold and silver was he in the sunshine. The little gem dropped into the thicket, with quivering wings that never again would bear their owner upward. Quickly my little companion darted forward to tear the vines apart to get at the bird which lay upon the ground beneath.

He had hardly forced his hand through, when he uttered a shriek of terror and fell back, then ran quickly to me and clung to my legs, trembling and weeping. Pointing to the bushes, he faintly murmured, "*Fer de Lance.*"

Cautiously approaching, I saw a wicked-looking head, belonging to a snake as large around as my arm. It was broad, triangular in shape, and flat, with gleaming eyes, and thrust itself toward us savagely, murder in its every look and motion. My gun was charged for another humming-bird, and the load of small shot I fired into the snake did not cause its death, and it unwound itself and crawled rapidly toward us, its eyes flashing fire, intent upon striking us with its fangs, one blow of which would cause certain death. When he got within reach of a stout cudgel my boy handed me, I mauled him so severely that he gave up the ghost after a short but severe fight; for the "*Fer de Lance*" is no coward, and, like the rattlesnake, will fight even fire.

I soon had the satisfaction of seeing him hanging limp and lifeless from my stick, drops of deadly poison dripping from his jaws. Between shot and cudgel he got badly mangled, and made a sorry specimen for preservation; I substituted for him a smaller one, killed later in the day, to send to Washington. Nothing could induce my boy to retrieve the bird, and, relying upon his sagacity, I did not myself make the attempt.

Finally, about eleven o'clock, we reached the summit of the hill overlooking the valley toward the bay. I sat down upon a grassy knoll, beneath the shade of a small tulip-tree, and feasted my eyes upon the prospect. The sea was like glass, upon the bay rested the three little islets which give the bourg of *Trois-Ilets* its name. Beyond the bay, five miles away, lay Fort de France, and yet farther were the extinct volcanoes of the *Trois Pitons*, and away east, just a hint of the Atlantic. Below me rolled hill and valley, enclosing in their embrace La Pagerie, birthplace of Josephine.

Never was scene more peaceful, nor solitude more sweet. Little wonder that Josephine should recur to it in memory again and again, when surrounded by the pomp and magnificence of courts. An hour passed, I lay in silent musing, gazing on the waving fields and shimmering sea:

" 'Tis the fervid tropic noontime ; faint and low the sea-waves beat ;
Hazy rise the inland mountains through the glimmer of the heat."

From this day-dream I was rudely awakened by a tremor of the earth beneath me; it seemed to tremble, to vibrate; and then ensued that feeling of uncertainty that one experiences when, at the crest of a mighty wave, he is about to descend into abysmal depths, with his heart in his mouth.

Sadly I retraced my steps, not so much in love, I fear, with this beautiful spot, as an hour before the shock.

That afternoon, the river came down from the mountains a roaring torrent, washing away a bridge and a great deal of cane along its banks; and my host lamented the loss of several hundred francs the flood had cost him. That night, another earthquake occurred, which awoke me all too rudely and caused me to reflect upon the strength of the thin strips of bamboo, above my head, that had supported the heavy tiles for a hundred years.

My little garcon went with me to the boat at early morn, and wept bitterly because I would not take him with me; and I left him, regardless of my douceur of silver, a picture of rags and melancholy.

CHAPTER XIX.

ASCENT OF THE GUADELOUPE SOUFRIERE.

POINT A PITRE. — THE RIVIERE SALEE. — USINES. — EARTHQUAKE, FIRE AND HURRICANE. — A LIVING BULWARK. — THE CARAVELS OF COLUMBUS. — OUR LADY OF GUADELOUPE. — THE CARIBS. — BASSE TERRE. — LE PERE LABAT. — ORPHANS. — THE CHOLERA PLAGUE. — A PERMIS DE CHASSE. — MIXED. — A HORSE WITH POINTS. — GOVERNMENT SQUARE. — THE CONVENT. — A SUMMER RETREAT. — MATOUBA. — MY THATCHED HUT. — DOCTOR COLARDEAU. — THE COOLIE. — THE COFFEE PLANTATION. — FIRST COFFEE IN THE WEST INDIES. — ITS CULTIVATION. — TEMPERATURE OF THE COFFEE REGION. — BLOSSOMS AND FRUIT. — PICKING AND PREPARING. — THE HIGH WOODS. — THEIR GRANDEUR. — GIANT TREES. — HUGE BUTTRESSES. — LIANAS, ROPES AND CABLES. — EPIPHYTES AND PARASITES. — AERIAL GARDENS. — THE SULPHUR STREAM. — THE CONE. — THE SUMMIT. — THE PORTAL. — BLASTS OF HOT AIR. — NATURE'S ARCANA. — SULPHUR CRYSTALS. — ERUPTIONS. — A GRAND VIEW. — IMPENETRABLE FORESTS. — AN EXTINCT BIRD. — JUAN PONCE DE LEON. — THE FOUNTAIN OF YOUTH. — THE DESCENT INTO GLOOM.

IT was in the height of the "hurricane season," in August, that I left Isle of Martinique, the birthplace of Josephine, for Guadeloupe. At four o'clock, one calm morning, we steamed into the harbor of Point à Pitre, Guadeloupe's metropolis, and fired a gun. It was very dark; only the light-house lamp sent its gleam abroad; but in an hour the water about us was alive with boats.

Guadeloupe is separated into two islands, one of volcanic origin, uneven and mountainous, the other low and flat, without even a hill. A narrow creek divides them — a shallow, salt passage, called the Rivière Salée. The banks of this creek are lined with mangroves; and it is one of the hottest places in the West Indies, as my shooting excursions verified. Point à Pitre is situated at the southern mouth of this

POINT A PITRE.

salt river. It is regularly built, with broad, straight streets, with a fountain in the center of a square, a fine cathedral, and many good houses. Here is, also, one of the largest *usines*, or factories for making sugar, in the world, second only to the largest known — that of the khedive of Egypt.

What strikes the visitor with surprise is the *new*

appearance of all the buildings, and the scarcity of trees. The explanation of this is found in the records of the city; it is just recovering from the effects of a destructive fire. Within the past few years Point à Pitre has passed through at least four trying ordeals by the elements. First, it was shaken down by an earthquake; then all the buildings were of stone, large and massive. Rebuilding their city, these indomitable Frenchmen constructed their houses of wood. It was not long, not many years, before, in the language of my informant, "there came along the tallest kind of a hurricane, and tumbled their wooden houses into ruins." To add to the horrors, a fire broke out, which swept their city clean. The wise men cogitated, how to build to escape earthquake, fire, and hurricane. The result was the adoption of the present system of construction, with strong iron frame, filled in with brick or composite. The loss of life in these successive disasters has been fearful, but these courageous creoles have faith in the future of their city; and I doubt if they once give a thought to the mighty power against which they are contending, or that they are fighting forces controlled by Nature's laws, that always will operate in the same way and place, without regard to the little doings of mankind.

But it was not to remain in Point à Pitre that I came here; the blue mountains forty miles away beckoned me to their cool retreats, and before night I had engaged passage on board a little schooner, the "Siren," for Basse Terre, at the foot of the mountains. I left Point à Pitre in the evening — the sea like glass, the mosquitoes like fiends. For many hours we drifted aimlessly. The cabin was a black hole full of merchandise, and I was obliged to sleep on deck, which was covered with negroes. With a bulwark of fat and garrulous negroes, men and women, on either side of me, I stretched myself upon a narrow ledge and fell asleep. If those blacks had given way, I would have been lost. To their credit be it said, they did not, but sat there the livelong night, and soothed me to sleep with the musical numbers of their patois. The night was dark, the sky black, with stars, shining in it as through holes in a vaulted roof. In the middle of the night there came up a rain-storm, driving, pitiless. Awakened by the plashing of drops in my face, I drew my rubber poncho over me and fell asleep again to the murmur of their patter on the waves.

These are historic waters. I was coasting a shore along which sailed the caravels of Columbus; but even the consciousness of this fact could not induce me to go to the rail and peer into the darkness for some ancient landmark. Spite of historic reminiscence, and in spite of my odorous enclosure of natives, I slept the sleep of the just man who is taking his second night's rest in his clothes; thanks to years of camp life.

I have said that this was historic ground, this island of Guadeloupe, and fraught with deeds dear to America's existence, these waters that lave its shores. Let me quote, in confirmation, the words of Irving as he describes the second voyage of Columbus: "The islands among which Columbus had arrived were a part of that beautiful cluster called by some the Antilles, which sweep almost in a semicircle from the eastern end of Porto Rico to the coast of Paria on the Southern continent. . . . . During the first day that he entered this archipelago, Columbus saw no less than six islands of different magnitude. After seeking in vain for good anchorage at Dominica, he stood for another of the group, to which he gave the name of his ship, Marigalante. Here he landed, displayed the royal banner, and took possession of the archipelago in the name of his sovereigns. The island appeared to be uninhabited; a rich and dense forest overspread it; some of the trees were in blossom, others laden with unknown fruits, others possessing spicy odors, among which was one with the leaf of the laurel and the fragrance of the clove. Hence they made sail for an island of larger size, with a remarkable mountain; one peak, which proved afterward the crater of a volcano, rose to a great height, with streams of water gushing from it." [This is the volcano I hope to reach by and by.] "As they approached within three leagues, they beheld a cataract of such height that, to use the words of the narrator, it seemed to be falling from the sky. As it broke into foam in its descent, many at first believed it to be a stratum of white rock. To this island, which was called by the natives *Turuqueira*, the admiral gave the name of Guadeloupe, having promised the monks of Our Lady of Guadeloupe, in Estremadura, to call some newly-discovered place after their convent. Landing here on the 4th of November, 1493, they visited a village near the shore, the inhabitants of which fled in affright, leaving their children behind in their terror and confusion. The island on this side extended for a distance of five-and-twenty leagues, diversified with lofty mountains and broad plains."

This was the first island in which Columbus saw

the wonderful *Caribs*, of whom he had heard so much in Hispaniola. The account he gave of their neat villages, of the finding here of the fragment of a vessel, and the first pine-apple, is extremely interesting, as are all descriptions of first things, or the discovery of things previously unknown, to us of the present day.

And this coast, which I later saw in all its grandeur of lofty cliffs and towering mountains, in its loveliness of curving bays and palm-bordered beaches, this coast was right abeam, hidden behind the impenetrable wall of night. A second time I sought a landing on Guadeloupe shore before daylight. We sailed into the roadstead of Basse Terre, on the open sea at the southern end of the island. Darkness covered everything; a few cocks commenced crowing, a few lights gleamed out. At five, a gun boomed out from the fort, and the cathedral bell commenced at once, as if from the vibration, tolling for early mass. Daylight crawled slowly in and revealed the open market by the landing, already crowded with people, the noise of whose wrangling had reached us long since.

Basse Terre is the seat of government of Guadeloupe, as Fort de France is that of Martinique. Like Fort de France, also, it is chosen by these far-seeing Frenchmen as the dépôt of government property, that other towns, like that of Point à Pitre, and St. Pierre of Martinique, may not, by their superior advantages for commerce and trade, draw all the population thither. To this end, the distribution of wealth, and the better cultivation of the soil, the French have covered both their islands with roads, in striking contrast to the rough bridle-paths of the English islands equally mountainous. The government buildings are in the upper part of the town between two rivers, behind a large stone fort. They surround three sides of a square bordered by mighty palmistes, and with an elegant fountain of bronze as center-piece. North and east of the town tower the mountains, the land commencing to rise to their summits at its very outskirts; its upper streets lead into the hills. The houses are built of stone, but are not large or pretentious. The streets are straight, parallel with the shore, and at right angles with it. In the center of the town is an open market-place, in which is a fountain fed from the mountains, around which is a row of tamarind trees. All the serving-women of the place come to this fountain to fill their jars with the cool water that perpetually drips from the bronze lips of the basin. The cathedral, or more properly the *Basilique*, is a good old structure of stone, dating from the time of Le Père Labat.

As the founder of this town, and an author of note, whose valuable book on the Antilles contains the most comprehensive account of these islands, this worthy père deserves especial notice. Born in Paris in 1663, he joined the Dominican friars in 1685, and two years later was appointed professor of mathematics and philosophy at Nancy. In 1693, while in Paris, he saw letters from the Superior of that order in Martinique to the Brothers in France, imploring them to send out missionaries to replace those who had died from contagious disease. Seizing this opportunity for consecrating himself to mission work, and carrying out a resolution he had a long time cherished, he departed for Martinique, arriving there in January,

1694. Two years later he was sent to Guadeloupe. Later, returning to Martinique, he found his place occupied by another, and was, as a mark of confidence, appointed *procureur général* of the mission. In this capacity he visited all the isles of the Antilles, French, English, and Dutch; but passed the greater portion of his time in Martinique and Guadeloupe. In 1703 he founded the town of Basse Terre, and took an active part in the defence of the island against the attack of the English, in March of the same year. The "Bellicose *Père Blanc*," as he was called by the people of the island, could not prevent his monastery from being burned, by which disaster he lost all his books, manuscripts, and instruments. He returned to France in 1705, resided in Paris and Rome, and in the former city prepared his different voyages for publication. He there died in 1738. His most important work, "*Nouveau Voyage aux Iles d'Amérique*," is as valuable as it is at the present time rare. It was published in Paris in 1722. He wrote, besides, six large works of travel, chiefly from the manuscripts of other travelers. A genus of plants, containing a species indigenous to Cuba and one to Cayenne, was named, in his honor, *Labatia*. The old Basilique remains, in defiance of earthquakes and hurricanes, a monument to the activity and zeal of this good father. Its front, however, was rebuilt a few years ago.

During my stay in Basse Terre I was struck by the number of children fatherless and motherless, and upon inquiry was told that these orphans, whose sweet faces so appealed to one's sympathy, were survivors of the great cholera plague not many years since, in which some fifteen thousand persons, I believe, were swept away. Outside the town, but a few minutes' walk along the bluff, lies the cemetery, where crosses and quaint tombs mark the last resting-places of many poor souls. Beyond, below this place of sepulchre, is a depression in the hillside, which, I was told, was once a deep ravine, into which were cast the bodies of those who died of the plague. So rapidly were they stricken down that people enough could not be found to bury them, and the living hardly sufficed to take away the dead. Finally vessels were employed, which, laden with corpses, departed one after the other into the offing with their freight of death. There was scant ceremony in the carrying away of these stricken ones from the place where once they had enjoyed life to be given over to the dwellers of the deep! For many months the corpses strewed the strand, and fish from the sea were banished from the tables of the island for a twelvemonth after. What is remarkable in this plague is, that it extended to the higher and generally healthy mountain villages, and killed as ruthlessly as along the heated coast.

The heat in town was intense, and I was glad to be allowed to depart for the mountains, after having been compelled to wait for my permit to shoot. Every one desirous of shooting in these islands is compelled to pay ten francs for a *permis de chasse*, which the French official, with characteristic courtesy to a stranger, gave me without the usual fee. It was a lengthy document, exceeding in size my American passport from the Secretary of State; and, in the comparison of the two papers, each of which affects to describe me accurately, there is much food for reflection upon the fallibility of passport-makers. Indeed, were I furnished with a few more *accurate* descriptions, I should certainly lose my identity and wander about in a maze of uncertainty, feeling, like those immortal twins, decidedly mixed. My American description gives my eyes as brown, mouth small, nose straight, hair brown, and face oval. To this a justice of the peace has affixed hand and seal. A French official, in the name of the governor, positively asserts that eyes and eyebrows are black, mouth large (*bouche grande*), nose aquiline, "*visage ovale*," and complexion *blanc*— which is supposed to be light. To avoid any unpleasantness with the numerous *gendarmes* who patrol the country, I carried both papers.

Armed, then, with my *permis de chasse*, and sped on my way with a hearty *bon voyage* from the chief of police, I turned my horse's head toward the mountains. He was a picturesque animal, that horse; and when I say picturesque, I use the term in its most artistic sense, for by no other can I do justice to his many projecting points, bold features, and rough angularities. He, indeed, was a horse of many points — good ones, too, perhaps, in a certain sense. Hanging my umbrella from one of his shoulder-blades, and grasping his mane with one hand, I vaulted into the dilapidated saddle, deeply sunken between loins and withers. With a groan he started forward, putting in motion his somewhat formidable array of joints, and I ascended the hills to the rattle of bones.

Beyond the government buildings is the Convent of Versailles, where the girls of the island are educated; and higher up, occupying a broad plateau some fifteen hundred feet above the sea, is the summer camp of the governor and the troops. Spacious buildings, including a hospital, barracks, and governor's house, are almost hidden by trees, among which the palmiste towers conspicuous with its gray column and green coronet. Passing these, my road led me to a little hamlet on the mountain-side overlooking the Caribbean Sea, called *Matouba*. Nearly all its little thatched houses were full, as the people of Basse Terre, all who can afford it, come up here at this, the sickly season, to enjoy the baths and the cool air. Through the kindness of a friend I was able to hire a small room, one of two, in a little thatched hut eighteen feet by fourteen. The other half, separated by a partition, over which I could easily make a hand-spring, was occupied by the owner of the house, his wife, brother, and three children. Contentedly I swung my hammock from two corners of the room, thanking a good Providence that I could enjoy all by myself as much room as sufficed for the other six.

For ten days I remained in Matouba, roaming over the coffee plantations and climbing the hills in quest of birds. Many streams dash hurriedly down from the mountain, and there are waterfalls and cascades, and high up the hill is the *bain chaud*, a warm spring difficult of access. Tired of the continual rain, and wishing for the society of some one speaking my own language, I set off one morning, under guidance of my boy "Co-co," to find the mayor of a neighboring commune — the commune of St. Claude — who could, I was told, speak English. Passing through the little village, I entered a higher region devoted to coffee plantations, and climbed to a spur of the Soufrière, right beneath the volcano itself, where I found a comfortable little country house, was greeted in English by the proprietor, who had heard of me before, and welcomed. A delightful week was passed here, for my host, Monsieur Colardeau, was a graduate of Yale College, and had lived in America, practicing his profession of physician, for eighteen years. He was a naturalist withal, and the remainder of that day was devoted to the animal life of the mountains, and especially the birds.

The "hurricane season," from July through October, is one of calms, tempests, and rains, and it was several days before the weather cleared sufficiently for me to undertake the ascent of the Soufrière. At last, one night, just before the sun dipped beneath the sea, the jagged outlines of the volcano showed against a clear sky, and my friend predicted a fair day for the morrow. At daybreak, the Indian provided by my friend came for me; not an Indian native to the island, they were long since extinct, but one from the far East, the land to which Columbus in his voyages thought he was discovering a shorter route — an Indian under indenture, a coolie from Calcutta. He brought a knapsack full of provisions which Madame Colardeau had provided the night before, and he carried upon his head my photographic apparatus, and marched before me into the mists of the morning which came pouring down from the mountain-tops. After drinking a cup of black coffee, I seized my gun and followed my guide.

Behind the house, far up the slope, stretched a broad area of coffee-trees, an inheritance, this coffee estate, from the ancestors of Monsieur Colardeau, who in no particular allowed it to deteriorate from its pristine vigor of a century ago. Coffee-trees of many years' growth grew by the side of young plants set out to replace the aged and enfeebled ones. The plantation is divided into small squares a few hundred feet in length, by long rows of quick-growing trees called *pois douce*, *pomme rose*, and oleander. This is to protect the tender coffee-plants from the wind, and from the hurricanes which sometimes ravage these islands. These long rows of high trees give the coffee estates a striated appearance at a distance. The coffee-tree is allowed to grow to a height of but six or eight feet, as this insures more perfect berries and renders the gathering easier. The younger plants are further protected and shaded by plantains and bananas, which attain a great height in a twelvemonth.

Coffee was early introduced into the West Indies. It is said that, of three plants entrusted to the captain of the first vessel bringing it, two died, and that the remaining one was only kept alive by water withheld from a famishing crew. The first coffee was grown in Martinique; hence, though that island does not raise enough for its own consumption at the present time, all coffee exported from Guadeloupe is known as "Martinique coffee." Its cultivation is easy and pleasant, although somewhat expensive and difficult during the first years of its growth. Being generally situated on the mountains, the coffee plantations are considered as the most healthy and desirable places of residence in the West Indies. At the height of two thousand feet, in the mountains of Guadeloupe, the temperature varies from fifty-five degrees, Fahrenheit, during the winter months, to eighty degrees during the hottest days of August. A few miles below, on the sea-shore, it reaches one hundred degrees.

The coffee-plants are raised from seeds generally sown in beds. When from fifteen to eighteen months old, the plants are transplanted from the nurseries into the fields at a distance of six feet apart each way. The young trees sometimes give a light crop in the third year from setting out, and increase in yield from that time for several years. A coffee-tree is in its full strength and beauty at the age of twenty years, and will last a century. The tree blossoms, generally, every month from February to May. The fruit ripens from August to January, and is picked carefully by hand, there being ripe and green berries on the same branches, and, indeed, often blossoms also. As soon as the berries are all removed, the trees commence blossoming again, and so on for many years. The fruit, or "berry," as it is called, is red, and somewhat resembles a cherry, and is quite sweet. The kernel, which is the coffee, is divided into two parts with their flat sides adhering.

After having been picked from the trees, the berries are passed through a mill made for the purpose, which divides the red pulpy skins from the kernel. These last, which are the only parts saved, after a slight fermentation of a few hours, in order to remove the mucilaginous coating with which they are covered, are washed freely in cold water and then dried in the sun. They are still covered, after being dried, with a tough, yellowish pellicle, which is removed by placing the coffee in large mortars with ovoidal bottoms, made of hard wood or iron, and under the action of heavy rounded pestles, working like the fulling-mills of woolen factories. Beneath these pestles, which are generally worked by water-power, the pellicles are broken off into small scales, like bran, and the coffee liberated. The whole is then carried to the fanning-mill, from which the coffee comes out freed from the chaff. Lastly, the coffee is spread upon large tables, and all the black, brown, or broken grains removed by hand; though this is done only for the superior article called *café bonifieur*, which has a local value of two cents more per pound than that not thus treated.

Nearly all the coffee raised in the island goes to France, where it is much sought after; but it is expensive, its value being, in the island itself, from twenty-three to twenty-six cents, when purchased from the producers. Mocha coffee is raised only in small quantities, but it is of excellent quality. In order to increase the cultivation of coffee, the colonial government has lately offered a premium of forty dollars for every new *hectare* (two acres) thus planted. The coffee plantations do not interfere with the sugar estates, as they are generally on the mountains, while the latter occupy land near the seashore. There are, at present, nine hundred and sixty-five coffee estates in Guadeloupe. This description of coffee-culture was given me by Monsieur Colardeau.

From the glossy green leaves gleamed berries, yellow and red, giving a beautiful effect. In one of the squares I observed a large bed of strawberries, the only ones I have seen in these islands. Higher up I found a species of *rubus*, a raspberry found only in high altitudes, and the only representative of its family in these wilds. Beyond the limits of the coffee grove we came upon the borders of the high-woods, where one must go to see the vegetation of the tropics in its greatest perfection of growth and luxuriance.

There is a suggestiveness of giant trees and a refreshing thought of cool retreats in the appellation, universal throughout these islands, bestowed upon these high forests, to distinguish them from those of the lowland. As you set foot over the sharply-defined line of demarkation, you leave the sun with his scorching beams behind, and enter a gloomy arch beneath a canopy of leaves. The trail is sinuous and slippery, and winds beneath huge trees, which we feel — for we cannot see their crowns — rear their heads aloft. Overhead is a leafy vault, through which the sun cannot send a gleam, save now and then a needle ray; and through this vaulted roof are thrust up the trunks of mighty trees, with a diameter, from buttress to buttress, of twenty feet. And these broad buttresses, which spread out on every side as supports to the main trunk, are studies in themselves. In the spaces between them there is room to pitch a tent. Fifty, sixty feet up, begin the broad-armed limbs, which spread over a vast area; and from these limbs depend attractive and wonderful ropes and cordage of nature's making, which descend from out the canopy above as from the zenith of heaven, and touching the earth, climb again into space, no one knows where, no one knows how. They are of all sizes, and twisted into every conceivable shape — some like huge hawsers and cables, and others small as basslines and stretched as straight and taut as the rigging of a ship. Surrounded by the net-work of lianes and lialines alone, the trunks would be barely visible; but this is not all. Up their rough circumference creep vines and climbing-plants, clinging closely and firmly by multitudinous rootlets, hung with broad and pendulous leaves. Attached again to the vines and lianes are groups and clusters of epiphytic and parasitic plants, some like pine-apples, some large as cabbages, some like huge callas; and among them ferns and tillandsias, scores of species, piled, plant after plant, one above the other, in seeming confusion, each striving for a foothold in its aerial world. Now and then there will be a great spike of blossoms, crimson, scarlet, or pure white, at which a humming-bird will dart, fluttering up and down, the whole scene reminding one of those lines in "Evangeline," where the vines —

"Hung their ladder of ropes aloft, like the ladder of Jacob,
On whose pendulous stairs the angels, ascending, descending,
Were the swift humming-birds, that flitted from blossom to blossom."

No sound broke the solemn stillness of this mountain forest save the cooing of a distant wood-pigeon, and nothing showed itself except an occasional *perdrix*, or mountain partridge, as it flitted like a ghost across our path. Up and higher we ascended; the trees diminished in size, and there came to our ears the murmur of falling water, which we could not see, from the rankness of the vegetation. *Balisiers*, or wild plantains, with broad green leaves and spikes of crimson and golden cups, now lined the trail, and glorious tree-ferns, in majesty of beauty unsurpassed, spread their leaves above them.

We reached the stream, and found it warm — so

hot that vapor arose on this not too cool atmosphere. It was sulphur-impregnated, also, as the discolored leaves abundantly testified, and flowed over a bituminous bed. The luxuriance of the vegetation here was marvelous, and pen of mine cannot describe the beauty of the ferns, orchids, and parasites, arches and bridges of tropical trees and ferns, that overhung and spanned this tepid stream. A few rods farther up we came upon a basin of colorless water, walled off with blocks of lava, the overflow of which formed the stream. At it I cast a wistful glance, but could only stop to feel its warmth with my hand and note the beauty of the banks of ferns above it. Here we left my apparatus, plunged anew into a depth of greenwood, and commenced an ascent that, for steepness, left all former paths behind. We had to lift ourselves up by successive broad steps, and cling to roots and trees for aid.

Emerging from the darkness of this tunnel-like passage, we came upon another zone of vegetation, where the trees were dwarfed to shrubs, and so intertwined and matted together that a path had to be cut with the cutlass. Every native laborer of these islands carries a large and ugly-looking *machete*, or cutlass, nearly two and a half feet long and two inches broad, which serves them in a variety of ways. There we found the path washed into deep, cistern-like cavities, down which we descended on one side only to climb out at the other. After much hard work this rough road was gone over, and we came abruptly upon a plain of small extent, and, looking up, saw the cone whose side we fain would climb. Straight before us was the trail of former tourists, which climbed directly up the mountain-side, so steep it seemed impossible to ascend it. There was no vegetation now to obstruct the view. All about us the plain and steep acclivity was covered with a matted carpet of coarse grass. Immediately above us towered an immense rock, so delicately poised and so far-jutting, that it appeared ready to fall. Undoubtedly, the next earthquake will dislodge and hurl it below, to join its fellows that thickly stud the plain beneath. For an hour and a half, with many stops for breath, we mounted upward, and made a final pause beneath the rock to gather strength to meet the tempest of wind that howled above. Here my taciturn guide pointed out a narrow ledge where a man died of exhaustion, and was found at midnight by my informant, who was sent in search of him, on his knees, with his face covered with his hands.

Imagine an immense pyramid, truncated by some internal force that has rent the sides at the same time, leaving the summit-plane strewn with huge rocks, and reft in twain by a mighty chasm, and you have the Soufrière of Guadeloupe at the present day. We followed a narrow path over sounding rocks that told of caverns beneath, and entered, through a great portal formed by two adjacent rocks, upon a plateau covered with a carpet of sphagnum and lycopodium, spangled with pink blossoms, wild hemp, and yellow, trumpet-shaped flowers. Narrow trails crossed and recrossed this little track, like rivers on a map. It was now eleven o'clock, and we stopped to lunch at the portal, — for, since my coffee, I had not tasted food that day, — then pursued our way across the plateau. We reached a dark chasm, made as though

ASCENT OF THE GUADELOUPE SOUFRIERE. 341

THE SOUFRIERE OF GUADELOUPE.

some Titan had rent the solid rock asunder — so deep that we could not see the bottom of the dark abyss until we stood upon a narrow bridge of rock that spanned the central space. The southern end is a perpendicular wall, running down into depths the eye cannot penetrate. From a fissure near its base arose blue fumes which stained the face of the cliff a long way up, as though away down in the earth's center, where the Vulcans are at work, there burned a very hot coal fire.

We crossed the bridge and scaled the opposite cliff, and were greeted, at the top, with loud blasts and snorts, like those of a high-pressure steamer, and volumes of vapor blown in our faces. Following this, I found an aperture in a mound of stones, sulphur-lined, only a few inches in diameter, through which was forced a column of steam with noises so loud that we could not hear each other speak. This aperture is in the center of a desolate area, having on its borders numerous openings, whence issue blasts of hot air that taint the atmosphere for many feet around. I peered into one, arched like an oven, and it was like a glimpse into the arcana of nature, — into the miniature palace of a *génie*, — for the whole interior was encrusted with sulphur crystals glistening like yellow topaz; and a small black passage led down into unknown depths, whence issued rumblings, groans, and grumblings. Up from this black throat came such blasts of old Vulcan's fetid breath, that I was glad to escape with only a few crumbling crystals for my pains. Ravines seam the sides of the cone in every direction, some spanned by natural bridges of rock; but that to which I constantly recurred was that central gorge, with its wicked-looking throat, from which there have been two eruptions recorded — one in 1797, the other in 1815. Doubtless it will again, at some future time, act as the vent for the internal ebullitions of mother earth.

According to Humboldt, the summit is over five thousand feet above the sea, and the view afforded me, as an occasional rift occurred in the masses of mist, was grand beyond description. Climbing to an elevated rock, I obtained shelter from the terrific gale that nearly swept me off my feet, and awaited a break in the cloud of mist. It came: I looked upon a scene well worth a year of common life to view. Beneath me, in full view, were those six islands discovered by Columbus on that memorable November day in 1493. Far away, east by north, lay Désirade, the first land seen by Columbus on his second voyage, a low, table-surfaced rock. South by east lay Dominica, looking like a glorious vision of cloud-land, the first of the Caribbees at which Columbus touched; and east, right below, the island of Marigalante, where first in this archipelago the royal banner of Spain was displayed. I looked down to the eastward, over a sloping plain of verdure, upon forest almost as impenetrable and wide-spreading as on that day, nearly four centuries ago, when it resounded to the blasts of trumpets and the firing of arquebuses. For, the second day of his arrival here, one of the captains of the great admiral's fleet strayed into the forest with some men and was lost. For several days they wandered in trackless forest so dense as almost to exclude the light of day. "Some, who were experienced seamen, climbed the trees to get a sight of the stars by which to govern their course, but the spreading branches and thick foliage shut out all view of the heavens." A party sent in search wearied themselves in wading the many streams, which number, at this day, more than fifty.

Almost under the cliffs of the volcano lay the Saintes, a cluster of rocky islets discovered on All-Saints' Day. There is a significance and poetic meaning attached to every name bestowed by Columbus on these islands, as witness those already mentioned. With but few exceptions, fortunately, they retain his perfect appellations. Away north is the triple crown of Montserrat, and I fancied I could discover the dim outlines of St. Kitts, an island named probably for the good giant who bore his lord aloft, rather than for the great navigator who discovered it. Farther yet, and forty miles out of sight, lies St. Eustatius, where the American flag was *first* saluted by a foreign power; and a few miles beyond is Saba, a single volcanic peak, ending on the north this chain of volcanic islands. The Virgin Isles, named for St. Ursula and her ten thousand virgins, yet farther lie obscured. Nearer is Antigua, but low and dim. The curtains of mist again drew together, and I prepared to descend.

This mountain was once the home of a bird of ill-omen, (described in former pages,) the *Diablotin*, or "Little Devil," which lived in holes in the rocks, and was hunted with dogs by the planters in olden time. Its discovery was my principal motive for ascending the Soufrière; but I returned without finding a trace of its existence. Fatigued, and bathed in perspiration, I arrived at the hot bath, on the borders of the high-woods, and plunged into its limpid waters; but half an hour's immersion in its tepid current removed every trace of weariness, and I floated blissfully until the sinking sun warned me to be on the march again.

Years ago — three hundred and sixty-five — there landed upon this island of Guadeloupe, Juan Ponce de Leon, noblest and gentlest of all those old *conquistadores*, fresh from his discovery of Florida. But two years previously he had sailed in quest of that wonderful fountain of youth, lured on by the tales of the Indians of Cuba. And who knows but that he was still seeking that fountain of rejuvenescence when he essayed to explore these wilds and met with disastrous defeat from the Caribs? I have floated on the glassy surface of the wonderful spring of Wakulla, in Florida, and one winter's day sailed down the bright waters of Silver Spring, and do not wonder that the simple natives should invest these mysterious creations with occult power. But it is a pity that the old Spaniard could not have found this mountain spring, one dip in which were worth a month's immersion in those of Florida.

A velvet-backed humming-bird came down from the odorous banks above me — a tiny bird, with a Latin name too long to mention here — and danced in the sunlight, his garnet throat glowing like a coal in the departing beams, as I bade farewell to this enchanted spot and descended into the deep gloom of the high-woods.

APPENDIX.

From Proceedings of United States National Museum.

A General Catalogue of the Birds noted from the Islands of the Lesser Antilles visited by Frederick A. Ober; with a Table showing their Distribution, and those found in the United States.

By George N. Lawrence.

		Birds of the Lesser Antilles.	Barbuda.	Antigua.	Guadeloupe.	Dominica.	Martinique.	St. Vincent.	Grenada.	United States.
	*1	Turdus nigrirostris, Lawr							X	
	2	Turdus caribbæus, Lawr							X	X	
	3	Turdus?					X				
	4	Margarops herminieri (Lafr.)			X	X	X	X		
	5	Margarops densirostris (Vieill.)		X	X	X	X	X		
	6	Margarops montanus (Vieill.)			X	X	X	X		
	7	Ramphocinclus brachyurus (Vieill.)					X			
	8	Cinclocerthia ruficauda, Gould	X		X	X		X		
	9	Cinclocerthia gutturalis, Lafr						X		
	10	Mimus gilvus, Vieill							X	X	
	11	Myiadestes genibarbis, Sw				X	X			
	12	Myiadestes sibilans, Lawr						X		
	13	Thryothorus rufescens, Lawr				X	X			
	14	Thryothorus musicus, Lawr						X		
	15	Thryothorus grenadensis, Lawr							X	
	16	Thryothorus martinicensis, Scl.					X			
	17	Siurus nævius (Bodd.)		X	X	X				X
	18	Siurus motacilla (Vieill.)		X						X

* New Species in small capitals.

Catalogue of Birds. — Continued.

		Birds of the Lesser Antilles.	Barbuda	Antigua	Guadeloupe	Dominica	Martinique	St. Vincent	Grenada	United States
Wood warblers	19	Dendrœca virens (Gm.)				X				X
"	20	DENDRŒCA PLUMBEA, Lawr			X	X				
"	21	Dendrœca petechia var. ruficapilla (Gm.)	X	X						
"	22	DENDRŒCA PETECHIA VAR. MELANOPTERA, Lawr			X	X				
"	23	Dendrœca rufigula, Baird						X		
Wren	24	LEUCOPEZA BISHOPI, Lawr						X		
Hyacinthy Greenlet	25	Setophaga ruticilla (Linn.)		X	X	X	X	X	X	X
"	26	Vireosylvia calidris (Linn.)		X						
"	27	VIREOSYLVIA CALIDRIS VAR. DOMINICANA, Lawr			X	X	X	X	X	
Martin	28	Progne dominicensis (Gm.)				X	X	X	X	
Swallow	29	Hirundo horreorum, Barton			X					
Sugar Bird	30	Certhiola dominicana, Taylor	X	X	X	X				
"	31	CERTHIOLA SACCHARINA, Lawr						X		
"	32	CERTHIOLA ATRATA, Lawr						X	X	
"	33	Certhiola martinicana, Reich					X			
Tanager	34	Euphonia flavifrons (Sparm.)			X	X	X	X	X	
Tanager Bird	35	CALLISTE VERSICOLOR, Lawr						X	X	
Tanager	36	Saltator guadeloupensis, Lafr			X	X				
Finch	37	Loxigilla noctis (Linn.)	X	X	X	X	X	X	X	
Finch	38	Phonipara bicolor (Linn.)	X	X	X	X	X	X	X	
Kingbird	39	QUISCALUS LUMINOSUS, Lawr					X			
"	40	Quiscalus inflexirostris, Sw					X			
	41	QUISCALUS GUADELOUPENSIS, Lawr			X					
Hang nest	42	Icterus bonana (Linn)				X				
Tyrant Shrike	43	Elainea martinica (Linn.)			X	X	X	X	X	
"	44	MYIARCHUS OBERI, Lawr	X			X	X	X	X	
"	45	MYIARCHUS SCLATERI, Lawr					X			
"	46	BLACICUS BRUNNEICAPILLUS, Lawr				X				
Tyrant Shrike	47	Tyrannus rostratus, Scl	X	X		X	X	X		
"	48	Tyrannus melancholicus, Vieill							X	
	49	Glaucis hirsutus (Gm.)							X	
Hummingbirds	50	Eulampis jugularis (Linn.)			X	X	X	X		
"	51	Eulampis holosericeus (Linn.)	X	X	X	X	X	X	X	
"	52	Thalurania wagleri (Less.)				X				
"	53	Orthorhynchus exilis (Gm.)	X	X	X	X				
"	54	Orthorhynchus ornatus, Gould						X		
"	55	Orthorhynchus cristatus (Linn.)							X	
Swallow	56	CHÆTURA DOMINICANA, Lawr				X				
"	57	Chætura sp. ?						X	X	
"	58	Chætura sp. ?							X	
"	59	Swift sp. ?					X			

APPENDIX.

Catalogue of Birds. — Continued.

		Birds of the Lesser Antilles.	Barbuda.	Antigua.	Guadeloupe.	Dominica.	Martinique.	St. Vincent.	Grenada.	United States.
Bett Swift	60	Cypseloides niger (Gm.)			X					
Woodpecker	61	Melanerpes l'herminieri (Less.)			X					
Kingfisher	62	Ceryle alcyon (Linn.)			X	X	X	X	X	
"	63	Ceryle torquata (Linn.)			X					
Cuckoo	64	Coccyzus mioor (Gm.)	X	X	X	X	X	X	X	X
"	65	Crotophaga ani, Linn						X	X	
Parrot	66	Chrysotis augusta (Vig.)				X				
"	67	Chrysotis guildingi (Vig.)						X		
"	68	Parrot sp.?				X				
Owl	69	STRIX FLAMMEA VAR. NIGRESCENS, Lawr.				X		X	X	
	70	SPEOTYTO AMAURA, Lawr		X						
Osprey	71	Pandion baliætus (Linn.)			X			X	X	
Buzzard	72	Buteo pennsylvanicus (Wils.)			X			X	X	X
Eagle	73	Uribitioga anthracina (Nitzsch.)?				X				
Hawk	74	Falco communis var. anatum, Bp.?	X	X						X
"	75	Tinnunculus sparverius var. antillarum (Gm.)	X	X	X	X	X		X	X
Frigate bird	76	Fregata aquila (Linn.)	X	X		X	X	X	X	X
Tropic bird	77	Phæthon æthereus (Linn.)			X			X	X	
	78	Phæthon flavirostris, Brandt			X	X		X		X
Pelican	79	Pelecanus fuscus (Linn.)	X	X		X	X	X	X	X
Booby	80	Sula fiber (Linn.)		X				X	X	
Heron	81	Ardea herodias, Linn	X	X			X	X	X	X
"	82	Herodias egretta (Gm.)	X							X
"	83	Garzetta candidissima (Gm.)		X		X		X	X	X
	84	Florida cœrulea (Linn.)		X		X		X	X	X
Whimbrel	85	Butorides virescens (Linn.)	X	X	X	X	X	X	X	X
Night	86	Nyctiardea violacea (Linn.)			X				X	X
Spoonbill	87	Platalea ajaja (Linn.)						X	X	X
Pintail	88	Dafila bahamensis (Linn.)	X	X						
Duck	89	Clangula glaucion (Linn.)	X							X
Pigeons	90	Columba corensis, Gm.			X	X	X	X		
"	91	Columba leucocephala, Linn	X	X						
"	92	Zenaida martinicana, Bp.	X	X	X	X	X	X		
"	93	Chamæpelia passerina (Linn.)	X	X	X	X	X	X		X
"	94	Geotrygon montana (Linn.)			X	X	X	X	X	
	95	Geotrygon mystacea (Temm.)				X				
Guinea fowl	96	Numidia meleagris (Linn.)	X							
Quail	97	Ortyx virginianus (Linn.)		X						X
Rail	98	Rallus crepitans, Gm.	X	X	X					X
"	99	Porzana?							X	
Snake	100	Porphyrio martinicus (Linn.)				X		X		X

Catalogue of Birds. — Continued.

		Birds of the Lesser Antilles.	Barbuda.	Antigua.	Guadeloupe.	Dominica.	Martinique.	St. Vincent.	Grenada.	United States.
Coot Gallinule	101	Gallinula galeata (Licht.)			×				×	×
Coot	102	Fulica ?	×	×					×	×
Plover	103	Squatarola helvetica (Linn.)						×		×
"	104	Charadrius virginicus, Borkh.	×	×	×	×		×		×
Ring Plover	105	Ægialitis semipalmata (Bp.)	×		×			×		×
Plover	106	Strepsilas interpres (Linn.)				×		×		×
Oystercatcher	107	Himantopus nigricollis (Vieill.)	×	×				×		×
Snipe	108	Gallinago wilsoni (Temm.)	×	×				×		×
Sandpiper	109	Tringa minutilla, Vieill. . .						×		×
	110	Tringa maculata (Vieill.)				×				×
Sanderling	111	Calidris arenaria (Linn.)						×		×
Sandpiper	112	Ereunetes petrificatus (Ill.)	×	×	×	×				×
Snipe	113	Symphemia semipalmata (Gm)	×	×						×
	114	Gambetta flavipes (Gm.)	×					×		×
Yellow shanks	115	Gambetta melanoleuca (Gm.)		×				×		×
Salmon Bill	116	Rhyacophilus solitarius (Wils.)	×	×	×			×		×
Sandpiper	117	Tringoides macularius (Linn.)				×	×	×	×	×
Curlew	118	Numenius longirostris (Wils.)						×		×
"	119	Numenius hudsonicus (Lath.)	×	×					×	×
Duck	120	Anous stolidus (Linn.)				×			×	×
Tern	121	Sterna maxima, Bodd.	×	×	×			×	×	×
"	122	Sterna dougalli, Mont.		×		×	×		×	×
'	123	Sterna antillarum (Less.)				×				×
,	124	Sterna fuliginosa (Gm.)			×	×			×	×
"	125	Sterna anæstheta, Scop.				×				×
Gull	126	Larus atricilla (Linn.)	×	×	×				×	×
Petrel	127	Æstrelata ?					×			
Diver	128	Podilymbus podiceps (Linn.) ?	×					×	×	×

The separate catalogues comprised in the above general one are all published in the "Proceedings of the United States National Museum," Washington, Vol. I., that of the Birds of Dominica occupying pp. 46–69; that of St. Vincent, pp. 185–198; those of Antigua and Barbuda, pp. 232–242; that of Grenada, pp. 265–278; that of Martinique, pp. 349–360; that of Guadeloupe, pp. 449–462.

New York, March 20, 1879.

[From the Annals of the New York Academy of Sciences.]
BY GEORGE N. LAWRENCE.

DESCRIPTION OF NEW SPECIES OF BIRDS. ISLAND OF DOMINICA.

AN exploration of some of the least known of the West India islands, for the purpose of elucidating their natural history, has been undertaken by Mr. Fred. A. Ober, of Beverly, Massachusetts, under the auspices of the Smithsonian Institution.

He has already sent every species heretofore obtained in Dominica, with twenty-three additional ones. His first collection consists of one hundred and fifty specimens, embracing thirty-one species, three of which I consider new and have described below. Of this collection he writes as follows: " The first collection was made in the mountains of the Caribbean side of Dominica, though it includes also birds of the lower hills and valleys, there seeming to be but few kinds of the low lands that do not ascend to the mountains; though there are many birds of the mountains and upper valleys that never descend into the low country near the coast."

Besides the three species of humming-birds well known as inhabitants of the island, I was greatly surprised to find another species in the collection, viz., *Thalurania Wagleri*, of which there are seven specimens — all males. The only locality heretofore given for it is Brazil, and it is considered rather rare; it looks now as if its headquarters were Dominica, yet it seems strange that none are recorded from any intermediate place. It would appear to be not uncommon, as more specimens were sent than of *Eulampis holosericeus* and *Orthorhyncus exilis*, which are abundant species. *Eulampis jugularis* was sent in large numbers. On the label of one of the examples of *T. Wagleri* is, " Sulphur lake, 2,300 feet above the sea."

The second collection was made on the eastern or Atlantic side of the island; it contains eighty-two specimens, and has in it ten additional species, but no novelties. There are two specimens of that fine and rare species of parrot, *Chrysotis augusta*.

1. *Thryothorus rufescens.* " Rosignol."

MALE. Entire plumage rufous, much deeper in color above, of a lighter and brighter shade underneath; tail dark rufous, regularly and closely crossed with narrow bars of black; the coloring of the under part of the tail is duller, but is barred in a similar manner; inner webs of quills blackish-brown, outer webs and both webs of the innermost secondaries dark rufous, with distinct narrow bars of black; upper mandible dark-brown, the under yellowish-white; feet pale brown.

Length, $4\frac{7}{8}$ in.; wing, $2\frac{1}{8}$; tail, $1\frac{5}{8}$; tarsus, $\frac{11}{16}$; bill from front, $\frac{9}{16}$; from rictus, $\frac{3}{4}$.

Type in National Museum, Washington.

2. Dendrœca plumbea.

MALE. The whole of the upper plumage is dark plumbeous; a narrow white line extends from the bill, over and beyond the eye, and there is a white mark on the lower eyelid; the lores are black; the under plumage is of a lighter plumbeous than that of the upper; the chin, middle of the throat and of the breast intermixed with white, center of abdomen white; the two middle tail-feathers, and the outer webs of the others, are like the back in color; the inner webs are blackish slate-color; on the inner web of the outer tail-feather, at the end, is a spot of white; on the next feather is a smaller one, and the next two have only a terminal edging of white; the middle and greater wing-coverts have their outer webs of the color of the back, and their inner webs black; they end conspicuously with white, forming two bars across the wings; quills with their outer webs like the back, and their inner blackish slate-color; under wing-coverts and axillars white; upper mandible black, the under light horn-color; tarsi and toes light brown.

Length (skin), $5\frac{1}{4}$ in.; wing, $2\frac{7}{16}$; tail, $2\frac{1}{4}$; tarsus, $\frac{3}{4}$; bill from front, $\frac{7}{16}$.

The female is above of a dark greenish olive; it has black lores, with a white stripe over the eye and on the lower eyelid, just as in the male; below it is of a much lighter or grayish-olive, the chin, middle of the throat and of the breast mixed with pale yellowish-white, the middle of the abdomen is pale yellow; the ends of the wing-coverts, the under wing-coverts, and the axillars, are white, with just a tinge of yellow; the spots at the ends of the tail-feathers, as in the male, but less distinct; bill and feet of the same color as those of the male.

Types in National Museum, Washington.

3. Vireosylvia calidris, var. Dominicana.

[Dominica Catalogue, p. 55.]

4. *Myiarchus Oberi*. "Sunset Bird."

MALE. Pileum, nape, and sides of the head dark umber-brown, upper plumage dark olive-brown, upper tail-coverts edged with dull ferruginous : two middle tail-feathers blackish brown, the other feathers are colored the same, except on the outer two-thirds of the inner webs, where they are bright ferruginous; outer web of lateral feather and ends of the others, ash color; quills brownish black, the primaries narrowly edged with dark ferruginous; the outer secondaries are margined with very pale rufous, and the other secondaries with pale yellowish white; wing-coverts dark-brown, ending with pale ashy tinged with rufous; under wing-coverts pale, dull yellow, inner margins of quills light salmon-color; lores, throat, upper part of breast, and sides, clear bluish-gray, lower part of breast, abdomen, and under tail-coverts, pale yellow; bill and feet deep black.

Length, $8\frac{1}{4}$ in.; wing, $3\frac{7}{8}$; tail, $3\frac{5}{8}$; tarsus, $\frac{7}{8}$; bill from front, $1\frac{3}{8}$. The female does not differ in plumage from the male.

Types in National Museum, Washington.

REMARKS. This is a large species, exceeding *M. crinitus* in size; the fourth quill is longest, the third and fifth nearly as long, and equal; the bill is large and strong, and of a deep black throughout; the upper plumage is dark, much like that of *M. tyrannulus*, but is even darker.

In the collection are seven specimens. They agree closely in plumage; two only differ from the type in the dimensions of the wing, one having it three and three-quarters, and the other four inches in length.

Mr. E. C. Taylor (Ibis, 1864) records a species of *Myiarchus* from Dominica, which was for a good while undetermined. In a List of Birds from St. Lucia, given by Mr. Sclater (P. Z. S., 1871, p. 271), he refers it to *M. erythrocercus*.

I have a specimen of this species from Bahia (verified by Mr. Sclater); on comparison I find the two birds to differ very decidedly.

M. erythrocercus is smaller; above it is of a lighter brown, more ochreous, especially on the crown; the bill is weaker and more depressed; they are somewhat alike in the coloration of the tail-feathers, but the line of contact of the two colors is more decided in *M. Oberi*.

I do not determine that this is the same as the species obtained by Mr. Taylor; possibly the two forms may exist in Dominica.

I have named this species in compliment to Mr. Fred. A. Ober, who has so industriously worked up the avifauna of Dominica.

5. *Blacicus brunneicapillus*.

Blacicus Blancoi, Lawr., nec Gundlach.

MALE. The plumage above is of a clear olive-brown, assuming an ochreous cast on the rump; the crown is of a much darker brown, forming a decided cap; tail and quill-feathers brownish-black; the tertials are edged with very pale fulvous; the throat is gray with just a tinge of fulvous on the lower part; middle of breast, abdomen, and under wing-coverts reddish-ochreous, under tail-coverts of the same color, but paler; sides of the breast olivaceous; upper mandible black, the under pale yellowish-white; tarsi and toes brownish-black.

Length (fresh), $5\frac{3}{4}$ inches; wings, $2\frac{7}{8}$; tail, $2\frac{5}{8}$; tarsus, $\frac{5}{8}$.

Habitat, Dominica. Mr. Ober says: "Everywhere abundant in the ravines and dark valleys of the mountains."

Type in National Museum, Washington.

REMARKS. In "A Provisional List of the Birds of Dominica," published in 'Forest and Stream,' December 6, 1877, this bird was put as *Blacicus Blancoi*, Gundlach. Wishing to make a comparison with the type, I desired Dr. Gundlach to loan it to me for that purpose, with which request he kindly complied. The specimen was received quite recently, and I found that, though closely allied, the two birds are quite distinct.

B. Blancoi is from Porto Rico; the specimen sent is mounted, and is of somewhat smaller dimensions than the bird from Dominica; the wing measures $2\frac{5}{8}$ inches; the tail, $2\frac{1}{2}$; the tarsus, $\frac{9}{16}$. The crown is olive-brown, which color gradually merges into the greenish-olive of the back and rump. In the new species the crown is deep brown, and the upper plumage olive-brown; it also differs in having the throat gray, which in the other is light fulvous; the color of the abdomen is rather paler than it is in *B. Blancoi*.

In another specimen of the new species, a female, "in young of the year plumage," the feathers of the wings and back are strongly marked with rufous, yet the upper plumage is as decidedly brown as in the adult, and the throat gray.

6. *Strix flammea*, var. *nigrescens*.

[Dominica Catalogue, p. 64.]

APPENDIX. 355

7. *Chætura Dominicana.* "Hirondelle."

Chætura poliura, Lawr. (nec Temm.), Proc. U. S. National Museum, page 62.

MALE. Upper plumage smoky-black; lores black; rump dark ash; upper tail-coverts brownish-black, just edged with whitish; tail glossy black, the spines fine and projecting for nearly a quarter of an inch; wings glossy black; throat dark grayish-ash; breast and abdomen of a warm smoky-brown; under tail-coverts brownish-black; bill black; feet yellowish-brown.

Length (fresh), $4\frac{2}{3}$ inches; wing, $4\frac{1}{2}$; tail, $1\frac{2}{3}$.

The female is similar to the male in plumage.

Habitat, Dominica.

Types in National Museum, Washington.

REMARKS. In my Catalogue of the Birds of Dominica (Proc. U. S. Nat. Mus. 1878), I referred this species provisionally to *C. poliura*, Temm., being partly induced to do so because that species was noted from Tobago, comparatively a not very distant point. I then stated that it agreed quite well with the measurements given of that species by Mr. Sclater, in his Notes of the Cypselidæ (Proc. Zool. Soc., 1865, p. 593), but that the wing was shorter. The measurement of $3\frac{1}{4}$ inches, given by me, was taken from Mr. Ober's note, and is clearly an error, as, in the four specimens sent, the wings of each measure $4\frac{1}{2}$ inches.

Quite lately I received a collection made in Tobago by Mr. Ober, and found in it an example of *C. brachyura*, Jard., which Mr. Sclater says, "Does not seem to be decidedly different from *C. poliura*, Temm., although the tail is rather shorter and the upper coverts are much produced, so as to reach nearly to the end of the rectrices." In Mr. Ober's example from Tobago, the upper coverts reach quite to the end of the tail-feathers.

The species from Dominica is very distinct, and I think is undescribed. The Tobago bird is blacker above, and has the abdomen also black; it is at once distinguished by its light ashy upper tail-coverts.

The only other species requiring notice, if it really does, is the *Hirundo acuta*, Gm., from Martinique, which does not seem to be recognized by late writers, and is not noticed by Mr. Sclater in his Notes of the Cypselidæ. The locality given for it, Martinique, is what has induced me to allude to it.

Gmelin's name is based upon the "Sharp-tailed Swallow" of

Latham, who gives the size as that of a wren, "length three inches and eight lines;" he cites Buffon and Brisson. It is "L'Hirondelle noire acutipenne de la Martinique" of Buffon, Pl. Enl., No. 544. He describes it as being very small, the size of a wren, the length 3 inches and 8 lines; the whole upper part of the body without exception black, etc., the wings extending beyond the tail eight lines. Boddaert refers this to *H. pelasgia*, Linn., but they do not agree in size or color.

8. *Dendrœca petechia*, var. *melanoptera*.
[Guadeloupe Catalogue, p. 453.]

9. *Quiscalus Guadeloupensis*.
[Guadeloupe Catalogue, p. 457.]

NEW SPECIES OF OWL, FROM ANTIGUA.
10. *Speotyto amaura*.

"Owl. Length, ♂, 8½ in.; alar extent, 21½; wing, 6¾.

"Length, ♀, 8½ in.; alar extent, 21; wing, 6¼.

"Iris bright yellow. Called here, 'coo coo,' from its hoot at night. I considered it for a time as almost mythical, reports concerning its existence were so conflicting. Some described it as a large Bat, others asserted that it was (judging from the size of its eyes) as large as a 'Guinea Bird'; all agreed that it was a night-bird, that it lived in old drains, holes in the cliffs, and ruined walls: and that its hoot would strike terror to the stoutest heart.

"Like its congener of Dominica, it has a bad name; and though it may not be called here, as in Dominica, the 'Jumbie Bird,' or bird of evil spirits, — the name implies more than that, — still it has the reputation of being a bad character. The blacks declare that it will not hesitate to tear the eyes out of any individual unfortunate enough to meet it at night. 'Me rudder see de debbil, any time,' is their forcible way of testifying to the powers, supernatural and otherwise, possessed by this poor owl. Finding it impossible to shoot one, I offered a reward of two shillings for the first owl brought me, and within three hours had three living birds which the men dug out of a cliff in the Chalk-hills. One that I kept two days gave frequent utterance to a chattering cry, especially if any one approached, but it did not hoot. It feeds upon lizards and mice, it is said."

MALE. Upper plumage of a fine deep brown color, marked with roundish spots of light fulvous; the spots are smallest on the crown, hind neck, and smaller wing-coverts; they are conspicuously large on the other wing-coverts, the dorsal region, scapulars, and tertials; the quills are blackish-brown with indented marks of pale reddish fulvous on the outer webs of the primaries, and large roundish paler spots on the inner webs; under wing-coverts reddish fulvous, sparsely mottled with black; tail dark brown, of the same color as the back, crossed with four bars (including the terminal one), of light reddish fulvous, which do not quite reach the shaft on each web; bristles at the base of the bill black, with the basal portion of their shafts whitish; front white, superciliary streak pale fulvous; cheeks dark brown, the feathers tipped with fulvous; upper part of throat pale whitish buff, the lower part grayish-white, with a buffy tinge, separated by a broad band of dark brown across the middle of the throat, the feathers of which are bordered with light fulvous; the sides of the neck and the upper part and sides of the breast are dark brown, like the back, the feathers ending with fulvous, the spots being larger on the breast; the feathers of the abdomen are pale fulvous, conspicuously barred across their centers with dark brown; on some of the feathers the terminal edgings are of the same color; the flanks are of a clear light fulvous, with bars of a lighter brown; under tail-coverts fulvous, with indistinct bars of brown; thighs clear fulvous, with nearly obsolete narrow dusky bars; the feathers of the tarsi are colored like the thighs and extend to the toes; bill clear light yellow, with the sides of the upper mandible blackish; toes dull yellowish-brown.

Length (fresh), $8\frac{1}{2}$ in.; wing, $6\frac{3}{4}$; tail, $3\frac{1}{8}$; tarsus, $1\frac{1}{4}$.

The female differs but little from the male in plumage; the bars on the abdomen appear to be a little more strongly defined, and at the base of the culmen is a small red spot. There are two females in the collection, the other also having the red spot; in one the tarsi are feathered to the toes, in the other only for two-thirds their length.

Length of one (fresh), 8 in.; wing, $6\frac{1}{2}$; tail, $2\frac{7}{8}$; tarsus, $1\frac{1}{4}$.

Length of the other, $8\frac{1}{2}$; wing, $6\frac{1}{2}$; tail, 3; tarsus, $1\frac{1}{4}$.

Mr. Ridgway suggested a comparison with his *S. guadeloupensis*, the type of which belongs to the Boston Natural History Society, and by the courtesy of Dr. Brewer I have been able to make it.

Compared with *guadeloupensis*, the prevailing color is dark brown, instead of a rather light earthy-brown, and the spots on the interscapular region are much larger; it is more strikingly barred below, the other having the breast more spotted; the bars on the tail are four instead of six. In the Antigua bird each feather of the breast is crossed with but one bar, while those of the other are crossed with two.

11. *Myiarchus Sclateri.*

[Martinique Catalogue, p. 357.]

DESCRIPTIONS OF SEVEN NEW SPECIES OF BIRDS FROM THE ISLAND OF ST. VINCENT, WEST INDIES.

WHEN Mr. Ober had completed his investigations in Dominica he proceeded to St. Vincent; but unfortunately, while there, he had two attacks of fever, one early in October, from which he soon recovered, but in December he had a relapse; by this he was completely prostrated, and it was not until the end of January that he was convalescent.

There were also constant rains, and consequently his collecting was seriously interfered with. He thinks, however, that the specimens obtained, and the birds observed, complete quite thoroughly the avifauna of the island.

He left for the island of Grenada about the 1st of March, at which time he forwarded to the Smithsonian the collection made in St. Vincent. There are only ninety specimens, representing thirty-five species; seven of these I consider new to science, and their descriptions are given below. Besides the species sent, he enumerates twenty-four others, which he either saw, or had named to him as undoubtedly frequenting the island : making the total number fifty-nine.

12. *Turdus nigrirostris.*

FEMALE. Front, crown, and occiput dark warm brown, each feather of the crown and occiput with a shaft-stripe of dull pale rufous; upper plumage reddish olivaceous brown, deeper in color on the upper part of the back and on the wing-coverts; the latter have their ends marked with small spots of bright rufous, which possibly may be an evidence of the example not being fully mature ; the tail is of a dark warm brown, the shafts black; inner webs of quills blackish-brown; the outer webs reddish-brown, of the same color as the tail-feathers ; the shafts are glossy-black; under lining of wings clear cinnamon red; under plumage light brownish ash, with the middle of the abdomen and the crissum white ; on the upper part of the breast a few feathers end with dark reddish-brown, forming an irregular narrow band ; the throat unfortunately is soiled with blood, but as well as I can judge, it has stripes colored like the breast, and the feathers edged with whitish ; the thighs are dull fulvous; the bill is large and strong, the upper mandible is black, the under also, but showing a brownish tinge ; tarsi and toes dark brown.

Length (fresh), $9\tfrac{1}{4}$ in.; wing, $4\tfrac{1}{2}$; tail, $3\tfrac{1}{2}$; tarsus, $1\tfrac{1}{4}$; bill from front, $\tfrac{7}{8}$.

Type in National Museum, Washington.

REMARKS. There is but one specimen in the collection ; in the section (*Planesticus*) which this species comes under, the sexes do not differ.

In the distribution of colors on the under plumage, it is much like *T. albiventris*, but the color of the breast and sides is darker, and the upper plumage is of a much deeper and richer brown. The strong black bill is a striking feature.

Mr. Ober says: "Not abundant; obtained in Rutland Vale, January 25, 1878."

13. *Myiadestes sibilans.* "Soufrière Bird."

The upper plumage is black; the front, lores, and sides of the head for a short distance under the eye, are intense black; the crown, occiput, hind neck and ear coverts are deep black ; the upper part of the back is not quite so deep in color, as it has a slight smoky tinge ; the lower part of the back, rump, and upper tail-coverts have a wash of dull olivaceous, the latter terminate with black ; the ear-coverts have their shafts narrowly streaked with white, less striking than in *M. genibarbis;* the lower eyelid is pure white ; the chin and the anterior part of the rictal stripe are white, the posterior part of the latter is cinnamon-red; a very distinct black moustachial line starts from the under mandible, and joins the black of the side of the neck, separating the rictal stripe from the bright cinnamon-red color of the throat; the breast and upper part of the abdomen are of a clear plumbeous gray ; the middle and lower part of the abdomen and the under tail-coverts are of a rather paler cinnamon-red than the throat ; the thighs are blackish plumbeous, some of the feathers ending with light-red; the quills are black, the edge of the wing and bases of the quill-feathers are white ; the tail-feathers, except the outer two, are brownish slate-color, marked transversely with black bars, which are not very conspicuous ; the first lateral feather has the inner web grayish-white, with a blackish diagonal mark at the base, the outer web is black for one quarter of its length from the base, the remaining part of a dusky ash-color ; the second feather is blackish, except that it has for half its length, on the inner web, an elongated white mark along the shaft, widening out to the end; the bill is black; tarsi and toes very pale yellow, claws black; "iris bright hazel."

Length (fresh), 7¼ in.; wing, 3¾; tail, 3; tarsus, 1.

The sexes do not differ in plumage.

Types in National Museum, Washington.

REMARKS. This differs from all the West India species in its black upper plumage. The color of the throat is much lighter than in *M. genibarbis* and *solitarius;* in both of these the color is of a deep chestnut red; it has the black moustachial line as in *M. genibarbis*, but it is more defined.

M. armillatus (according to the description and plate) differs in being of a lighter color above, slate-gray (*gris ardoise*); in having the red of the under plumage darker, brownish-red (*brun roux*); it has no moustachial line, and the eye is encircled with white; but it varies especially in having the feathers of the thigh terminating in bright yellow.

Mr. Ober writes: "This bird has been an object of search for fifty years, and has so long eluded the vigilance of naturalists and visitors to the mountains, that it is called the 'invisible bird.' From being seen only on the Soufrière Mountain, it has acquired the name of 'Soufrière-bird.'"

Mr. Ober is entitled to great credit for unraveling the mystery connected with this bird. By his indomitable perseverance, and camping out on the top of the mountain for several days, he secured seven specimens.

14. *Thryothorus musicus.* "Wall-Bird."

MALE. Above of a dark ferruginous, somewhat darker on the crown and brighter on the rump; lores, and a line running back from the eye, white tinged with rufous; the exposed portions of the wings are dark rufous, conspicuously barred with black; the inner webs of the primaries are blackish-brown; under wing-coverts white; the tail-feathers are dark-rufous, barred with black; the entire back and upper tail-coverts are marked inconspicuously with narrow transverse dusky lines; the feathers of the rump have concealed white shaft-stripes, which become wider toward the ends of the feathers; the feathers of the back, also, have the basal portion of their shafts marked with white; the throat, breast, and middle of the abdomen are white, the latter tinged with rufous; the sides are light ferruginous; the under tail-coverts are rufous, each feather marked with a subterminal round black spot; upper mandible black; the under whitish, with the end dusky; tarsi and toes light brownish flesh-color.

Length (fresh), 5¼ in. ; wing, 2½ ; tail, 1⅛⅜ ; tarsus, ¾.

There are three male specimens in the collection, but no female; one example is evidently not mature ; in this, the white dorsal and rump spots are wanting, and the crissum is immaculate; the sides are dull rufous, the under plumage is tinged with rufous, and marked with faint narrow, dusky bars. This specimen was killed February, 1878.

Types in National Museum, Washington.

REMARKS. In its white under plumage, this species somewhat resembles *T. mesoleucus*, Scl., from St. Lucia ; but it is bright rufous above, instead of earthy-brown, and the flanks are light ferruginous instead of fulvous : it is also of larger dimensions. The transverse markings on the back, and the round black spots on the crissum, are strong characteristics.

Mr. Ober states that it is common, and is known as the "House wren" and "Wall bird," breeding in holes in houses and trees. He says : "The sweet warble of this lively little bird may be heard morning, noon, and night, about the houses and sugar mills, as well as far up the mountain-sides and valleys."

15. *Certhiola atrata*.

MALE. The entire plumage is black ; on the head and throat it is of a deeper color ; the breast, upper part of abdomen, and rump, on a side view, show a just perceptible tinge of greenish olive ; bill and feet black.

Length (fresh), 4⅞ in. ; wing, 2¾ ; tail, 1¾; tarsus, ¾.

The female differs only in being smaller.

Length (fresh), 4 in. ; wing, 2¼; tail, 1⅜ ; tarsus, ⅝.

Types in National Museum, Washington.

REMARKS. This is certainly a remarkable departure from the regular pattern of coloration, which prevails so uniformly in this genus. Had there been only a single example, I should have considered it as probably a case of abnormal coloring; but it seems to be the representative form of the genus in this island. Mr. Ober says it is very abundant, and "seems to have almost entirely replaced the black and yellow one of Dominica," &c. He has sent four specimens, two of each sex. But what is surprising is, that there is likewise found in St. Vincent a species of the usual style of coloration, of which he sends but two specimens, stating that it is not abundant. This I have described as a new species also.

16. *Certhiola saccharina.* "Molasses Bird."

FEMALE. Crown, occiput, lores, and sides of the head glossy black; back of a dull grayish or smoky black; rump dull greenish-yellow; a very conspicuous white superciliary stripe runs from the bill to the hind neck; tail black, the first two lateral feathers have a small patch of dull white on their inner webs at the end, the third feather has the end narrowly white; wings black, with a white patch at the base of the primaries; these have their outer webs narrowly margined with white; edge of wing light yellow; under wing-coverts white; throat dark plumbeous, breast and upper part of abdomen, clear light yellow, the sides and lower part of the abdomen are light ashy-olive, under tail-coverts yellowish-white; bill and feet black.

Length (fresh), $4\frac{1}{2}$ in.; wings, $2\frac{1}{2}$; tail, $1\frac{9}{16}$; tarsus, $\frac{5}{8}$. Two specimens are in the collection; one, marked ♂, has the plumage greatly soiled; the other is marked as a ♀ with a ?; this I have taken for the type, the plumage being in a much better condition.

The male measures, length, $4\frac{5}{8}$ in.; wing, $2\frac{1}{2}$; tail, $1\frac{3}{4}$; tarsus, $\frac{3}{4}$.

Types in National Museum, Washington.

REMARKS. This, in appearance, comes nearest to *C. Portoricensis*, but differs in the superciliary stripe being wider and extending farther back, in the throat being many shades darker in color, in having the flanks of a darker olive, and the yellow on the rump darker and duller. The color of the breast and rump in *C. Portoricensis* is of a deeper yellow.

17. *Leucopeza Bishopi.*

MALE. The general plumage is smoky-black, rather darker on the head; the sides are blackish cinereous; a circle of pure white surrounds the eye; a large roundish spot on the middle of the throat, the upper part of the breast, and the middle of the abdomen, are dull white, somewhat mixed with blackish on the throat and with cinereous on the abdomen; a very small spot on the chin, and the tips of the feathers on the upper part of the throat, are dull white; the black on the upper part of the breast has the appearance of a broad band, separating the white of the throat from that of the lower part of the breast; the under tail-coverts are cinereous-black at base, ending largely with dull white; wings and tail black, the outer two tail-feathers have a small white spot, triangular in shape, on their inner webs at the end; bill black; tarsi and toes very pale yellowish-brown, perhaps much lighter colored in the living bird, nails also pale.

Length (fresh), 5¾ in. ; wing, 2⅝ ; tail, 2¼ ; tarsus, ⅞.
Two specimens marked as females do not differ in plumage from the males.
Length (fresh), 5½ in. ; wing, 2⅝ ; tail, 2⅝ ; tarsus, ⅞.

Another specimen, marked male, and of quite different colors, I have no doubt is the young of this species ; though Mr. Ober, in his notes, says of it (No. 428) : " The quickest to respond to my call on the Soufrière, was this little bird. It seems an associate of the preceding species (*L. Bishopi*), though I never saw them closely together ; yet in general shape and habits, especially in search for insects, they resembled one another. As I have got both male and female of the other, it precludes the possibility of its being the adult of the former. That there may be no doubt, I have preserved one in rum."

The color of this specimen (No. 428) is of a dark olive-brown above, lighter below, and where the white markings are in the adult, it is of a pale dull rufous ; on the throat showing some white, and around the eye partially white ; the marks on the ends of the tail-feathers are precisely as in the black specimens ; the quills are dark brown ; the tail-feathers are black. But what I consider conclusive evidence of its being the young of *L. Bishopi* is, that on the crown the black feathers are beginning to appear. Had it not been marked as a male, I should have taken it for the female of this species. But according to Mr. Ober, the sexes are alike.

Types in National Museum, Washington.

REMARKS. This is a remarkable species, and at first I was at a loss where to place it properly ; I determined it to be a Sylvicoline form, yet unlike any of that family in coloration. On comparing it with the description and plate of *Leucopeza Semperi*, Mr. Sclater's new form from St. Lucia (P. Z. S., 1876, p. 14), I determined it to be a second species of that peculiar genus, and, like that species, having long and light-colored tarsi.

Mr. Ober requested that I would bestow the name of our friend Mr. Nathaniel H. Bishop on some West India bird of his procuring, if the opportunity offered ; and it gives me much pleasure to connect his name with so remarkable a species.

The habits of this bird would seem to be like those of the wren, as Mr. Ober has on the labels, "Wren?" He states that they are "very rare and very shy, and found in the crater and dark gorges of the Soufrière."

Three specimens were obtained in November, 1877, and one in February, 1878.

18. *Calliste versicolor.* "Sour-sop Bird."

MALE. Front, crown, and occiput of a bright deep chestnut-red; upper plumage golden fawn-color, clearest on the sides of the neck and on the rump, in some positions showing a pale greenish-silvery gloss; upper tail-coverts bluish-green; lores and partly under the eye black; sides of the head and ear-coverts dull dark-green; tail-feathers black, except the two middle ones, which, with the outer margins of the others, are bluish-green; quills black, conspicuously edged with bluish-green; wing-coverts black, with their exposed portions bluish-green; under wing-coverts of a light salmon color; the under plumage is changeable according to position; viewed from the bill downward it is of a light bluish-lilac, the blue color deepest on the lower part of the throat and the upper part of the breast; on a side view the abdomen is of a purplish-red; the feathers of the upper part of the throat are tipped with gray; the under tail-coverts are bright cinnamon color; upper mandible black; the under, light brownish horn color; tarsi and toes black.

Length, $6\frac{1}{4}$ in.; wing, $3\frac{3}{8}$; tail, $2\frac{1}{2}$; tarsus, $\frac{13}{16}$.

The female differs in having the top of the head of a lighter chestnut color, and the upper plumage of a pale green; the under plumage has the same colors as the male, but much subdued; the abdomen, sides, and under tail-coverts are of a light cinnamon color; the wings and tail are black, but margined with a paler bluish-green; the markings about the head and on the throat are similar to those of the male, "iris hazel."

Length, 6 in.; wing, $3\frac{1}{4}$; tail, $2\frac{1}{2}$; tarsus, $\frac{13}{16}$.

Types in National Museum, Washington.

REMARKS. This fine new species belongs to the group which contains *C. vitriolina, cayana, cyanolæma,* and *cucullata*; it somewhat resembles the latter, a species I have never seen, but according to the plate (Mon. of Calliste, Scl.), the colors of the present bird are generally darker, with no tendency to ochreous-yellow above, as in *C. cucullata,* and the abdomen is purple instead of reddish ochreous; the crown is of a clearer and brighter chestnut-red. It is larger than any of its allies; and a strikingly different character is its very large and stout bill, exceeding in size that of any of them I am acquainted with, being fully as large as the bill of *Tanagra cana.*

No species of Calliste appears to be on record before from any of the West India islands proper. There are five specimens in the collection, three ♂ and two ♀, procured in February, 1878. "Frequents the mountain ridges and valleys."

Descriptions of Supposed New Species of Birds from the Island of Grenada, West Indies.

19. *Turdus Caribbæus.*

MALE. Upper plumage dark-olive, with the forehead dull reddish-brown; tail dark brownish-olive; quills dark-brown; lower part of throat, upper part of breast and sides, clear ash; lower part of breast, middle of abdomen, and under tail-coverts white; upper part of throat white, with distinct narrow stripes of ashy-brown; the under wing-coverts are pale cinnamon; upper mandible blackish for two-thirds its length, the end yellow; the under is yellow, with the base black; tarsi and toes brown; "iris red, naked skin around the eye orange."

Length (fresh), $9\frac{1}{4}$ in.; wing 5; tail, $4\frac{1}{2}$; tarsus, $1\frac{8}{18}$.

There are two specimens in the collection, both males; the length given of the other is $9\frac{1}{2}$ inches; the tarsi are blackish-brown.

Habitat, Grenada. Mr. Ober says: "Rather numerous, but shy." Type in National Museum, Washington.

REMARKS. This species has a naked space around the eye, similar to that of *T. gymnopthalmus;* but it is of larger dimensions and differently colored from that species. The upper plumage of the new bird is clear deep olive, not at all brownish as in the other; the under plumage is of a lighter ash, and has a much greater extent of white; the striations on the throat are darker and more clearly defined.

20. *Thryothorus Grenadensis.* "God Bird."

FEMALE. Upper plumage of a rather bright ferruginous, a little inclining to brownish on the head and hind neck, and brighter on the rump; lores whitish tinged with rufous; a light rufous stripe extends over the eye to the hind neck; tail dull rufous, barred with black; the primary quills have their outer webs of a dull light rufous, with broad black bars; the inner webs are brownish-black; the wing-coverts and tertials are rufous with narrower black bars; under wing-coverts pale rufous; the throat is very pale rufous, inclining to whitish; the breast light rufous; the middle of the abdomen is of a rather paler shade; the sides and under tail-coverts are of a bright darker ferruginous; the upper mandible brownish-black; the under pale yellow, dusky at the tip; tarsi and toes hazel-brown.

Length (fresh), $4\frac{3}{4}$ in.; wing, $2\frac{1}{4}$; tail, $1\frac{1}{2}$; tarsus, $\frac{4}{8}$; bill from front, $\frac{11}{18}$.

There is also a specimen of the male, but as it was in poor condition, I chose the female as the type, from which it does not differ in plumage; its measure is given; length, 5 in.; wing, $2\frac{1}{4}$; tail, $1\frac{1}{2}$.

Habitat, Grenada. "Abundant."
Type in National Museum, Washington.

REMARKS. This species differ from *T. rufescens*, from Dominica, in having the coloring lighter throughout, especially below, the entire under plumage of *T. rufescens* being of a dark rufous; there are subterminal black markings on the under tail-coverts of *T. rufescens*, whereas those of the new species are immaculate.

T. musicus, from St. Vincent, is at once distinguished by its white under plumage.

21. *Quiscalus luminosus.* "Bequia-Sweet."

MALE. The general plumage is of a lustrous dark bluish-violet; the upper and under tail-coverts are dull dark green; tail dark glossy green; tertials, outer webs of larger quills, and the middle and larger wing coverts, glossy-green like the tail; the inner webs of the larger quills are black; smaller wing-coverts the color of the back; under wing-coverts black; the bill and feet are black; "iris yellow."
Length (fresh), $10\frac{1}{4}$ in.; wing, 5; tail, $4\frac{1}{2}$; tarsus, $1\frac{1}{4}$; bill, $1\frac{1}{4}$.

FEMALE. Upper plumage of a fine dark brown, light on the crown, the feathers of which are margined with dull pale rust-color; the tail is blackish-brown, with a wash of greenish, quills dark-brown; the under plumage is dark brownish-ash, lighter on the throat and breast, and fuliginous on the flanks, lower part of abdomen, and under tail-coverts; on the lower part of the neck is a wash of dull rust-color; bill and feet black; "iris yellow."
Length (fresh), $9\frac{3}{4}$ in.; wing, $4\frac{3}{4}$; tail, 4; tarsus, $\frac{3}{16}$; bill, $1\frac{1}{8}$.

Habitat, Grenada.
Types in National Museum, Washington.

REMARKS. The male of this species, in dimensions and general appearance, somewhat resembles *Q. brachypterus* from Porto Rico, but is of a brighter and more uniform violet; it may be at once known by its upper and under tail-coverts being green, the other having the upper coverts colored like the back, and the under ones black. The females are totally unlike, — that sex in *Q. brachypterus* being black like the male, only duller.

9 CASTLE STREET,
EDINBURGH, *April* 1880.

LIST OF BOOKS
PUBLISHED BY DAVID DOUGLAS.

ADAMSON—On the Philosophy of Kant.
By ROBERT ADAMSON, M.A., Professor of Logic and Mental Philosophy, Owen's College ; formerly Examiner in Philosophy in the University of Edinburgh. Ex. fcap. 8vo, 6s.

"Within less than two hundred pages they convey to the intelligent reader a fair knowledge of Kant's method and doctrines. The notes indicate wide reading, and form an admirable appendix to the text."—*Theological Quarterly.*

BAILDON—Morning Clouds:
Being divers Poems by H. B. BAILDON, B.A. Cantab., Author of "Rosamond," etc. Ex. fcap. 8vo, 5s.

"Their tremulous beauty, delicate fancies, and wealth of language, recall the poetry of Shelley."—*Literary World.*

Bible Readings.
Extra fcap. 8vo, 2s.

BISHOP—Four Months in a Sneak-Box.
A Boat Voyage of 2600 Miles down the Ohio and Mississippi Rivers, and along the Gulf of Mexico. By N. H. BISHOP. With Maps and Plates. 8vo, 10s. 6d.

BISHOP—The Voyage of the Paper Canoe.
A Geographical Journey of 2500 Miles, from Quebec to the Gulf of Mexico, during the year 1874-75. By N. H. BISHOP. With Maps and Plates, 10s. 6d.

"There are some capital stories in this book, with a racy American flavour; and Mr. Bishop especially shines in his delineation of the liberated and enfranchised negro."—*Pall Mall Gazette.*

"Cruises of 'Rob Roy' or of 'Nautilus' seem tame when compared with such enterprises as that recorded in Mr. Bishop's 'Voyage of the Paper Canoe.' One thing is certain, Mr. Bishop did a very bold thing, and has described it with a happy mixture of spirit, keen observation, and *bonhommie.*"—*Graphic.*

"We may say that this voyage is most instructive and amusing, and the first few of the maps of the eastern coast of the States are, for their size, the most perfect in detail and execution which we have ever met. We cannot close the volume without paying a fitting tribute of its worth, by stating that we do not care how soon particulars of his last voyage are presented to us."—*Land and Water.*

"This well-known traveller, who, at the age of seventeen, walked one thousand miles across South America, and presented the world with a graphic account of his performance, now presents us with one of the most interesting works on modern travel and adventure that it is possible to conceive. Were we to be obliged to name volumes of travel equal in interest to Mr. Bishop's, we could only name one, and that is Captain Burnaby's 'Ride to Khiva.'"—*Sporting and Dramatic News.*

BLACKIE—Lyrical Poems.
By JOHN STUART BLACKIE, Professor of Greek in the University of Edinburgh. Crown 8vo, cloth, 7s. 6d.

BLACKIE—The Language and Literature of the Scottish Highlands. In 1 vol. crown 8vo, 6s.

"The way to a mother's heart is through her children; the way to a people's heart is through its language."—*Jean Paul Richter.*
"Ein Buch, das ich auch deutschen Lesern, und zwar in einem beträchtlich weitem Umfange, nicht angelegentlich genug empfehlen kann."—*Dr. R. Pauli.*

BLACKIE—Four Phases of Morals:
Socrates, Aristotle, Christianity, and Utilitarianism. Lectures delivered before the Royal Institution, London. Ex. fcap. 8vo, Second Edition, 5s.

BLACKIE—Songs of Religion and Life. Fcap. 8vo, 6s.

"The poems in this volume may be regarded as a Second Edition of the second part of my 'Lays and Legends of Ancient Greece,' which has long been out of print, along with other Poems not hitherto published, and a few from a volume of 'Lyrical Poems' previously published, all having one common object, viz. 'the cultivation of religious reverence without sectarian dogmatism, and of poetical sentiment tending not so much to arouse the imagination or to take the fancy, as to purify the passions and to regulate the conduct of life.'"—*Preface.*

BLACKIE—On Self-Culture:
Intellectual, Physical, and Moral. A *Vade-Mecum* for Young Men and Students. Twelfth Edition. Fcap. 8vo, 2s. 6d.

"Every parent should put it into the hands of his son."—*Scotsman.*
"Students in all countries would do well to take as their *vade-mecum* a little book on self-culture by the eminent Professor of Greek in the University of Edinburgh."—*Medical Press and Circular.*
"An invaluable manual to be put into the hands of students and young men."—*Era.*
"Written in that lucid and nervous prose of which he is a master."—*Spectator.*
"An adequate guide to a generous, eager, and sensible life."—*Academy.*
"The volume is a little thing, but it is a *multum in parvo* . . . a little locket gemmed within and without with real stones fitly set."—*Courant.*

BLACKIE—On Greek Pronunciation. Demy 8vo, 3s. 6d.

BLACKIE—On Beauty. Crown 8vo, cloth, 8s. 6d.

BLACKIE—Musa Burschicosa.
A Book of Songs for Students and University Men. Fcap. 8vo, 2s. 6d.

BLACKIE—War Songs of the Germans. Fcap. 8vo, price 2s. 6d. cloth; 1s. paper.

BLACKIE—Political Tracts.
No. 1. GOVERNMENT. No. 2. EDUCATION. Price 1s. each.

BLACKIE—Homer and the Iliad.
In three Parts. 4 vols. demy 8vo, price 42s.

BOWEN—"Verily, Verily," The Amens of Christ.
By the Rev. GEORGE BOWEN of Bombay. Small 4to, cloth, 5s.

BOWEN—Daily Meditations by Rev. G. Bowen of Bombay.
With Introductory Notice by Rev. W. HANNA, D.D. Author of "The Last Day of our Lord's Passion." New Edition, small 4to, cloth, 5s.; or limp roan, red edges, 7s. 6d.

> "Among such books we shall scarcely find another which exhibits the same freshness and vividness of idea, the same fervour of faith, the same intensity of devotion. ... I count it a privilege to introduce in this country a book so fitted to attract and to benefit."—*Extract from Preface.*
>
> "These meditations are the production of a missionary whose mental history is very remarkable. ... His conversion to a religious life is undoubtedly one of the most remarkable on record. They are all distinguished by a tone of true piety, and are wholly free from a sectarian or controversial bias."—*Morning Post.*

BROWN—John Leech and other Papers.
By JOHN BROWN, M.D., F.R.S.E. Crown 8vo. [*In the Press.*

BROWN—Locke and Sydenham, and other Papers.
Extra fcap. 8vo, 7s. 6d.

BROWN—Horæ Subsecivæ.
Ninth Edition. Extra fcap. 8vo, 7s. 6d.

BROWN—Letter to the Rev. John Cairns, D.D.
Second Edition. Crown 8vo, sewed, 2s.

BROWN—Arthur H. Hallam;
Extracted from "Horæ Subsecivæ." Fcap. sewed, 2s.; cloth, 2s. 6d.

BROWN—Rab and his Friends;
Extracted from "Horæ Subsecivæ." Fiftieth thousand. Fcap. sewed, 6d.

BROWN—Rab and his Friends.
Cheap Illustrated Edition. Square 12mo, ornamental wrapper, 1s.

BROWN—Rab and his Friends.
With India-proof portrait of the Author after Faed, and seven India-proof Illustrations after Sir G. Harvey, Sir J. Noel Paton, Mrs. Blackburn, and G. Reid, R.S.A. Demy 4to, cloth, price 9s.

BROWN—Marjorie Fleming: a Sketch.
Fifteenth thousand. Fcap. sewed, 6d.

BROWN—Our Dogs;
Extracted from "Horæ Subsecivæ." Nineteenth thousand. Fcap. sewed, 6d.

BROWN—"With Brains, Sir;"
Extracted from "Horæ Subsecivæ." Fcap. sewed, 6d.

BROWN—Minchmoor.
Fcap. sewed, 6d.

BROWN—Jeems the Doorkeeper: a Lay Sermon.
6d.

BROWN—The Enterkin.
6d.

BROWN—The Capercaillie in Scotland, by J. A. Harvie
BROWN. Etchings on Copper, and Map illustrating the extension of its range since its Restoration at Taymouth in 1837 and 1838. Demy 8vo, 8s. 6d.

LIST OF BOOKS

BRUCE—Memories: a Tale, and other Poems.
By WM. BRUCE, D.D. 4s. 6d.
"Written with a delicacy of sentiment and correctness of taste which are worthy of praise'. . . . the graceful thoughts and delicate expressions which the author gives us."—*Courant.*

CAMPBELL—My Indian Journal,
Containing descriptions of the principal Field Sports of India, with Notes on the Natural History and Habits of the Wild Animals of the Country. By Colonel WALTER CAMPBELL, Author of "The Old Forest Ranger." 8vo, with Illustrations by Wolf, 16s.

CUMMING—Wild Men and Wild Beasts.
Adventures in Camp and Jungle. By Lieut.-Colonel GORDON CUMMING. With Illustrations by Lieut.-Col. BAIGRIE and others. Second Edition. Demy 4to price 24s.

Also, a cheaper edition, with *Lithographic* Illustrations. 8vo, 12s.

CHALMERS—Life and Works of Rev. Thomas Chalmers, D.D., LL.D.
MEMOIRS OF THE REV. THOMAS CHALMERS. By Rev. W. HANNA, D.D., LL.D. New Edition. 2 vols. crown 8vo, cloth, 12s.
DAILY SCRIPTURE READINGS. Cheap Edition. 2 vols. crown 8vo, 10s.
ASTRONOMICAL DISCOURSES, 1s.
COMMERCIAL DISCOURSES, 1s.
SELECT WORKS, in 12 vols., crown 8vo, cloth, per vol., 6s.
    Lectures on the Romans. 2 vols.
    Sermons. 2 vols.
    Natural Theology, Lectures on Butler's Analogy, etc. 1 vol.
    Christian Evidences, Lectures on Paley's Evidences, etc. 1 vol.
    Institutes of Theology. 2 vols.
    Political Economy, with Cognate Essays. 1 vol.
    Polity of a Nation. 1 vol.
    Church and College Establishments. 1 vol.
    Moral Philosophy, Introductory Essays, Index, etc. 1 vol.

CHALMERS—George Paul Chalmers, R.S.A.
By ALEXANDER GIBSON and J. F. WHITE. With Portrait Etched by RAJON and Illustrations by GEORGE REID, R.S.A. Royal 8vo, 21s.

CHIENE—Lectures on Surgical Anatomy.
By JOHN CHIENE, Surgeon, Royal Infirmary, Edinburgh. In 1 vol. 8vo. With numerous illustrations drawn on Stone by BERJEAU. 12s. 6d.
"Dr. Chiene has succeeded in going over the most important part of the ground, and in a pleasant readable manner. . . . They (the plates) are well executed, and considerably enhance the value of the book."—*Lancet.*

CONSTABLE—Archibald Constable and his Literary Correspondents: a Memorial. By his Son, THOMAS CONSTABLE. 3 vols. 8vo, 36s., with Portrait.
"The cream of a generation of interesting men and women now gone from among us—these are the subjects of this important memoir."—*Saturday Review.*
"These three volumes are decidedly additions to our knowledge of that great and brilliant epoch in the history of letters to which they refer."—*Standard.*
"He (Mr. Constable) was a genius in the publishing world. . . . The creator of the Scottish publishing trade."—*Times.*

"These three volumes are of a singular and lasting interest."—*Nonconformist.*
"The third volume (Sir Walter Scott) of this elaborate and interesting history is almost an independent work."—*Athenæum.*
"We heartily commend this book to the notice of all readers."—*Guardian.*

DASENT—Burnt Njal.
From the Icelandic of the Njal's Saga. By Sir GEORGE WEBBE DASENT, D.C.L. 2 vols. demy 8vo, with Maps and Plans, 28s.

DASENT—Gisli the Outlaw.
From the Icelandic. By Sir GEORGE WEBBE DASENT, D.C.L. Small 4to, with Illustrations, 7s. 6d.

DASENT—Tales from the Norse.
By Sir GEORGE WEBBE DASENT, D.C.L. Third Edition, with Introduction and Appendix. In 1 vol. demy 8vo. [*In the Press.*

DAVIDSON—Inverurie and the Earldom of the Garioch.
A Topographical and Historical Account of the Garioch from the Earliest Times to the Revolution Settlement, with a Genealogical Appendix of Garioch Families flourishing at the Period of the Revolution Settlement and still represented. By the Rev. JOHN DAVIDSON, D.D., Minister of Inverurie. In 1 vol. 4to, 25s.

DITTMAR—A Manual of Chemical Analysis.
Ex. fcap. 8vo, 5s.

DITTMAR—Tables for Do.
Demy 8vo, 3s. 6d.

DUN—Veterinary Medicines; their Actions and Uses.
By FINLAY DUN. Fifth Edition, revised and enlarged. 8vo, 14s.

DUNBAR—Social Life in Former Days;
Chiefly in the Province of Moray. Illustrated by Letters and Family Papers. By E. DUNBAR DUNBAR, late Captain 21st Fusiliers. 2 vols. demy 8vo, 19s. 6d.

ERSKINE—Letters of Thomas Erskine of Linlathen.
Edited by WILLIAM HANNA, D.D., Author of the "Memoirs of Dr. Chalmers," etc. Third edition. In 1 vol. crown 8vo, 9s.

"Here is one who speaks out of the fulness of a large living human heart; whose words will awaken an echo in the hearts of many burdened with the cares of time, perplexed with the movements of the spirit of our time, who will speak to their deepest needs, and lead them to a haven of rest."—*Daily Review.*
"It does one good to come in contact with so saintly a man, and Dr. Hanna has certainly conferred a benefit on the Church at large by editing this volume."—*Edinburgh Courant.*
"'How high must that peak have been which caught the light so early,' were the words with which a writer in the *Contemporary Review*, in sketching the life of Thomas Erskine, shortly after his death, characterised his position, his spirit, and his influence."—*Nonconformist.*
"They exhibit much felicitous power of expression, as well as depth and seriousness of thought."—*Guardian.*
"We have a delightful picture of a circle of friends, belonging chiefly to the untitled aristocracy of Scotland, bound together by ties of kindred and friendship, as well as by those of strong religious sympathy. In the midst of them stands Erskine, like Agamemnon, taller by the head than any of his comrades, and to all, guide, teacher, and friend. . . . The real charm of the book lies in its exhibition of a Christian character."—*Theological Review.*
"The influence of his (Erskine's) thoughts has been far reaching and profound.' --*Argus.*

ERSKINE—The Internal Evidence of Revealed Religion.
Crown 8vo, 5s.

ERSKINE—The Unconditional Freeness of the Gospel.
New Edition, revised. Crown 8vo, 3s. 6d.

ERSKINE—The Spiritual Order,
And other Papers selected from the MSS. of the late THOMAS ERSKINE of Linlathen. Second Edition. Crown 8vo, 5s.

"It will for a few have a value which others will not the least understand. But all must recognise in it the utterance of a spirit profoundly penetrated with the sense of brotherhood, and with the claims of common humanity."—*Spectator.*

"Very deserving of study."—*Times.*

Vide BIBLE READINGS and FRAGMENTS OF TRUTH.

ERSKINE—The Doctrine of Election,
And its Connection with the General Tenor of Christianity, illustrated especially from the Epistle to the Romans. Pp. xxiv. and 348. Second Edition. Crown 8vo, 6s.

ERSKINE—The Brazen Serpent:
Or, Life coming through Death. Third Edition. 5s.

FINLAY—Essay
On the best Means of Improving the Relations between Capital and Labour. By JAMES FAIRBAIRN FINLAY, M.A. Demy 8vo, 1s.

FLETCHER—Autobiography of Mrs. Fletcher
(Of Edinburgh), with Letters and other Family Memorials. Edited by her Daughter. Second Edition. Crown 8vo, 7s. 6d.

"This is a delightful book. It contains an illustrative record of a singularly noble, true, pure, prolonged, and happy life. The story is recounted with a candour, vivacity, and grace which are very charming."—*Daily Review.*

FLEURY—L'Histoire de France.
Par M. LAMÉ FLEURY. New Edition. 18mo, cloth, 2s. 6d.

FORBES—The Deepening of the Spiritual Life.
By A. P. FORBES, D.C.L., Bishop of Brechin. Fifth Edition. 18mo, cloth, price 1s. 6d. ; or paper covers, 1s. ; calf, red edges, 3s. 6d.

FORBES—Kalendars of Scottish Saints,
With Personal Notices of those of Alba, etc. By ALEXANDER PENROSE FORBES, D.C.L., Bishop of Brechin. 1 vol. 4to, price £3:3s. A few copies for sale on large paper, £5:15:6.

"A truly valuable contribution to the archæology of Scotland."—*Guardian.*

"We must not forget to thank the author for the great amount of information he has put together, and for the labour he has bestowed on a work which can never be remunerative."—*Saturday Review.*

"His laborious and very interesting work on the early Saints of Alba, Landonia, and Strathclyde."—*Quarterly Review.*

Fragments of Truth.
Being the Exposition of several Passages of Scripture. Third Edition. Extra fcap. 8vo, 5s.

FRASER—Alcohol: its Function and Place.
By THOMAS R. FRASER, M.D., F.R.S., Professor of Materia Medica in the University of Edinburgh. With Diagrams and Tables. 8vo, 1s.

GAIRDNER—On Medicine and Medical Education.
By W. T. GAIRDNER, Professor of the Practice of Medicine in the University of Glasgow. Three Lectures, with Notes and an Appendix. 8vo, 3s. 6d.

GAIRDNER— Clinical and Pathological Notes on Pericarditis. By W. T. GAIRDNER, Professor of the Practice of Medicine in the University of Glasgow. 8vo, sewed, 1s.

GEMMEL—The Renewal of the Soul;
Being an Exposition of the Third Chapter of the Gospel according to John. By JOHN GEMMEL, M.A., Minister of the Gospel at Fairlie. 1 vol. crown 8vo, 5s.

"Skilled in the art of interpreting Scripture by Scripture; and indications are not wanting that he is well read in classical, patristic, and Rabbinical literature." —*Scotsman.*

"The Sermons are full of spiritual insight, . . . and show a rare power of digesting and assimilating, and reproducing freshly, the results of much study." —*Daily Review.*

Gifts for Men.
By X. H. Crown 8vo, 6s.
"There is hardly a living theologian who might not be proud to claim many of her thoughts as his own."—*Glasgow Herald.*

GORDON—The Roof of the World;
Being the narrative of a journey over the high plateau of Tibet to the Russian Frontier, and the Oxus sources on Pamir. By Lieut.-Col. T. E. GORDON, C.S.I. With numerous Illustrations. Royal 8vo, 31s. 6d.

GORDON—The Home Life of Sir David Brewster.
By his Daugher, Mrs. GORDON. Second Edition. Crown 8vo, 6s.
"With his own countrymen it is sure of a welcome, and to the *savants* of Europe, and of the New World, it will have a real and special interest of its own."—*Pall Mall Gazette.*

By the same Author.

GORDON—Workers.
Fourth thousand. Fcap. 8vo, limp cloth, 1s.

GORDON—Work;
Or, Plenty to do and How to do it. Thirty-fifth thousand. Fcap. 8vo, cloth, 2s. 6d.

GORDON—Little Millie and her Four Places.
Cheap Edition. Fifty-fifth thousand. Limp cloth, 1s.

GORDON—Sunbeams in the Cottage;
Or, What Women may do. A Narrative chiefly addressed to the Working Classes Cheap Edition. Forty-fourth thousand. Limp cloth, 1s.

GORDON—Prevention;
Or, An Appeal to Economy and Common Sense. 8vo, 6d.

GORDON—The Word and the World.
Twelfth Edition. Price 2d.

LIST OF BOOKS

GORDON—Leaves of Healing for the Sick and Sorrowful.
Fcap. 4to, cloth, 3s. 6d. Cheap Edition, limp cloth, 2s.

GORDON—The Motherless Boy;
With an Illustration by Sir J. NOEL PATON, R.S.A. Cheap Edition, limp cloth, 1s.

"Alike in manner and matter calculated to attract youthful attention, and to attract it by the best of all means—sympathy."—*Scotsman*.

GORDON—Our Daughters.
An Account of the Young Women's Christian Association and Institute Union. Price 2d.

GORDON—Hay Macdowall Grant of Arndilly; his Life,
Labours, and Teaching. New and Cheaper Edition. 1 vol. Crown 8vo, limp cloth, 2s. 6d.

HANNA—The Life of our Lord.
By the Rev. WILLIAM HANNA, D.D., LL.D. 6 vols., handsomely bound in cloth extra, gilt edges, 30s.

Separate vols., cloth extra, gilt edges, 5s. each.
1. THE EARLIER YEARS OF OUR LORD. Fifth Edition.
2. THE MINISTRY IN GALILEE. Fourth Edition.
3. THE CLOSE OF THE MINISTRY. Sixth thousand.
4. THE PASSION WEEK. Sixth Thousand.
5. THE LAST DAY OF OUR LORD'S PASSION. Twenty-third Edition.
6. THE FORTY DAYS AFTER THE RESURRECTION. Eighth Edition.

HANNA—The Resurrection of the Dead.
By WILLIAM HANNA, D.D., LL.D. Second edition. One vol. fcap. 8vo, 5s.

HANNA—The Letters of Thomas Erskine.
Third Edition. Crown 8vo, 9s.

HANNA—Bowen's Daily Meditations.
New Edition. Square crown 8vo, 5s.

JENKIN—Healthy Houses.
By FLEEMING JENKIN, F.R.S., Professor of Engineering in the University of Edinburgh. Demy 8vo, 2s. 6d.

JERVISE—Epitaphs and Inscriptions from Burial-Grounds
and old Buildings in the north-east of Scotland. With Historical, Biographical, Genealogical, and Antiquarian Notes; also an Appendix of Illustrative Papers. By the late ANDREW JERVISE, F.S.A. Scot., Author of "Memorials of Angus and the Mearns," etc. With a Memoir of the Author. Vol. II. Cloth, small 4to, 32s.
Do. do. Roxburghe Edition, 42s.

JOASS—A Brief Review of the Silver Question, 1871 to 1879.
By EDWARD C. JOASS, Fellow of the Faculty of Actuaries, Edin. 8vo, 1s.

JOLLY—The Life of the Right Reverend Alexander Jolly,
D.D., Bishop of Moray. By Rev. W. WALKER, M.A., Monymusk. Crown 8vo, 2s. 6d.

"A valuable contribution to the history of Scottish Episcopacy. . . . Mr. Walker has done his work well."—*Scotsman.*

"Contains many racy anecdotes of a time and generation that have passed away."
—*Brechin Advertiser.*

"We congratulate Mr. Walker on the success he has achieved."—*Scottish Guardian.*

"Bishop Jolly was in every respect a remarkable man, whose memory deserves to be preserved by all who admire a pure and studious life."—*Dundee Advertiser.*

"Written by a loving hand, full of reverence, but with strong appreciation of Scottish humour."—*Guardian.*

JOLLY and GLEIG.
The Lives of Alexander Jolly, D.D., Bishop of Moray, and George Gleig, LL.D., Bishop of Brechin, and Primus of the Episcopal Church of Scotland. By the Rev. W. WALKER, M.A., Monymusk. Crown 8vo, 5s.

JOHNNY GIBB of Gushetneuk, in the Parish of Pyke-
tillim: with Glimpses of the Parish Politics about A.D. 1843. Fifth Edition, with a Glossary. Royal 8vo, with Portraits and Etchings from Drawings by George Reid, R.S.A. 31s. 6d.

Do., Fourth Edition, ex. fcap. 8vo, 2s.

"It is a grand addition to our pure Scottish dialect; . . . it is not merely a capital specimen of genuine Scottish northern *dialect*: but it is a capital specimen of pawky characteristic Scottish humour. It is full of good hard Scottish dry fun."—*Dean Ramsay.*

KENNEDY—Pilate's Question, "Whence art Thou?"
An Essay on the Personal Claims asserted by Jesus Christ, and how to account for them. By JOHN KENNEDY, M.A., D.D., London. Crown 8vo, 3s. 6d.

"Another able and seasonable little volume. . . . We earnestly commend this work as one of no ordinary power, and no ordinary usefulness at the present time."
—*Daily Review.*

"This treatise, written on a skilfully arranged plan, is unquestionably a powerful and eloquent vindication of the orthodox and catholic belief in opposition to rationalistic theories."—*Scotsman.*

"Dr. Kennedy is calm and measured, and singularly fair in his statements. . . . We would earnestly urge young people especially that they master the contents of this able and timely little volume."—*Contemporary.*

KER—Sermons by the Rev. John Ker, D.D., Glasgow.
Twelfth Edition. Crown 8vo, 6s.

"A very remarkable volume of sermons."—*Contemporary Review.*

"The sermons before us are of no common order;" among a host of competitors they occupy a high class—we were about to say the highest class—whether viewed in point of composition, or thought, or treatment.—*B. and F. Evangelical Review.*

KNIGHT—The English Lake District as interpreted in the
Poems of Wordsworth. By WILLIAM KNIGHT, Professor of Moral Philosophy in the University of St. Andrews. Ex. fcap. 8vo, 5s.

KNIGHT—Colloquia Peripatetica (Deep Sea Soundings);
Being Notes of Conversations with the late John Duncan, LL.D., Professor of Hebrew in the New College, Edinburgh. By WILLIAM KNIGHT, Professor of Moral Philosophy in the University of St. Andrews. Fifth Edition, enlarged. 5s.

LIND—Sermons.
By Rev. ADAM LIND, M.A., Elgin. Ex. fcap. 8vo, 5s.

LAING—Lindores Abbey, and the Burgh of Newburgh;
Their History and Annals. By ALEXANDER LAING, LL.D., F.S.A. Scot. 1 vol. small 4to. With Index, and thirteen Full-page and ten Woodcut Illustrations 21s.

"This is a charming volume in every respect."—*Notes and Queries.*
"The prominent characteristics of the work are its exhaustiveness and the thoroughly philosophic spirit in which it is written."—*Scotsman.*

LANCASTER—Essays and Reviews.
By the late HENRY H. LANCASTER, Advocate; with a Prefatory Notice by the Rev. B. JOWETT, Master of Balliol College, Oxford. Demy 8vo, with Portrait, 14s.

LAURIE—On the Philosophy of Ethics. An Analytical
Essay. By S. S. LAURIE, A.M., F.R.S.E., Professor of the Theory, History, and Practice of Education in the University of Edinburgh. Demy 8vo, 6s.

"Mr. Laurie's volume now before us is in substance, though not in form, a reply to Mr. Mill's Utilitarianism. Mr. Laurie has the metaphysical head and the metaphysical training of his countrymen, and has brought both to bear with great force on the problem proposed."—*Saturday Review.*

LAURIE—Notes on British Theories of Morals.
Demy 8vo, 6s.

"His criticisms are candid and highly instructive, *e.g.* those of the views of Bentham, Mill, and Bain. He manifests great aptitude in detecting radical defects, in exposing logical inconsistencies, and in detecting the legitimate tendencies of philosophical systems."—*British Quarterly.*

Life among my Ain Folk.
By the Author of "Johnny Gibb of Gushetneuk." 12mo, cloth, 2s. 6d.

LINDSAY—A Gold Standard without a Gold Coinage in
England and India a step towards an International Monetary System. By A. M. LINDSAY. Demy 8vo, 1s.

A Lost Battle.
A Novel. 2 vols. Crown 8vo, 17s.

"This in every way remarkable novel."—*Morning Post.*
"We are all the more ready to do justice to the excellence of the author's drawing of characters."—*Athenæum.*
"The story is altogether a most enjoyable one."—*Scotsman.*
"The characters throughout, even down to the least important one, are well drawn."—*Pall Mall Gazette.*
"It possesses almost every requisite of a good novel."—*Vanity Fair.*
"Very few of our best veteran writers of fiction have given to the world a prettier story, or one told in a purer style and with a healthier moral."—*Standard.*
"The book is pleasantly free from affectation; the working out of the plot . . . is, on the whole, managed with much cleverness, and most of the characters are natural and consistent."—*Saturday Review.*
"It combines literary grace and constructive fancy with purity of tone, and even an elevated *morale*."—*Standard.*
"A story which is pure and lofty from beginning to end, and has not a dull page in it."—*Spectator.*
"We may fairly rank it among the most promising works of fiction which have been given to the public within recent years."—*Literary World.*
"The secret of its fascination, so far as it can be explained, perhaps lies in the combination of perfect ease and naturalness with perfect refinement, not only of tone, but of thought and sentiment, and with that pure and true feeling for beauty in character and situation, which shows that the author has the soul of the artist."—*Contemporary Review.*

PUBLISHED BY DAVID DOUGLAS.   13

"The characters are carefully conceived and consistently developed, without the faintest straining after sensational effect, while the story never flags, and is exceedingly good and well worth reading, having the rare merit of improving up to the end."—*Inverness Courier.*

"Many a happy phrase, and even far-reaching expression, convinces us that we are in the hands not only of a shrewd and genial observer, but of a thoughtful writer."—*Daily Review.*

"The women in it are real women, and the types selected are all interesting . . . She has breathed into them a genuine life, and given them deep social interest."—*Courant.*

MACLAGAN—Nugæ Canoræ Medicæ.
Lays of the Poet Laureate of the New Town Dispensary. Edited by Professor DOUGLAS MACLAGAN. 4to. With Illustrations, 7s. 6d.

MAIR—Records of the Parish of Ellon.
By THOMAS MAIR. In 1 vol. demy 8vo, 7s. 6d.

MAXWELL—Antwerp Delivered in MDLXXVII.;
A Passage from the History of the Netherlands, illustrated with Facsimiles of a rare Series of Designs by Martin de Vos, and of Prints by Hogenberg, the Wierixea, etc. By Sir WILLIAM STIRLING-MAXWELL, Bart., K.T. and M.P. In 1 vol. folio. 5 guineas.

"A splendid folio in richly ornamented binding, protected by an almost equally ornamental slip-cover. . . . Remarkable illustrations of the manner in which the artists of the time 'pursued their labours in a country ravaged by war, and in cities ever menaced by siege and sack.'"—*Scotsman.*

MICHIE—History of Loch Kinnord.
By the Rev. J. G. MICHIE. Demy 8vo, 2s. 6d.

"It is throughout a piece of genuine, honest, literary workmanship, dealing thoroughly with its subject on the basis of careful study and personal inquiry and labour."—*Aberdeen Free Press.*

MILN—Researches and Excavations at Carnac (Morbihan),
The Bossenno, and Mont St. Michel. By JAMES MILN. In 1 vol., royal 8vo, with Maps, Plans, and numerous Illustrations in Wood-Engraving and Chromolithography. 42s.

"Mr. Miln has made some interesting discoveries, and his record of them is simply and modestly written. He seems to have spared no pains either in making his excavations, or in writing and illustrating an account of them. . . . Mr. Miln has thus an opportunity worthy of an ambitious archæologist, and he has succeeded in using it well."—*Saturday Review.*

"This elegant volume, one of those which are the luxury of art, is the work of an enthusiastic and well-informed antiquary."—*British Quarterly.*

MOREHEAD—Memorials of the Life and Writings of the
Rev. ROBERT MOREHEAD, D.D., formerly Rector of Easington, Yorkshire, and previously Dean of Edinburgh. Edited by his Son, CHARLES MOREHEAD, M.D. Crown 8vo, 7s. 6d.

M'CRIE—John Calvin, a Fragment by the Late Thomas
M'Crie, Author of "The Life of John Knox." Demy 8vo, 6s.

MACFARLANE—Principles of the Algebra of Logic, with
examples, by ALEX. MACFARLANE, M.A., D. Sc. (Edin.), F.R.S.E. 5s.

MACKAY—Memoir of Sir James Dalrymple, First Viscount Stair. A Study in the History of Scotland and Scotch Law during the Seventeenth Century. By Æ. J. G. MACKAY, Advocate. 8vo, 12s.

MACPHERSON—Omnipotence belongs only to the Beloved.
By Mrs. BREWSTER MACPHERSON. 1 vol., extra fcap., 3s. 6d.

MACLAGAN—The Hill Forts, Stone Circles, and other Structural Remains of Ancient Scotland. By C. MACLAGAN, Lady Associate of the Society of Antiquaries of Scotland. With Plans and Illustrations. 1 vol. fol., 31s. 6d.

"We need not enlarge on the few inconsequential speculations which rigid archæologists may find in the present volume. We desire rather to commend it to their careful study, fully assured that not only they, but also the general reader, will be edified by its perusal."—*Scotsman.*

M'LAREN—The Light of the World.
By DAVID M'LAREN, Minister of Humbie. Crown 8vo, extra, 6s.

"We are conscious of having but very inadequately represented this valuable book, and can only hope that what we have said may lead all who have the opportunity to study it for themselves."—*Literary World.*

"In this modest and unpretending volume we have collected together some of the wisest and best essays upon Christ, His mission and His character, His sayings and His doings, that we have met for a long time."

"It is difficult to exaggerate the wise common sense which breathes in every page of the writer's work."—*Courant.*

"This is a welcome volume."—*Dundee Advertiser.*

"The work is pervaded by a healthy moral tone, and characterised throughout by breadth and liberality of sentiment."—*Scotsman.*

"... The fine spirit of the volume. ... It is excellent for thought, and for knowledge also."—*Nonconformist.*

MITCHELL—Our Scotch Banks:
Their Position and their Policy. By WM. MITCHELL, S.S.C. Second Edition, fcap., 2s. 6d.

MOLBECH—Ambrosius:
A play, translated from the Danish of Christian K. F. Molbech by ALICE BERRY. Extra fcap. 8vo, 5s.

NAPIER—"The Lenox of Auld:"
An Epistolary Review of "The Lennox, by William Fraser." By MARK NAPIER. With Woodcuts and Plates. 1 vol. 4to, 15s.

Notes and Sketches Illustrative of Northern Rural Life in the Eighteenth Century, by the Author of "Johnny Gibb of Gushetneuk." In I vol. fcap. 8vo, 2s.

"This delightful little volume. It is a treasure. ... We admire the telling simplicity of the style, the sly, pawky, Aberdonian humour, the wide acquaintance with the social and other conditions of the northern rural counties of last century, and the fund of illustrative anecdotes which enrich the volume. The author has done great service to the cause of history and of progress. It is worth a great many folios of the old dry-as-dust type."—*Daily Review.*

OBER—Camps in the Caribbees: Adventures of a Naturalist in the Lesser Antilles. By FREDERICK OBER. Illustrations, sm. 8vo, 12s.

OGG—Cookery for the Sick and a Guide for the Sick-Room.
By C. H. OGG, an Edinburgh Nurse. Fcap. 1s.

PATRICK, R. W. COCHRAN—Records of the Coinage of
Scotland, from the earliest period to the Union. Collected by R. W. COCHRAN-PATRICK of Woodside. Only two hundred and fifty copies printed. Now ready, in 2 vols. 4to, with 16 Full-page Illustrations, Six Guineas.

"The future Historians of Scotland will be very fortunate if many parts of their materials are so carefully worked up for them and set before them in so complete and taking a form."—*Athenæum.*

"When we say that these two volumes contain more than 770 records, of which more than 550 have never been printed before, and that they are illustrated by a series of Plates, by the autotype process, of the coins themselves, the reader may judge for himself of the learning, as well as the pains, bestowed on them both by the Author and the Publisher."—*Times.*

"The most handsome and complete Work of the kind which has ever been published in this country."—*Numismatic Chronicle,* Pt. IV., 1876.

"We have in these Records of the Coinage of Scotland, not the production of a *dilettante,* but of a real student, who, with rare pains and the most scholarly diligence, has set to work and collected into two massive volumes a complete history of the coinage of Scotland, so far as it can be gathered from the ancient records."
—*Academy.*

PATRICK—Early Records relating to Mining in Scotland:
Collected by R. W. COCHRAN-PATRICK. Demy 4to, 31s. 6d.

"The documents contained in the body of the work are given without alteration or abridgment, and the introduction is written with ability and judgment, presenting a clear and concise outline of the earlier history of the Mining Industries of Scotland."—*Scotsman.*

"The documents . . . comprise a great deal that is very curious, and no less that will be important to the historian in treating of the origin of one of the most important branches of the natural industry."—*Daily News.*

"Such a book . . . revealing as it does the first developments of an industry which has become the mainspring of the national prosperity, ought to be specially interesting to all patriotic Scotchmen."—*Saturday Review.*

Popular Genealogists;
Or, the Art of Pedigree-making. Crown 8vo, 4s.

"We have here an agreeable little treatise of a hundred pages, from an anonymous but evidently competent hand, on the ludicrous and fraudulent sides of genealogy. The subject has a serious and important historical character, when regarded from the point of view of the authors of *The Governing Families of England.* But it is rich in the materials of comedy also.

"The first case selected by the writer before us is one which has often excited our mirth by the very completeness of its unrivalled absurdity. Nobody can turn over the popular genealogical books of our day without dropping on a family called Coulthart of Coulthart, Collyn, and Ashton-under-Lyne. The pedigree given makes the house beyond all question the oldest in Europe. Neither the Bourbons nor Her Majesty's family can be satisfactorily carried beyond the ninth century, whereas the Coultharts were by that time an old and distinguished house.

"We are glad to see such a step taken in the good work as the publication of the essay which has suggested this article, and which we commend to those who want a bit of instructive and amusing reading."—*Pall Mall Gazette.*

RENTON, W.—Oils and Water Colours.
By WILLIAM RENTON. 1 vol. fcap. 5s.

"The book is obviously for the Artist and the Poet, and for every one who shares with them a true love and zeal for nature's beauties."—*Scotsman.*

"To have observed such a delicate bit of colouring as this, and to have written so good a sonnet in the 'strict style,' as that we have quoted, shows that our author has no common powers either as an observer or a writer."—*Liverpool Albion.*

"To those minds that really hold this joy in beauty, Mr. Renton's book will undoubtedly give delight."—*Northern Ensign.*

ROBERTSON—Historical Essays,

In connection with the Land and the Church, etc. By E. WILLIAM ROBERTSON, Author of "Scotland under her Early Kings." In 1 vol. 8vo, 10s. 6d.

ROBERTSON—Scotland under her Early Kings.

A History of the Kingdom to the close of the 13th century. By E. WILLIAM ROBERTSON. In 2 vols. 8vo, cloth, 36s.

"Mr. Robertson's labours are of that valuable kind where an intelligent and thorough sifting of original authorities is brought to bear upon a portion of history handed over hitherto, in a pre-eminent degree, to a specially mendacious set of Mediæval Chroniclers, and (not so long ago) to a specially polemical and uncritical class of modern historians. He belongs to the school of Innes and Skene and Joseph Robertson, and has established a fair right to be classed with the Reeves and Todds of Irish historical antiquarianism, and the Sharpes, and Kembles, and Hardys in England."—*Guardian.*

"Mr. Robertson, in the appendix to his 'Scotland under her Early Kings,' on the English claims, appears to the editor to have completely disposed of the claims founded on the passages in the Monkish Historians prior to the Norman Conquest. This paper is one of the acutest and most satisfactory of these very able essays."— *W. F. Skene in Preface to Chronicles of Picts and Scots.*

SCHIERN—Life of James Hepburn, Earl of Bothwell.

By Professor SCHIERN, Copenhagen. Translated from the Danish by the Rev. DAVID BERRY, F.S.A. Scot. Demy 8vo, 16s.

SHAIRP—Studies in Poetry and Philosophy.

By J. C. SHAIRP, LL.D., Principal of the United College of St. Salvator and St. Leonard, St. Andrews. Second Edition. 1 vol., fcap. 8vo, 6s.

SHAIRP—Culture and Religion.

By PRINCIPAL SHAIRP, LL.D. Fifth Edition. Fcap. 8vo, 3s. 6d.

"A wise book, and unlike a great many other wise books, has that carefully shaded thought and expression which fits Professor Shairp to speak for Culture no less than for Religion."—*Spectator.*

SHAIRP—On Poetic Interpretation of Nature.

By J. C. SHAIRP, LL.D., Principal of the United College of St. Salvator and St. Leonard, St. Andrews. Second Edition. In 1 vol., ex. fcap. 8vo, 6s.

"There is a real sense of relief and refreshment on turning from the news of the day to the unspeakable repose of nature, and in the sense of coolness, and stillness, and greenness, of which we become conscious as we follow Professor Shairp through these interesting and suggestive pages."—*Times.*

"The substance of Mr. Shairp's book was not originally delivered to a learned audience; but he is so essentially thoughtful and meditative, so rich in the facts and fruits of culture, so ably and suggestively critical, that Oxford has good reasons for expecting results of permanent value from her Professor of poetry."—*Guardian.*

"We have followed Mr. Shairp with much interest through his little volume, and heartily commend it to our readers. . . . We can promise a fresh pleasure in almost every page."—*Spectator.*

"Altogether, the book is one full of interest and instruction of a thoroughly elevating character."—*Aberdeen Free Press.*
"We can recommend no better, fresher, more helpful, more exhilarating exercise for the young lover of poetry, who has a real desire to know whereof he affirms—or ought to affirm—delight, when he reads a good poetical description, than to study these pages with attention, and to confirm or correct their criticisms by carefully examining the poets referred to for himself. He will learn to read them with new eyes, and will experience the same delight which he felt on turning to Tennyson after reading Brimley's essay."—*Courant.*

SHAIRP—Wordsworth's Tour in Scotland in 1803, in Company with his Sister and S. T. Coleridge; being the Journal of Miss WORDSWORTH, now for the first time made public. Edited by PRINCIPAL SHAIRP, LL.D. Second Edition. 1 vol., crown 8vo, 6s.

"If there were no other record of her than those brief extracts from Her Journal during the Highland Tour, which stand at the head of several of her brother's poems, these alone would prove her possessed of a large portion of his genius."—*North British Review.*

SHAIRP—Kilmahoe, a Highland Pastoral,
And other Poems. Fcap. 8vo, 6s.

SIMPSON—The Near and the Far View,
And other Sermons. By Rev. A. L. SIMPSON, D.D., Derby. 1 vol. ex. fcap. 8vo, 5s.

"Very fresh and thoughtful are these sermons."—*Literary World.*
"Dr. Simpson's sermons may fairly claim distinctive power. He looks at things with his own eyes, and often shows us what with ordinary vision we had failed to perceive. . . . The sermons are distinctively good."—*British Quarterly Review.*

SKENE—The Four Ancient Books of Wales,
Containing the Cymric Poems attributed to the Bards of the sixth century. By WILLIAM F. SKENE. With Maps and Facsimiles. 2 vols. 8vo, 36s.

"Mr. Skene's book will, as a matter of course and necessity, find its place on the tables of all Celtic antiquarians and scholars."—*Archæologia Cambrensis.*

SKENE—The Coronation Stone.
By WILLIAM F. SKENE. Small 4to. With Illustrations in Photography and Zincography. 6s.

SKENE—Celtic Scotland.
A History of Ancient Alban. By WILLIAM F. SKENE. Vol. I. Book I. History and Ethnology. Illustrated with Maps. 15s.

"It is a book of solid and good work, and which ought to be thankfully welcomed by all who are engaged in any minute study of the early history of Britain."—*Pall Mall Gazette.*
"This volume is the first instalment of a work which will bring the early history of Scotland out of the clouds and mists of artificially constructed systems of history, exaggerated tradition, and legendary fiction, and into a real, if still somewhat dim, historic light."—*Edinburgh Courant.*
"Da ist es denn in der That ein Fortschritt, wenn ein Gelehrter, der sich die schwierigen, aber unerlässlichen Sprachkenntnisse erworben und seit Jahren mit Sichtung der vertrauenswerthen Ueberlieferung von den Truggebilden, welche alles Keltische so leicht bedecken, befasst hat, die bedeutende Aufgabe in die Hand nimmt nach strenger Methode die wirklichen Thatsachen jener Anfangsjahrhunderte hinzustellen. Er hat sich gründlich mit der einheimischen Literatur von Wales und Irland bekannt gemacht und steht durch Kenntniss des Deutschen in Verbindung mit den Fortschritten der sprachvergleichenden Wissenschaft über-

haupt. . . . Ungemein lehrreich mit Hülfe einiger Kärtchen, deren wissenschaftliche Begründung wohl verdient von der neuen Ausgabe des Historischen Atlas von Spruner-Menke für die britannische Abtheilung ernstlich in Betracht gezogen zu werden, ist Alles, was ein so genauer Kenner seiner Heimath, wie Skene es ist, hinsichtlich der physikalischen und ganz besonders der geschichtlichen, Geographie derselben beibringt. . . . Linguistik, Ethnographie, Topographie und Kritik der historischen Quellen greifen für diese wichtige Epoche des Ueberganges wirkungsvoll in einander, wie es meines Wissens bisher in keinem anderen Werke geschehn ist."—*Göttingische gelehrte Anzeigen.*—Dr. R. PAULI.

SKENE—Celtic Scotland.

A History of Ancient Alban. Vol. II. Book II. Church and Culture. In 8vo, with Maps, 15s.

"He brings to the consideration of his subject a thoroughly unprejudiced mind. . . . He has waited till every source of information seems to have been exhausted, and then he gives us the result of his investigations in a calm and carefully weighed narrative. . . . To thank Mr. Skene for a work like this might almost savour of impertinence. It stands alone in a field of labour in which others have not been idle."—*Academy.*

"We are glad now to welcome the second volume of the work, an instalment which will be found equally valuable with the first. . . . It is a work of the highest value; and our opinion of it is by no means to be measured by the brief mention to which we are limited here."—*Westminster Review.*

". . . The second volume of Mr. Skene's learned and valuable work on Celtic Scotland. . . . Mr. Skene is unimpeachably impartial."—*Saturday Review.*

"Mr. Skene bears himself . . . with a serene impartiality. . . . He is no mere polemic, using history as a weapon for controversial purposes. . . . Instead of building with materials derived from cloudland he proceeds according to the best methods of historic criticism. . . . Such are his fairness no less than his facility of suggestion, his painstaking enthusiasm no less than the minute fidelity of his erudition, his reverent spirit no less than his ingenuity and power of synthesis, that his views may be trusted assuredly to prevail. Most readers will instinctively detect in him qualities that suffice to protect novelty from the accusation of paradox."—*Spectator.*

SKENE—Celtic Scotland.

A History of Ancient Alban. Vol. III. Book III., Land and People.

[*In the Press.*

SMALL—Scottish Woodwork of the Sixteenth and Seventeenth centuries. Measured, Drawn, and Lithographed by J. W. SMALL, Architect. In one folio volume, with 130 Plates, Four Guineas.

"Guided by competent knowledge, the compiler of this work would appear to have had ample access to desirable examples, and has thus been enabled to make a selection well fitted at once to gratify the connoisseur and to afford valuable suggestions to the designer or the craftsman. . . . The lithograph plates are beautifully executed, and the volume altogether brought out in capital style."—*Scotsman.*

"Mr. J. W. Small's very admirable volume, illustrative of ancient Scottish woodwork. . . . It is impossible to over-estimate the value of the minute details that abound in Mr. Small's admirable work. Very opportunely has Mr. Small come to the rescue of art furniture with his admirable work, of which it is impossible to speak in unduly eulogistic terms."—*Furniture Gazette.*

SMITH—Shelley: a Critical Biography.

By GEORGE BARNETT SMITH. Ex. fcap. 8vo, 6s.

"One of the kindest, if not exactly one of the acutest estimates that has ever been written of a poet about whose life, genius, and works, many writers have greatly differed, and about whom future writers will continue to differ."—*Scotsman.*

"Mr. Barnett Smith may be congratulated upon having undertaken a noble and manly task, and having done it well. . . . The monograph, taken as a whole, is scarcely susceptible of improvement."—*Morning Post*.

"Mr. Smith's Critical Biography strikes us as being singularly fresh-hearted in feeling, verified by a noble and unaffected sympathy with all that is spiritually beautiful in nature and man."—*Telegraph*.

"Mr. Smith's Biography is eminently suggestive, and while worthy of his acknowledged critical taste, it is rendered deeply interesting by the psychological questions it broaches."—*Courant*.

"We are grateful to him for enabling us to think more kindly of the author of two such magnificent poems as 'The Cenci,' and 'Prometheus Unbound.'"—*Guardian*.

"Mr. Barnett Smith has done good service to the memory of Shelley."—*Contemporary Review*.

"The criticism of the poems is thoughtful, keen-sighted, and in every way valuable, displaying an accurate knowledge of Shelley, and of his place in English literature. Mr. Smith's own style is fluent, pithy, and frequently brilliant. . . . The essay, as a whole, is powerfully written, and . . . will prove a welcome contribution to the study of this great poet."—*Freeman*.

SMITH—The Sermon on the Mount.
By the Rev. WALTER C. SMITH, D.D. Crown 8vo, 6s.

SMITH—Answer to the Form of Libel before the Free
Presbytery of Aberdeen. By W. ROBERTSON SMITH, Professor of Oriental Languages and Exegesis of the Old Testament in the Free Church College, Aberdeen. 8vo, 1s.

"He has shown it to be possible to maintain devoutness of spirit, and a hearty acceptance of the dogmatic forms of belief, with a thorough application to the Scriptures of the ordinary methods of philological criticism."—*Rev. T. A. Cheyne* in *Academy*.

SMITH—Additional Answer to the Libel,
With some Account of the Evidence that parts of the Pentateuchal Law are later than the Time of Moses. By W. ROBERTSON SMITH, Professor of Oriental Languages and Exegesis of the Old Testament in the Free Church College, Aberdeen. 8vo, 1s.

"The freshness and intimate acquaintance with the position of criticism which these eighty-eight pages display, justify us in commending this pamphlet to the attention of all Biblical students. There is nothing startling in it except indeed its moderation."—*Academy*.

SMITH—Answer to the Amended Libel, with Appendix
containing Plea in Law. By W. ROBERTSON SMITH. 8vo, 6d.

SMYTH—Life and Work at the Great Pyramid.
With a Discussion of the Facts ascertained. By C. PIAZZI SMYTH, F.R.SS.L. and E., Astronomer-Royal for Scotland. 3 vols., demy 8vo, 56s.

SOUTHESK—Saskatchewan and the Rocky Mountains.
Diary and Narrative of Travel, Sport, and Adventure, during a Journey through part of the Hudson's Bay Company's Territories in 1859 and 1860. By the EARL OF SOUTHESK, K.T., F.R.G.S. 1 vol., demy 8vo, with Illustrations on Wood, by WHYMPER, 18s.

SOUTHESK—Herminius.
A Romance. By L. E. S. Fcap. 8vo, 6s.

SPENS—Should the Poor-Law in all Cases Deny Relief to
the Able-bodied Poor? By WALTER COOK SPENS, Advocate, Sheriff-Substitute of Lanarkshire. Demy 8vo, 1s.

STEVENSON — Christianity Confirmed by Jewish and
Heathen Testimony, and the Deductions from Physical Science, etc. By THOMAS STEVENSON, F.R.S.E., F.G.S., Member of the Institution of Civil Engineers. Second Edition. Fcap. 8vo, 3s. 6d.

STRACHAN — What is Play?
A Physiological Inquiry. Its bearing upon Education and Training. By JOHN STRACHAN, M.D., Jun. In 1 vol. fcap., 1s.

"We have great pleasure in directing the attention of our readers to this little work . . . bearing as it does on one of the most important aspects of physiological medicine, as well as on education in the highest sense of the word."—*Lancet*.
"A very interesting, and, in the main, a wise little book."—*Mind*.
"It is so seldom that so much sound sense, clear reasoning, and able development of ideas, which will probably be new to the majority of readers, are compressed into a hundred duodecimo pages, as Dr. Strachan has contrived to put into his little treatise *on Play*."—*Scotsman*.

TAIT — Sketch of Thermodynamics.
By O. G. TAIT, Professor of Natural Philosophy in the University of Edinburgh. Second Edition, revised and extended. Crown 8vo, 5s.

TEIGNMOUTH — Reminiscences of Many Years.
By LORD TEIGNMOUTH. 2 vols., demy, 8vo, 28s.

WILSON — The Botany of Three Historical Records:
Pharaoh's Dream, The Sower, and the King's Measure. By A. STEPHEN WILSON. Crown 8vo, with 5 plates, 3s. 6d.

"The book is useful as affording illustrations of Scripture incident and teaching."—*Inverness Courier*.
"The writer deserves credit for the pains he has taken in making his researches, and by means of well-designed woodcuts he has so illustrated the work as to make his arguments as clear as is possible."—*Courant*.

WILSON — Reminiscences of Old Edinburgh.
By DANIEL WILSON, LL.D., F.R.S.E., Professor of History and English Literature in University College, Toronto, Author of "Prehistoric Annals of Scotland," etc. etc. 2 vols. post 8vo, 15s.

"We have only been able to single out some specimens at random from a book that is essentially discursive; but we have found the whole very enjoyable reading, and there is no lack of variety of incidents. The illustrations, which are after pen-and-ink sketches by the author where he is not indebted for them to the irrepressible Mr. Sharpe, are equally clever and characteristic."—*Pall Mall Gazette*.
"Professor Wilson has given us a book for which we may be thankful, especially in these days of slipshod learning and superficial display. He knows his subject thoroughly, and writes about it with the ease of a master. We must not omit to notice the exceedingly graceful and accurate pen-and-ink sketches by the author himself, reproduced with rare fidelity by photozincography, and the two laughable caricature vignettes by C. K. Sharpe, which are exceedingly characteristic."—*Edinburgh Courant*.

WYLD — Christianity and Reason:
Their necessary connection. By R. S. WYLD, LL.D. Extra fcap. 8vo, 3s. 6d.

BOOKS ON SPORT AND NATURAL HISTORY.

I.
Shortly will be Published,
In one Very Handsome Folio Volume,

Sport and Photography in the Rocky Mountains.
BY ANDREW WILLIAMSON.

With Eighteen Full-Page Illustrations, taken on the spot, of the Grisly Bear, Wapiti, etc. etc.

II.
Saskatchewan and the Rocky Mountains. Diary
and Narrative of Travel, Sport, and Adventure, during a Journey through part of the Hudson's Bay Company's Territories in 1859 and 1860. By the EARL OF SOUTHESK, K.T., F.R.G.S. 1 Vol., Demy 8vo, with Illustrations on Wood by WHYMPER, 18s.

III.
The Roof of the World; being the Narrative of
a Journey over the High Plateau of Thibet to the Russian Frontier on the Oxus Sources on Pamir. By Lieut.-Colonel T. E. GORDON, C.S.I. In 1 Vol., Royal 8vo, with Illustrations and Maps, 31s. 6d.

IV.
My Indian Journal. Containing Descriptions of
the Principal Field Sports of India, with Notes on the Natural History and Habits of the Wild Animals of the Country. By Colonel WALTER CAMPBELL, Author of "The Old Forest Ranger." 8vo, with Illustrations by WOLF, 16s.

V.
Wild Men and Wild Beasts. Adventures in
Camp and Jungle. By Lieut.-Colonel GORDON CUMMING. With Illustrations by Lieut.-Colonel BAIGRIE and others. Second Edition. Demy 4to, Price 24s.

Also a Cheaper Edition with *Lithographic* Illustrations. 8vo, 12s.

BOOKS ON SPORT AND NATURAL HISTORY—*Continued.*

VI.

The Capercaillie in Scotland. By J. A. HARVIE BROWN.
With Etchings on Copper, and Map illustrating the extension of its range since its Restoration at Taymouth in 1837 and 1838. Demy 8vo, 8s. 6d.

"A carefully prepared and exhaustive monograph of the Capercailzie in Scotland, which ought to be perused by every proprietor of an estate, forester, and naturalist in the country."—*Journal of Forestry.*

VII.

Four Months in a Sneak-Box. A Boat-Voyage
of 2600 Miles. By NATHANIEL H. BISHOP. In 1 Vol., Demy 8vo, with Maps and Plates, Price 10s. 6d.

"The Author of the interesting 'Voyage of the Paper Canoe,' noticed in these columns twelve months ago, has just published a companion volume under the curious title of 'Four Months in a Sneak-Box.' It is a relation of a second cruise to the Gulf of Mexico by a somewhat different route from the one he previously followed. The most striking difference, however, consisted in the boat used on this occasion, which was a staunch little craft, twelve feet in length, built upon a purely American model, recently introduced by the bay men of the New Jersey coast to wild-fowlers. In it the author rode more than 2600 miles down the Ohio and Mississippi rivers."—*Live Stock Journal.*

"The Maps illustrating the work are done after a fashion we do not remember to have seen before, being printed upon tracing paper, with wonderfully good effect."

VIII.

By the same Author.

Voyage of the Paper Canoe. From Quebec to
the Gulf of Mexico. In 1 Vol.; Demy 8vo, with Maps and Plates, Price 10s. 6d.

IX.

Veterinary Medicines; their Actions and Uses.
By FINLAY DUN. Fifth Edition, revised and Enlarged. 8vo, 14s.

DAVID DOUGLAS, 9 Castle Street, Edinburgh.

www.ingramcontent.com/pod-product-compliance
Lightning Source LLC
Chambersburg PA
CBHW030604300426
44111CB00009B/1102